RAILS 4

FOR STARTUPS USING MOBILE AND SINGLE PAGE APPLICATIONS

Complete Guide to Architecting and Deploying a Scalable Mobile Website with a Single Page Application and Rails

By Anthony O'Leary

© Copyright 2014 Anthony O'Leary

Licence Notes

This eBook is licensed for your personal enjoyment only. This eBook may not be re-sold or given away to other people. If you would like to share this book with someone else, please purchase an additional copy for each recipient. If you're reading this book and did not purchase it, or it was not purchased for your use only, then please return to Smashwords.com and purchase your own copy. Thank you for respecting the hard work of this author

About Author

Anthony O'Leary works as a mobile software architect. Freelanced as a developer contractor around the world working with companies such as Apple, and Ericsson. Experienced with high performance scalable architecture, and mobile native iOS/android applications.

Contact: oleary.anthony@gmail.com

TABLE OF CONTENTS

Introduction 1
    Development Environment 2
    Requirements 2
Ruby Overview 3
    Advantages of static typed languages such as Java/C++ 3
    Different Ruby programs 4
    Installation 4
    Object orientated language 5
    Functional programming 33
    Object orientated Programming 34
    Composition 40
    Method visibility : public, private, protected 42
    Design patterns 47
    Modules 48
    Threads 50
    Background jobs 54
    Gems 56
    Manage ruby versions 58
    Development Tools 58
Rails Overview 60
    Environments 60
    Create a new Rails application 62
    Rails server 63
    Version control 66

- Testing 70
- Add boiler plate code for our dating app 71
- MVC 74
- Model 78
- Schema 82
- Useful rake db commands 84
- Concerns 89
- View 90
- Add side column for searching for members 103
- Template engines 105
- Controller 107
- Session 108
- Ajax 112
- Exceptions 114
- Logs 121
- Garbage collection 122
- Flash 124
- Asset pipeline 126
- Internationalisation 129
- Rake Task 130

Testing : unit, rspec, cucumber 134
- Testing Levels 134
- Blackbox, white box, grey box 135
- Software testing methodologies 135
- Fixtures 137
- Useful rake commands for running tests 138
- Integration tests 138
- Cucumber 139
- Number of QA people 140
- Native Mobile device testing 140

- Test Javascript 141
- Continuous integration 141
- Code metrics 142
- System tests 142
- Mobile debug tools 143

Caching 145
- Asset Pipeline Cache 146
- HTTP cache headers 147
- HTTP Header Time Based Cache 149
- HTTP Header Content Based Cache 150
- View Page Fragment caching 152

HTML5/CSS3 Overview 161
- HTML5 features 161
- CSS3 167
- Dating app boilerplate 169
- SASS/LESS 169
- Mobile Pixels 170

Javascript Overview 173
- Progressive enhancement 173
- Modernizer 174
- CoffeeScript 175
- Javascript loaders 175

Create the Dating Application 180
- Upload a photo 180
- Add the dating schema 182
- Send messages 193
- Store hobbies 196
- Add the ability to find other members 207
- Live streaming 220

Responsive Design 222

- Fluid versus adaptive and responsive design ... 225
- Responsive site versus mobile and responsive sites ... 228
- Network latency ... 229
- Grid frameworks ... 230
- Browser versus server side device detection ... 232
- Image rendering ... 240

General Mobile Optimisation Tips ... 247
- Pagespeed ... 247
- Add Icons for iPhone, iPad & Android to Your Website ... 247
- Viewport ... 248
- Accessing native mobile functionality ... 250

Fonts ... 251
- Chrome font resizing ... 251
- Pixel (px) ... 252
- ems ... 253
- Font size suggestions ... 255
- Font types ... 256

UX Overview ... 258
- MVP ... 258
- Do mobile first ... 259
- UX Design Steps ... 261
- Rapid prototyping ... 270
- UX usability study ... 274

Make the Dating Site Responsive ... 279
- UX process ... 279
- Sketch ... 280
- Low fidelity mockup ... 282

RUBY RAILS SEO ... 288
- Sitemap ... 288
- Valid HTML ... 288

- Breadcrumbs 289
- Page URL slug name 289
- HTML5 markup 290
- Dynamic Meta Tags 291
- How responsive design affects SEO 292

Deployment 294
- nginx/apache 294
- Rails production server 295
- Database connections 295
- Security 296
- Rails deployment environment 298
- Application Hosting options 300
- Operations management 304
- Deployment Tools 305
- Server build tools 309
- How to enable features as you require them 312

Scalable Architecture 316
- How to loosely couple your application 317
- Sinatra services 328
- Database scalability 328

Single Page Applications (SPA) 331
- Who uses SPA 332
- Problems with SPA 332
- Single page application 'Perceived Page Load' 332
- Multi user server synchronization – live updates 336
- SPA Performance Monitoring 336
- Restful API versus Websocket Performance 336
- Feature Toggle 337
- SPA Grid Layout 338

Rewrite the dating app so far in backbone.js 339

- Turbolinks issues 339
- Reason to use a SPA 340
- SPA page Security 340
- RESTful API security 341
- Yeoman overview 344
- First Solution: Yeoman solution 345
- Second Solution 348
- Dating code 349
- Create SPA tests 354
- Debugging SPA 354
- Add extra backbone functionality 355
- Javascript templating engine 355
- Rewrite in angularjs 356

SPA SEO 357
- Google crawler 357
- Solution for SPA page crawler indexing 358
- SPA SEO Implementation 361
- Sitemaps 363

Convert to a Mobile App 364
- hybrid application 364

Big Data 368
- Data warehouse Versus Big Data 368
- Big Data work flow 369
- Hadoop Alternatives 369
- Column databases 371

Conclusion 373

INTRODUCTION

This book aims to give a practical guide to developing and scaling a Ruby Rails application with a focus on mobile devices and the issues with using a Single Page Application (SPA). Websites are getting more and more traffic from mobiles devices that it has become important to prioritise development to mobilise your web page, even for sites which also have native apps I have seen over 25% of web page users from mobile devices, and this is growing. We will cover enough Ruby Rails to get started and some advanced topics to give you an overview of the language capabilities. It is a practical guide but some wider concepts will be discussed so you have a broader view of topics when deciding the best architecture to use and general programming tips. For a startup some tips such as focusing on the minimum viable product and suggestions for deciding your technology stack. As a full stack developer people need to be aware of the full product cycle including UX and how images will render on for example the iPhone 6 Plus, development, deployment and even big data analysis. How do we prevent our app growing into one hugh monolithic mess of code, and how microservices can help decouple failure from other components.

I was leading a large mobile video streaming for a major mobile telco operator three years ago using a Java/Spring/hibernate stack with server side device detection supporting feature and smart mobiles. How the technology stack choices have changed since then. We will discuss is there a tipping point to start thinking about replacing Rails with a Java stack (or Scala, node.js etc).

We will develop a demo dating site for Web, later enhance it for tablet and phone devices. How to deploy and scale it will be discussed, and for a startup, most importantly how to do it all as cheap as possible and avoid mistakes. Then we will go through using a Javascript Single Page Application architecture with Rails, and how then to convert this to an iOS/android app.

Times have changed from the original famous 15 minute blog created by Rails, Single Page Applications now play a major part of any design consideration using just a backend Controller with no server side rendered view. This book shall discuss the technical issues involved with this approach.

Here's a question when you start building the front end: "SPA or standard Rails?" some point to consider are: SEO considerations, Caching, using a SPA for your front end forces you to develop a robust API. If you know you'll eventually need to build a number of different native clients, or if offering a public API is part of the core product, then starting with a SPA may make sense. I discuss Rails caching in detail to highlight what you will miss by not using Rails for your Views.

Development Environment

Typically for new team members as a development environment I standardise on the environment. This helps with getting a new developer up and running quickly, and to ensure local tests would be the same across all developers. For example I have seen Capybara tests fail on some different environments. Some options could be:

- Rebuild your computer with just Ubuntu as the Operating System so everyone wil use the same version of Linux.
- Allow Mac as a development machine.
- Vagrant with Chef to build the environment running as Ubuntu server on VirtualBox in an environment as close to production as possible.

Requirements

It will be required to install Ruby 2, Rails 4 minimum, and PostgreSQL database for the examples, rather than use the default SQLite as my aim is to enable you to have the ability to produce a production grade product.

For this book you should also install the Postgres gem: gem install pg

A useful link to configure your machine for Ruby Rails is with this script link. New developers on your team can have a standard environment then.

https://github.com/thoughtbot/laptop/blob/master/README.md

Thoughtbot use this Rails base setup: https://github.com/thoughtbot/suspenders

http://guides.rubyonrails.org/ is a good reference guide for Rails.

RUBY OVERVIEW

Yukihiro "Matz" Matsumoto created Ruby in 1993 and released it to the public in 1995, he quoted 'Ruby is designed to make programmers happy'.

Ruby is a interpreted **dynamic type language** like say PHP and Python, rather than say Java or 'C++' which is a compiled **static type language,** which means you can change the Ruby code and it will run without having to compile the code but the negative is that less coding errors are caught before you run the code, Static typing is great because it keeps you out of trouble. Dynamic typing is great because it gets out of your way and lets you get your work done faster.

In practice people can create good Rails applications without knowing the details of Ruby, job interviewing some programmers quickly reveals that. Unlike say Java people don't use as many software design patterns, or use the class protected/private declarations as proudly as in Java.

Advantages of static typed languages such as Java/C++

Static type compiled languages can prove the absence of certain run-time errors. For instance, they can prove properties like: booleans are never added to integers; private variables are not accessed from outside their class; functions are applied to the right number of arguments; only strings are ever added to a set of strings. But static type language will usually not detect all errors at compilation such as array bounds violations, or divisions by zero. Static type systems have therefore been dismissed by some as not being very useful. The argument goes that since such type languages can only detect simple errors, whereas unit tests provide more extensive coverage, why bother with static types at all? Although a static type language certainly cannot replace unit testing, it can reduce the number of unit tests needed by taking care of some properties that would otherwise need to be tested. Likewise, unit testing can not replace static typing. Testing can only prove the presence of errors, never their absence.So the compile time guarantees that static typing gives may be simple, but they are guarantees you get for free. A static type language provides a safety net that lets you make changes to a codebase with a high degree of confidence. Consider for instance a refactoring that adds an additional parameter to a method, Ruby would not detect this but a static type would at compile time.

Ruby compensates for being a dynamic type language by strongly focusing on creating tests as part of the development cycle. The fact that testing was so inbuilt with the Rails platform makes this a reason to use Ruby/Rails for many projects.

Different Ruby programs

MRI [Matz'a Ruby Interpreter], the inventor or Ruby, is the main tool for running Ruby, the 'offical' Ruby implementation. I normally check regularly for any new Ruby versions for the new language changes that come with them to be up to date on the latest features.

Other Ruby versions are:

- Ruby enterprise edition, http://www.rubyenterpriseedition.com, allows the ability to tune the garbage collection and better memory usage, the negative is that it is not up todate with the latest Ruby language features.
- JRuby, http://jruby.org/, is a high performance, stable, fully threaded Java implementation of the Ruby programming language.
- Rubinius, http://rubinis.us, is an implementation of Ruby designed for concurrency using native threads to run Ruby on all the CPU cores. It works well with the Puma Rails server. They created and maintain Rubyspec which is used to check any ruby interpreters are compatibility with MRI. Note:
- IronRuby, http://ironruby.net/, is an open source implementation of the Ruby programming language for. NET and Silverlight, heavily relying on Microsoft's Dynamic Language Runtime.
- MacRuby, http://macruby.org/, is an implementation directly on top of Mac OS X core technologies.

A reference for Ruby is http://www.ruby-doc.org/

Installation

Ruby is easiest to use on a Mac or Linux, if you have a Windows machine the easiest solution could be just to install VirtualBox and Ubuntu Server. Linux still will come in useful during production also as in practice most Ruby/Rails applications are deployed onto a Linux server. Once you download Ruby you can open a Ruby terminal console to test the language, firstly enter:

```
ruby -v
```

Then enter 'irb' to enter the console mode, it stands for Interactive RuBy, you can then enter your Ruby code and learn the language. People don't really use this for Rails development.

```
001> puts "Hello World"
Hello World
=> nil
```

'puts' is the basic command to print something out in Ruby. But then what's the => nil bit? That's the result of the expression. puts always returns nil.

create a file called test.rb, ruby files end in. rb, containing:

```
#!/usr/bin/ruby
print "Hello Ruby!\n"
print "Goodbye Ruby!\n"
```

and run it, easy as that.

```
ruby. /test.rb
```

Note: #!/usr/bin/ruby tells the program loader to use Ruby command to execute the file.

Object orientated language

Everything in Ruby is an Object, is something you'll hear rather frequently, every object has a class, and being a part of that class gives the object lots of useful methods. Being very object-oriented gives Ruby lots of power and makes your life easier. For Example a 'person' can be a class [also called an object] and 'bob' could be an instance of that class.

Ruby is true object orientated language, and everything appears to Ruby as an object. Even the most primitive things: strings, numbers and even true and false. Even a class itself is an object that is an instance of the Class class.

The number 12 is more than just a number, It is an object and Ruby lets you do all kinds of interesting things to it like adding and multiplying and asking it questions like:

```
irb> 12.class
=> Fixnum
```

or

```
irb> [].class
=> Array
```

Coding conventions

It is standard practice to write your code with naming conventions. The class name is always capitalised and, for multiple words, uses CamelCase (capitalised with no spaces).

Method names should start with a lowercase letter and use snake case, e.g. close_the_door. Variables use snake_case, are named where all letters are lowercase and words are separated by underscores, e.g. order_amount.

Variable scope

Scope is the formal term that represents when you can access a variable or method and when you can't. If your variable is "in scope" then it's available for use, otherwise it's "out of scope". Think of scope like a container of one-way glass around certain chunks of code. Inside that container, your variable or method can see (or use) anything in the world outside the container but the outside world can't see in.

```
def launch_longships(longships)
# We can use 'longships' because it was passed in.
launched_ships = 0
# Now launched_ships is in scope so we can use it
longships.each do |longship|
# Now 'longship' is in scope, so we can use it
longship_name = "#{longship.owner.name}"
# Now 'longship_name' is in scope so we can use it
```

```
longship.launch
launched_ships += 1
puts "#{longship_name} successfully launched!"
end

# Now we've exited the loop so `longship` and `longship_name`
# are no longer in scope so we cannot use them.
puts "Good news! We've launched #{launched_ships} ships!"
end
```

Methods

Methods help organise your code by keeping you from repeating yourself. Anything that you find yourself doing repeatedly should probably go in its own method. Methods should be short. If they're greater than 10 lines, you're probably doing too much. Every method returns something, even if it's just nil. Methods parameters can be called with no brackets. Bang Methods are finished with an exclamation point ! like #sort!, and they actually modify the original object.

```
> my_numbers = [1,5,3,2]
=> [1, 5, 3, 2]
> my_numbers.sort
=> [1, 2, 3, 5]
> my_numbers
=> [1, 5, 3, 2] # still unsorted
> my_numbers.sort!
=> [1, 2, 3, 5]
> my_numbers
=> [1, 2, 3, 5] # overwrote the original my_numbers object!
```

Methods ending with a question mark ? return true or false.

```
def empty?
@arr.empty? # Implicitly returned result
end
```

If you ever want to know what an object's methods are, just use the #methods method:

```
irb>12345.methods
```

In IRB, it will return a whole bunch of methods that you can try out on the number 12345. You'll also see that the basic operators like + and - and / are all methods too (they're included in that list). You can call them using the dot:

```
irb>1.+2
```

Ruby made some special shortcuts for them so you can just use them as you have been:

```
irb> 1+2
```

Sending messages

This syntax is not used very often. When you call methods, what we usually do is to use the standard dot notation:

```
irb>"cool".upcase
```

The dot operator is used to separate the message receiver ("cool") from the message (up-case), or another way to call it is:

```
irb>"cool".send(:upcase)
```

The send method uses a different syntax than dot notation, but the semantics are the same. In this example, the upcase message is sent to the receiver (i.e. the "cool" object) and the receiver responds by looking up a method with the same name as the message and invoking the appropriate code. If you want to call a method dynamically, then If the name of the method is in a variables can you invoke the method using this way.

How to create methods dynamically

You can define a method on the spot with Module#define_method(). Or else, you could use class_eval to define methods dynamically as well.

```
define_method(symbol, method)
#or
define_method(symbol) { block }
```

For example:

```
class Doctor
define_method("perform_checkup") do |argument|
"performing checkup on #{argument}"
end
```

```
end
doctor = Doctor.new
puts doctor.perform_checkup("throat")
```

Classes

Classes are the basic foundation that let us give an object general behaviours, which can contain data and methods. An object is an instance of a class. For example a customer class, remember one class and multiple objects can be created from this class.

```
#!/usr/bin/ruby
class Customer
def initialize(id, name)
@cust_id=id #create a session variable
@cust_name=name #create a session variable
end
def display_details()
puts "Customer id #@cust_id"
puts "Customer name #@cust_name"
end
end
```

```
irb> customer1=Customer.new("1", "Bob")
=> #<Customer:0x00000101124858 @cust_id="1", @cust_name="Bob">
irb> customer1.display_details()
Customer id 1
Customer name Bob
```

What was that random string in #<Customer:0x00000101124858>? That's the position in the computer's memory that the customer object is stored.

If you pass variables to your class when you create it with the 'new' method, they will be available to the #initialize method. Whenever Ruby creates a new object, it looks for a method named initialize and executes it. So one simple thing we can do is use an initialize method to put default values into all the instance variables or in the case above to pass in a parameter to initialise a value.

Instance variables begin with @ which will be unique per object.

Objects created from a class have access to the public methods of a class. These created objects are automatically deleted to free the memory when they are no longer referenced automatically by the garbage collector, as in Java.

If you want to give your customer some actions it can do, then give it some methods. Since these methods get called on an individual instance of the Customer class, they're called Instance Methods.

Accessing class variables

So if you want to know what customer1's cust_name is:

```
irb> customer1.cust_name
NoMethodError: undefined method `cust_name' for
#<Customer:0x00000101124858>
```

The instance variables are a part of customer1 but you can't access them from outside him because it's really nobody's business but his. So you have to create a method specifically to get that variable, called a getter method, and just name it the same thing as the variable you want:

```
def cust_name
@cust_name
end
```

```
> customer1.cust_name
=> "John"
```

What if you decide that you want to set that variable yourself? You need to create a setter method, which is similar syntax to the getter but with an equals sign and taking an argument:

```
def cust_name=(new_cust_name)
@cust_name = new_cust_name
end
```

You can imagine that you'll probably be writing a whole lot of those methods, so Ruby gives you a helper method called attr_accessor, which will create those getters and setters for you. Just pass it the symbols for whatever variables you want to make accessible and those methods will now exist for you to use. With Ruby you can just run this code and it appends to the the existing class code.

```
class Customer
attr_accessor :cust_name
end
```

attr_accessor uses Ruby's ability to create methods from within your script to set up #cust_name and #cust_name=(new_cust_name)

You should not make any data readable and certainly not writeable without a good reason. If you only want one or the other, Ruby gives you the similar attr_reader and attr_writer methods.

'self' explained

Because of your getters and setters, there are two different ways to access an instance variable from inside your class, either calling it normally using @cust_name or calling the method on the instance using 'self' which represents whatever object called a particular method. for example:

```
class Foo
attr_accessor :var
def bar1
var = 4
puts var
puts self.var
end
end

f = Foo.new
f.var = 3
f.bar1
```

Output

```
4
3
```

So, as we can see, 'var' is assigned without self keyword and, because of this, now there are two names var in the scope: local variable and instance attribute. Instance attribute is hidden by local variable, so if you really want to access it, use self.

Class variables

Just like you've got instance variables and instance methods, you also get class variables and class methods. Class variables begin with @@ and must be initialised before they can be used in method definitions. You can create class parameters to be shared with all classes :

```
class Triangle < Polygon
@@sides = 3
end
puts Triangle.sides # => 3
```

Class methods

You define a class method by preceding its name with 'self' such as def self.class_method or, identically, just the name of the class such as: def Customer.class_method.

There are two good reasons to use class methods: when you're building new instances of a class that have a bunch of known or "preset" features, or when you have some sort of utility method that should be identical across all instances and won't need to directly access instance variables.

The first case is called a factory method, and is designed to save you from having to keep passing a bunch of parameters manually to your #initialize method:

```
class Item
def self.show
puts "Class method show invoked"
end
end
```

Item.show

In def self.show, the keyword self denotes that the method show is being defined in the context of the Class itself, not its instances. Any method definition without the self qualifier is by default an instance method.

There is also another way to define class methods that you may come across in Ruby code:

```
class Item
class << self
def show
puts "Class method show invoked"
end
end
```

Numbers, operators

Because Ruby is so flexible, it lets you do some quirky things like multiplying completely different data types together in a way that you sort of think you should be able to but never expected to actually be able to do:

```
irb> "hi" * 3
=> "hihihihi"
```

Equal

= is for assignment, so it assigns a value to a variable,

== is for checking that two things are equal but don't have to be identical instances. You'll use this in most cases, especially when working with conditional statements.

```
> 1 + 1 == 2
=> true
```

When you start creating your own classes, you'll need to tell Ruby how to compare two class instances by writing your own version of this method.

=== can actually mean some different things (you can overwrite it easily). You will probably be sticking with == in most situations, but it's good to understand === as well, it typically asks whether the thing on the right is a member or a part or a type of the thing on the left. If the thing on the left is the range (1..4) and we want to know if 3 is inside there:

```
irb> (1..4) === 3
=> true
```

This also works for checking whether some object is an instance of a class:

```
irb> Integer === 3
=> true
```

What is nil

So What is nil? It represents nothing... literally. Before you assign a value to something, it starts as nil, for instance an item in an array or a variable:

```
irb> my_arr = []
=> []
irb> my_arr[3]
=> nil # hasn't been assigned yet
```

Sometimes you want to know if a value or variable is nil before doing something (because otherwise the operation would throw a bunch of errors at you). Use the method nil? to ask whether it's nil or not beforehand.

```
irb> nil.nil?
=> true
irb> [].nil?
=> false
```

Why is [] not nil? The array itself exists so it isn't nil... it just happens to contain no values yet so it's empty. If we asked for the first value of that array using [][0].nil?, that would be true. If you try to run a method on something that is nil, which you will inevitably do many many times by accident, you'll get the NoMethodError exception.

Blank/Empty

blank? and empty? are similar -- both basically check if the object has nothing in it -- but blank? will also ignore any whitespace characters. Note that blank? is a method provided by Rails and is not available in Ruby.

Constant

A Ruby constant is like a variable, except that its value is supposed to remain constant for the duration of the program. The Ruby interpreter does not actually enforce the constancy of constants, but it does issue a warning if a program changes the value of a constant. Constant names start with an uppercase letter followed by other characters. Constant objects are by convention named using all uppercase letters and underscores between words, e.g. THIS_IS_A_CONSTANT

```
irb> THIS_IS_A_CONSTANT = 10
=> 10
irb> THIS_IS_A_CONSTANT = 20
(irb):31: warning: already initialized constant A_CONST
(irb):30: warning: previous definition of THIS_IS_A_CONSTANT was here
=> 20
```

Outside the class or module, they may be accessed using the scope operator, :: prefixed by an expression that returns the appropriate class or module.

```
class FixedValues
PI = 3.14
end

>FixedValues::PI
=> 3.14
```

Strings

Strings are just made up of individual characters and denoted with quotes. Double Quotes are often interchangeable with Single Quotes. String Interpolation occurs when you want to insert something else into a string, like a variable. You'll find yourself using this a lot, for instance, when you make websites with dynamic text content that needs to change depending on who is logged in. Simply use the pound symbol and curly braces #{} to do so, and the output of whatever is within those curly braces will be converted to a string and you've got a new string:

```
irb> my_name = "Tiny Tim"
=> "Tiny Tim"
irb> my_name.class
=> String
irb> my_name.methods
#a list of methods
irb> my_string = "My name is #{my_name}!"
=> "My name is Tiny Tim!"
```

The key point here, though, is that interpolation only works inside DOUBLE quotes. Single quotes will simply escape every special character in the string and treat it like a normal letter (so the pound-curly-braces has no special meaning):

```
irb> my_name = "Tiny Tim"
=> "Tiny Tim"
```

```
irb> my_string = 'My name is #{my_name}!'
=> "My name is \#{my_name}!" # That's not what we wanted!
```

to_s is a method that will try to convert anything into a string, This method gets called a lot, anytime Ruby is outputting or rendering something (like a variable), it will call to_s on it to make it a nice friendly string first.

```
irb> 12345.to_s
=> "12345"
```

Combining Strings can be done using "concatenation", or basically just adding them together:

```
irb> my_name = "Tiny Tim"
irb> "hello" + " world" + ", say I, the great " + my_name + "!"
# => "hello world, say I, the great Tiny Tim!"
```

Instead of adding them with a plus +, you can also use the friendly shovel operator '<<' to append to a string (just like with arrays...):

```
irb> "hello " << "there"
=> "hello there
```

Symbols

Symbols are used a lot in Ruby, they are denoted with the colon before the name, e.g. :my_symbol instead of "my_string" The truth of the matter is that Symbols are Strings, just with an important difference, Symbols are immutable. A string is Mutable, meaning it can be added to. Whenever you have text that you want to play around with or use as regular text, just stick with strings.

But sometimes all you want is a name, like when you're using a hash key. In that case, it makes sense to use symbols. Symbols are immutable, so they don't change. They are also only stored in memory in one place, where as strings have a new place in memory each time you declare one:

```
> "hello".object_id
=> 70196107337380
> "hello".object_id
=> 70196107320960 # different
```

```
> :hello.object_id
=> 461128
> :hello.object_id
=> 461128 # same!
```

Iterations

A loop is really just code that will run a number of times until some condition is met. loop takes a block of code, denoted by either {...} or do... end (if it's over multiple lines):

```
i=0
while i < 5 do
print "#{i} "
i+=1
end
```

Things get more interesting when you realise that most of your loops will probably involve looping over each element in either an array or a hash of items. Ruby knows this and made it easy for you by specifying the #each method that you call directly on that array or hash. #each will automatically pass whichever item it is currently on into your code block. That item will be named whatever name you specify between the the pipes |..|:

```
guys = ["Bob", "Billy", "Joe"]
guys.each do |current_name|
print "#{current_name}! "
end
```

Parameters in loops

Parameters created in a loop are still accessible outside it:

```
i=0
while i < 5
print "#{i} "
i+=1
y=6
end
print "#{y}"
```

The blocks used by iterators (such as loop and each) are a little different. Normally, the local variables created in these blocks are not accessible outside the block.

Dates/Times

Ruby uses the Time class to let you work with dates and times, giving you some handy methods to find out about specific parts (like what day of the week it is) and to allow you to display them in a user-friendly fashion. To get the current time you just create a new Time object with no parameters or use Time.now, which is the same thing.

Use localtime to display the Time object in whatever your local system time is.

Time.utc returns Coordinated Universal Time (UTC) is used to synchronise time across internet networks.

Conditionals and flow control

You'll need to understand which types of things Ruby considers "true" and which ones it considers "false". In Ruby, it's simple: nil and false are 'false' and that's it. Everything else is 'true'.

'and' is the same as && but with lower precedence.

```
d = 1 && 2 && 3
puts "D is #{d}"
=> 3
e = 1 and 2 and 3
puts "E is #{e}"
E is 1
```

&& has more precedence than =, thus evaluated result is assigned to 'd'

'and' has less precedence than =, thus value of 'a' is directly assigned to 'e' which gets printed

Arrays

You'll be working with them all the time to help store data. Arrays begin life as empty containers waiting to be filled with objects or data. As items are added, they stay in whatever spot you put them, which is good because then you know exactly where to find them later. You can put anything in an array, Numbers, strings, objects, symbols.

Creating an Array can happen in many different ways. You can either create it empty, specify how many spaces it should have (still empty), or even fill it with default values:

```
> a = Array.new
=> [] # it's empty
> b = []
=> [] # still empty
> c = Array[]
=> []
> d = %w{ I am in london } # converts the string to an array
=> [ "I", "am", "in", "london" ]
> empty_array = Array.new(5)
=> [nil, nil, nil, nil, nil]
> simple_array = Array.new(3, "hi")
=> ["hi", "hi", "hi"]
```

And remember, you can store pretty much anything in there, even other arrays:

```
>complex_array = [1, 4, 8, "hello", simple_array]
=> [1, 4, 8, "hello", ["hi", "hi", "hi"]]
```

Accessing Items is easy, just start from 0

```
> arr = [1, 3, 5, 7, 2]
=> [1, 3, 5, 7, 2]
> arr[0]
=> 1
> arr[-1]
=> 2
> arr[1..3]
=> [3, 5, 7] # this returned an array!
> arr.slice(1..3)
=> [3, 5, 7] # same as using [1..3]
```

Modifying Items is as simple as accessing them is... just set them equal to a value:

```
> arr[0] = 42
=> 42
> arr
=> [42, 3, 5, 2] # changed it
> arr[0..2] = 99
=> 99
> arr
=> [99, 7, 2] # wiped out several values
```

What if you only want to add or subtract one single value? That's a very common operation with arrays, and Ruby has provided four handy methods that let you either pluck away or add onto the front or back of the array. First, the more common is to add or remove stuff from the END of the array, using #push or #pop:

```
> my_arr = [1,2,3]
=> [1,2,3]
> my_arr.push(747)
=> [1, 2, 3, 747]
> my_arr
=> [1, 2, 3, 747]
> my_arr.pop
=> 747
> my_arr.pop
=> 3
> my_arr
=> [1, 2]
```

The Shovel Operator, '<<' method is almost identical to push, since it just adds whatever's to its right into the array:

```
> my_arr = [1,2,3]
=> [1,2,3]
> my_arr << 3
=> [1, 2, 3, 3]
> my_arr << [4,5]
=> [1, 2, 3, 3, 4, 5]
```

Deleting Items from an array should be done carefully because, if you're deleting items inside a loop or something like that, it will change the index of the other items and you'll need to anticipate this or live to regret it. Delete an item at a specific index using #delete_at, which is sort of like popping but from anywhere you want:

```
> my_arr = [1,2,3]
=> [1, 2, 3]
> my_arr.delete_at(1)
=> 2
> my_arr
=> [1,3]
```

If you want to clear out the whole array, you can use #clear or, more easily, just set it equal to []:

```
> my_arr = [1,3,5]
```

```
=> [1,3,5]
> my_arr.clear
=> []
```

See if an array includes an item at all by using #include?, which, as you should see from the ? at the end, returns true or false:

```
> my_arr.include?(3)
=> true
> my_arr.include?(132)
=> false
```

To find where a specific item lives in the array, use #index but note that it only returns the first instance of this:

```
> [1,2,3,4,5,6,7,3,3,3,3,3].index(3)
=> 2 # Just the index of the first match
```

Strings are a lot like arrays, so much so that we can even convert an Array into a String, Just use #join and tell it what, if anything, you want in between each element (the "separator"):

```
> ["he", "llo"].join
=> "hello"
```

Hashes

Hashes may be a bit intimidating at first but they're actually pretty similar to arrays. They're basically just containers for data, like arrays, but instead of storing data based on numeric indices, you use "keys" which can be strings or symbols. This makes hashes more appropriate for storing data with a bit more depth to it.

A Hash is just a container for data where each piece of data is mapped to a Key. The data is called the Value. Keys can be either strings or symbols. Values can be anything, just like with arrays. A hash looks almost like an array, but with squiggly braces {} instead of hard ones [] There's no order to a hash (unlike an array)... you're accessing your data using strings anyway so it doesn't matter which order they're in. Make a new hash using several methods:

```
> my_hash = Hash.new
=> {}
or alternatively
> my_hash = {} # easier way
=> {}
```

You store data in a hash by matching a key with a value. Use the Hash Rocket => (not to be confused with the same symbol in our IRB examples which denotes the IRB output) if you're creating the hash, or just index into it like an array using hard brackets []:

```
> favorite_colours = { "eyes" => "blue", "hair" => "blonde"}
=> {"eyes"=>"blue", "hair"=>"blonde"}
> favorite_colours["eyes"]
=> "blue"
> favorite_colours["eyes"] = "green" # Changing an item
=> "green"
> favorite_colours
=> {"eyes"=>"green", "hair"=>"blonde"}
> favorite_colours["skin"] = "suburned" # Adding a new item
=> "sunburned"
> favorite_colours
=> {"eyes"=>"blue", "hair"=>"blonde", "skin"=>"sunburned"}
```

Hashes are useful for lots of reasons behind the scenes, how about a dictionary of words? Just store the words as keys and the meanings as values, if you so choose. When you're writing a program that needs to keep track of an object that has several different attributes but isn't terribly complex, a hash can be a perfect solution to avoid using a bunch of different variables to store the same data:

```
player_health = 100
player_name = "Player1"
player_speed = 7
```

or, better:

```
player = { "health" => 100, "name" => "Player1", "speed" => 7}
```

You see hashes all the time in Rails, including as a way of passing options or parameters to a method (since they can store all kinds of different things and be variably sized). Methods are often defined like:

```
def method_name arg1, arg2, arg3, options_hash
```

Allowing the user to specify any number of different parameters for that method.

Note that, when calling a method, if a hash is the last argument you are entering, you can skip the squiggly braces.

```
some_object.some_method argument1, argument2, :param1 => value1, :param2 => value2
```

Or, how about a real example from Rails, The link_to helper creates a link on the webpage and you can optionally assign it an ID and class (among other things like class and title attributes) by passing that in to the options hash:

```
link_to "click here!", "http://www.example.com", :id => "my-special-link", :class => "clickable_link"
```

This can also be written as

```
link_to "click here!", "http://www.example.com", id: "my-special-link", class: "clickable_link"
```

With Strings we use symbols as keys for hashes

```
> favorite_smells = { :flower => "rose", :cooking => "bacon" }
=> { :flower => "rose", :cooking => "bacon" }
```

Delete from a hash by just setting the value to nil or by calling the #delete method:

```
> favorite_smells[:flower] = nil
=> nil
> favorite_smells
=> {:cooking => "bacon" } # one deleted...
> favorite_smells.delete(:cooking)
=> "bacon"
> favorite_smells
=> {} #...and the other.
```

That's all pretty straightforward. What if we want to add two hashes together? Just use #merge. If there are any conflicts, the incoming hash (on the right) overrides the hash actually calling the method:

```
> favorite_beers = { :pilsner => "Peroni" }
=> { :pilsner => "Peroni" }
> favorite_colours.merge(favorite_beers)
=> {"eyes"=>"blue", "hair"=>"blonde", "skin"=>"sunburned", :pilsner => "Peroni"}
```

If you want to know what All the Keys are (more common) or All the Values are (less common) in a hash, just use the aptly named #keys and #values methods to spit them out as an array:

```
irb> favorite_colours.keys
=> ["eyes", "hair", "skin", :pilsner]
irb> favorite_colors.values
=> ["blue", "blonde", "sunburned", "Peroni"]
```

If you need a collection where the order does not matter, and the elements are guaranteed to be unique, then you probably want to use a set.

Enumerable

You've learned about Array and Hash, they each have their own methods for adding and deleting and accessing data and they both implement their own version of the #each method to iterate over their items but what makes them really powerful in Ruby is the ability to use Enumerable methods as well as the basic ones.

Reference: http://www.ruby-doc.org/core-2.1.2/Enumerator.html

"Enumerable" is actually a "module", which means it is just a bunch of methods packaged together that can (and do) get "mixed in", or included, with other classes (like Array and Hash. That means that Ruby programmers don't have to write all those methods many different times they just write them once, package them up as Enumerable, and tell Array and Hash to include them. As long as the class that wants to include Enumerable has its own #each method that Enumerable can use, it can get access to all the magic and joy of using the Enumerable methods by simply mixing it in. In this case, Enumerable contains really useful methods like #map and #each and #select.

Enumerable gives you lots of useful ways of doing something to every element of a collection object (an array or hash, for instance), which is a very common thing to do when you're building programs and websites.

#each is an iterator method that comes prepackaged with the Array and Hash and Range classes and it basically just goes through each item in the object you called it on and passes it to the block that you specified. It will return the original collection that it was called on:

```
irb> [1,2,3].each { |num| print "#{num}! " }
1! 2! 3! => [1,2,3]
```

Sometimes you also want to know what position in the array you are... so that sounds like a good chance to use Enumerable's #each_with_index, which will pass that position into the block as well:

```
> ["cool", "hot", "freeze"].each_with_index do |item, index|
> print "#{item} " if index%2==0
> end
Cool beans! => ["Cool", "freeze"]
```

What if I want to keep only the even numbers that are in an array? The traditional way would be to build some sort of loop that goes through the array, checks whether each element is even, and starts populating a temporary array that we will return at the end. It might look something like:

```
class Array
def keep_evens
result_array = []
for num in self
result_array << num if num % 2 == 0
end
return result_array
end
end
```

```
irb> my_array = [1,2,3,4,5,6,7,8,100]
irb> my_array.keep_evens
=> [2,4,6,8,100]
```

That's too much code when all you're doing is selecting certain items based on some criteria, better to use Enumerable's **#select** instead. It will run the block on every item of the object (whether array or hash or whatever) and return a new object that contains only those items for which the original block returned true:

```
irb> my_array.select{|item| item%2==0 }
=> [2,4,6,8,100] # that was easy.
```

What if instead of selecting only a few items we want to keep all items but modify them somehow? **#collect** will run your block and give you an object filled with whatever your block returned each time. Ruby has:

```
irb> my_array.collect{|num| num**2 }
=> [4,16,36,64,10000]
```

For **'map'**, It is the exact same method as collect, just called something different but 'map' is used more frequently, Collect is an alias to Map. Map and collect produce a new Array containing the results of the block applied to each element of the receiver:

Here's an example more like what you might see when you've got your own website built using Rails, where we may want to send only an array filled with our users' emails out to the webpage:

```
u = User.all
@user_emails = u.map { |user| user.email }
```

You can also use these methods on hashes as well, just remember that now you have two inputs to work with for your block:

```
irb> my_hash = {"Joe" => "male", "Pat" => "male", "Jane" => "female"}
irb> my_hash.select{|name, gender| gender == "male" }
=> {"Joe" => "male", "Pat" => "male"}
```

Up until now, all the methods we've seen run essentially independent operations on each element of our array or hash. What if we want to do something that keeps track of the result as we iterate, Like, say, summing up the elements of an array?

For that we need to use #inject (also called, #reduce), which passes not just the element but whatever was returned by the previous iteration into the block. You can either specify the initial value or it will just default to the first item of the array. It ultimately returns whatever the result of the last iteration is. Here's a way to sum an array:

```
irb>[1, 2, 3, 4].inject(0) { |result, element| result + element }
=> 10
```

Blocks, Procs, and Lambdas

One of the difficult parts of learning Ruby is understanding what blocks are and how they work. You have already seen them before... they are commonly used as inputs to some of the iterators like each or map.

Ruby Code blocks (called closures in other languages)

Blocks are just chunks of code that you can pick up and drop into another method as an input. They're often called "anonymous functions", as in javascript, because they have no name but behave much like functions. You declare a block using braces {} if it's on one line or do... end if it's on multiple lines (by convention... you can use either one.

```
>[1,2,3].each { |num| print "#{num}! " }
1! 2! 3! =>[1,2,3]
> [1,2,3].each do |num|
> print "#{num}!"
> end
1! 2! 3! =>[1,2,3] # Identical to the first case.
```

Just like methods, some blocks take inputs, others do not. Some return information, others do not. Blocks let you use the implicit return (whatever's on the last line) but not return, since that will return you from whatever method actually called the block.

Blocks are used as arguments to other methods (like #each), just like the normal arguments that you see between the parentheses... they just happen to always be listed last and on their own because they tend to take up multiple lines. Don't think of them as anything too special. The #each method isn't special either, it's just built to accept a block as an argument.

How does a method take a block then? Through the **yield** statement, which basically says "run the block right here". When you write your own methods, you don't even need to specially declare that you'd like to accept a block. It will just be there waiting for you when you call yield inside your method. If you want to ask whether a block was passed at all (to only yield in that case), use #block_given?, or rather: yield if block_given?

Blocks are code that can be implicitly passed to a method in Ruby. Any method can in fact be passed a block of code even if the method does not explicitly expect it. In the following example, the method test_blocks does not explicitly expect or do anything with a block, however, if called with a block the code will run printing "in test_blocks":

```
def test_blocks
```

```
puts "in test_blocks"
end

test_blocks { puts "in the block" }
```

Output:

```
in test_blocks
```

By simply adding the yield keyword to the method test_blocks the block will then be run causing the output to change:

```
def test_blocks
puts "in test_blocks"
yield
end

test_blocks { puts "in the block" }
```

Output:

```
in test_blocks
in the block
```

Procs

What if you want to pass two blocks to your function? What if you want to save your block to a variable so you can use it again later? That's a job for Procs. The block is sort of like a stripped-down and temporary version of a Proc that Ruby included just to make it really easy to use things like those #each iterators. A Proc is just a block that you save to a variable, thereby giving it a bit more permanence. Here is an example where we create a Proc object first and pass that into another method that expects a Proc:

```
def test_blocks(some_proc)
puts some_proc.call
end

some_new_proc = Proc.new { puts "in the Proc !" }
test_blocks(some_new_proc)

# Output:
# in the Proc !
```

another example is:

```
> my_proc = Proc.new { |arg1| print "#{arg1}! " }
```

Use that block of code (now called a Proc) as an input to a function by prepending it with an ampersand &:

```
> [1,2,3].each(&my_proc)
1! 2! 3! =>[1,2,3]
```

It's the same as passing the block like you did before.

When you create your own function to accept Proc's, you'll need to use #call instead of yield inside (because which Proc would yield run if you had more than one Proc passed in?). #call literally just runs the Proc that is called on. You can give it arguments as well to pass on to the Proc:

```
> my_proc.call("hello! ")  # note that this is the same `my_proc`
hello! => nil
```

Most of the time, using a block is more than sufficient. Once you start seeing the need for using a Proc (like passing multiple arguments or saving it for later as a callback), you'll have Procs there waiting for you.

Blocks and Procs are both a type of "closure". A **closure** is basically a formal, computer-science way of saying "a chunk of code that you can pass around but which hangs onto the variables that you gave it when you first called it". It's the blanket term used to refer to blocks and Procs and lambda's.

The main reason for having both block and Proc is:

- If we want to write Ruby like syntax when passing code to a method, and we only want to pass a single Proc we use blocks. This is very common pattern in Ruby code – especially with iterators.
- If we want to save a piece of code in a variable for reuse then use an explicit Proc object.
- If we want to pass multiple blocks of code to a method and invoke them, we also must use an explicit Proc object.

Lambda

There are two other similar closures to be aware of but about which you certainly don't need to be an expert because they're used in less typical applications. The first of these is a lambda. If Procs are sort of a more-fleshed-out version of blocks, then lambdas are sort of a more-fleshed-out version of Procs. They are one step closer to being actual methods themselves, but still technically count as anonymous functions. Lambda is very similar to a Proc. Let's first start off with an example:

```
def test_lambda(some_lambda)
some_lambda.call
end

some_new_lambda = lambda {puts "in the lambda" }
test_lambda (some_new_lambda)

# Output:
in the lambda
```

As you can see this looks exactly like the Proc example above, so what is the difference? The answer is in the way Ruby handles Procs and Lambda's. There are, in fact, two differences:

- Lambda's check the number of parameters passed into the call, Procs do not check the number of parameters.
- Lambda's return from the executing block but not from the lexically surrounding method call when they encounter a return keyword (in other words lambda behaves like calling a method which then calls return, whereas a Proc will return from the calling method too).

Here are a couple of examples to illustrate this. Firstly, the parameter handling differences:

```
def test_parameter_handling(code)
code.call(1,2)
end

l = lambda {|a,b,c| puts "#{a} is a #{a.class}, #{b} is a #{b.class}, #{c} is a #{c.class}" }
p = Proc.new {|a,b,c| puts "#{a} is a #{a.class}, #{b} is a #{b.class}, #{c} is a #{c.class}" }

test_parameter_handling (p)
```

output:

```
1 is a Fixnum, 2 is a Fixnum, is a NilClass
test_parameter_handling (1)
```

output:

```
ArgumentError: wrong number of arguments (2 for 3)
```

As you can see from the output of the example, the Proc does not care if we only call with two parameters when it's possible to use three parameters – it simply sets all unused parameters to nil. However, when passing a lambda to the method, Ruby throws an ArgumentError instead. So if you want your Proc (a lamdba is an instance of Proc, by the way) to be called with a specific set of parameters – no more and no less – then use lamdba.

Here is an example that demonstrates the differences how Proc and lambda behave when they encounter a return statement:

```
def return_using_proc
Proc.new { return "Hi from proc!"}.call
puts "end of proc call"
end
def return_using_lambda
lambda {return "Hi from lambda!"}.call
puts "end of lambda call"
end

puts return_using_proc
# Hi from proc!
puts return_using_lambda
# end of lambda call
```

When return_using_proc is called the method stops processing as soon as it encounters the return statement and we see "Hi from proc!" output. When return_using_lambda is called the return is encountered but does not cause the method to return and instead the method continues to run so we see "end of lambda call" output.

From ruby 1.9 there is a new shorter syntax for lambda:

- Ruby < 1.9
  ```
  p = lambda {a+b+c}
  p = lambda {|a,b,c| a+b+c}
  ```

- Ruby >= 1.9
  ```
  p = -> {a+b+c}
  p = -> a,b,c {a+b+c}
  ```

- Ruby < 1.9
  ```
  twice = lambda {|x| 2 * x }
  twice.call(5)
  # => 10
  ```

- Ruby >= 1.9
  can can written as
  ```
  twice = -> (x) { 2 * x }
  twice.call(5)
  # => 10
  ```

Just to focus on the differences between lambdas and Procs, a lambda acts more like a real method. What does that mean?

- A lambda gives you more flexibility with what it returns (like if you want to return multiple values at once) because you can safely use the explicit return statement inside of one.
- With lambdas, return will only return from the lambda itself and not the enclosing method, which is what happens if you use return inside a block or Proc.
- Lambda's are also much stricter than Procs about you passing them the correct number of arguments (you'll get an error if you pass the wrong number).

Blocks are unnamed little code chunks you can drop into other methods. Used all the time.

Procs are identical to blocks but you can store them in variables, which lets you pass them into functions as explicit arguments and save them for later. Used explicitly sometimes.

Lambdas are really full methods that just haven't been named. Used rarely.

Closure is just the umbrella term for all four of those things, which all somehow involve passing around chunks of code.

Functional programming

Functional programming is becoming more popular in part due to Scala, Clojure and Java 8. A major building block of functional programming is closures. Functional code is characterised by one thing: the absence of side effects. It doesn't rely on data outside the current function, and it doesn't change data that exists outside the current function. This is important in concurrent multi processor architecture.

In Ruby, a string is an array of characters. Characters in a string can be changed individually. For instance you can change a semicolon character in a string to a period inside the same string object. In Java and Scala, on the other hand, a string is a sequence of characters in the mathematical sense. Replacing a character in a string using an expression like s.replace(';', '.') gives a new string object, which is different from s. Another way of expressing this is that strings are immutable in Java. whereas they are mutable in Ruby. So looking at just strings, Java is a functional language, whereas Ruby is not. Immutable data structures are one of the cornerstones of functional programming.

Ruby closures

It's important to note that blocks, Procs and lambdas are all closures. Basically this means that they hold the values of any variables that were around when they were created. This is a very powerful feature of Ruby because if we wrap creating a block of code in a method call we can dynamically create different behaviour. For example:

```ruby
def create_multiplier(m)
lambda {|val| val * m}
end

two_times = create_multiplier(2)
three_times = create_multiplier(3)
puts two_times.call(1)
puts three_times.call(1)
```

Output:

```
2
3
```

Object orientated Programming

Object-Oriented Programming refers to a programming methodology based on objects, instead of just functions and procedures. These objects are organised into classes.

SOLID

It is good to be aware of the S.O.L.I.D. principles of design. SOLID is a set of five guiding principles that help developers design objects that are easy to maintain and use.

The Single Responsibility Principle

Single responsibility is the concept of a Class doing one specific thing (responsibility) and not trying to do more than it should.

The Open Closed Principle

Software entities (classes, modules, functions, etc.) should be open for extension, but closed for modification. "Open to extension" means that you should design your classes so that new functionality can be added as new requirements are generated. "Closed for modification" means that once you have developed a class you should never modify it, except to correct bugs. The reason behind this is that changing the code will mean that everything depending upon it will need to be retested as well.

The Liskov Substitution Principle

All this really means is that objects in a program should be replaceable with instances of their sub classes without altering the correctness of that program. In Ruby, the Liskov principle (LSP) works slightly differently because Ruby less rigidly enforces how types work (so-called **"Duck Typing"**) as opposed to a language like Java, where type safety is enforced by the compiler. If an object walks like a duck and talks like a duck, then the Ruby interpreter is happy to treat it as if it were a duck.

For example, if class "elephant" is a subtype of class "animal," then you should be able to use "elephant" where you use "animal," and the "walk" method of an elephant or animal will still "walk" (even though the implementation may be different), the "numberOfLegs" property will still return the number of legs (though again, it may be a different number from the base class), the "eat" method will not throw any exceptions that it would not throw in the "animal" class, and so on. It is much easier to make changes and test when you follow LSP.

A typical example that violates LSP is a Square class that derives from a Rectangle class. The Square class always assumes that the width is equal with the height. If a Square object is used in a context where a Rectangle is expected, unexpected behaviour may occur because the dimensions of a Square cannot (or rather should not) be modified independently.

in Ruby we don't declare the types of variables or methods - everything is just some kind of object. we rely less on the type (or class) of an object and more on its capabilities. Hence, Duck Typing means an object type is defined by what it can do, not by what it is. Duck Typing refers to the tendency of Ruby to be less concerned with the class of an object and more concerned with what methods can be called on it and what operations can be performed on it, or might simply pass an object to a method and know that an exception will be raised if it is used inappropriately.

Note: respons_to? is a Ruby method for detecting whether the class has a particular method on it. For example:

```
@member.respond_to?('upload_image')
```

Would return true if the Member class has an upload_image method on it.

The Interface Segregation Principle

This dictates that interfaces need to have as little functionality in them as possible. This allows the consumer to only deal with the functionality they are concerned with, which reduces testing needs and the impact of changes to the system.

Say, you have a class A and a class B, which is the client of class A. Suppose, class A has ten methods, of which only two are used by B. Now, does B need to know about all ten methods of A? Probably not - the principle of Information hiding. The more you expose, the more you create the chance for coupling. For that reason, you may insert an interface, call it C, between the two classes (segregation). That interface will only declare the two methods that are used by B, and B will depend on that Interface, instead of directly on A.

For example, if you have a class that has two objects using it:

```
class Car
def open
end
def start_engine
end
def change_engine
end
end

class Driver
def drive
@car.open
@car.start_engine
end
end

class Mechanic
def do_stuff
@car.change_engine
end
end
```

As you can see, our Car class has an interface that's used partially by both the Driver and the Mechanic. We can improve our interface like so:

```
class Car
def open
end

def start_engine
end
end

class CarInternals
def change_engine
end
end
```

```
class Driver
def drive
@car.open
@car.start_engine
end
end

class Mechanic
def do_stuff
@car_internals.change_engine
end
end
```

By splitting the interface into two, we can comply to the ISP.

The Dependency Inversion Principle

High-level objects are abstracted away from low-level objects. For example, let's say that you want to query a database and fill a data set. The temptation is to pass in the database connection information to the data set and let it make the connection. Instead, you pass in a connection that is already configured, and in this way, the database can change without needing to retest the entire data set object.

Inheritance

Inheritance is a core object orientated term. In Ruby, a class inherits from another class using the '<' notation. Unlike some other languages, a class can only have one parent.

Inheritance is the ability of one class to be a child of another class and therefore inherit all its characteristics, including methods and variables.

(Ruby 1.9 introduced BasicObject as Object's superclass.)

```
Class < Module < Object < BasicObject
```

An interesting exercise to try in Ruby is to use the method ::superclass to ask a class what its parent is. If you just keep on going and going, you'll see that everything eventually inherits from BasicObject, which originates most of the methods you have access to in the original object:For instance the number 1 is a class FixNum which inherits from Integer which inherits from Numeric which inherits from Object which inherits from BasicObject.

```
irb> 1.class.superclass
=> Integer
irb> 1.class.superclass.superclass
=> Numeric
irb> 1.class.superclass.superclass.superclass
=> Object
irb> 1.class.superclass.superclass.superclass.superclass
=> BasicObject
```

Or as we will later discuss exceptions:

```
irb>ZeroDivisionError.superclass
=> StandardError
irb>ZeroDivisionError.superclass.superclass
=> Exception
ZeroDivisionError.superclass.superclass.superclass
=> Object
> BasicObject.methods
=> # giant list of methods
```

Another example of using the parent method's in an inherited class.

```
class Mammal
def breathe
puts "inhale and exhale"
end
end

class Cat < Mammal
def speak
puts "Meow"
end
end

buddy= Cat.new
buddy.breathe
buddy.speak
```

Cat was defined as a subclass of Mammal. The subclass is sometimes also known as a derived or child class and the super-class as base or parent class). Cat will basically have the following inheritance hierarchy (the superclass links):

```
Cat < Mammal < Object < BasicObject
```

The reason to do all this inheritance is to keep our code as DRY as possible. It let's us not have to repeat a bunch of methods (say, #to_s, which is implemented in the Object class) for every different subclass. DRY - Don't Repeat Yourself is a common term used to basically mean to reuse as much code as possible, less code means less potential bugs.

There will be situations where certain properties of the super-class should not be inherited by a particular subclass. Though birds generally know how to fly, penguins are a flightless subclass of birds. you cannot say you only want to inherit some public methods and not other public methods. In this example we can override the fly method:

```
class Bird
def preen
puts "I am cleaning my feathers."
end
def fly
puts "I am flying."
end
end

class Penguin < Bird
def fly
puts "Sorry. I'd rather swim."
end
end

p = Penguin.new
p.preen
p.fly
```

Inheritance and instance variables

You can declare variable inside an instance of a class using @ which is only only used in this particular instance of the class:

```
class Dog
def initialize(breed)
@breed = breed
end

def to_s
"(#@breed, #@name)"
end
end
```

```
class Lab < Dog
def initialize(breed, name)
super(breed)
@name = name
end
end
```

Note:. to_s is called implicitly with any puts, print or p method.

```
puts Lab.new("Labrador", "Max").to_s
```

When you invoke **super()** with arguments, Ruby sends a message to the parent of the current object, asking it to invoke a method of the same name as the method invoking super - initialise in this case. super sends exactly those arguments.

The to_s method in class Lab references @breed variable from the super-class Dog. This code works as you probably expect it to:

```
puts Lab.new("Labrador", "Max").to_s
==> (Labrador, Max)
```

Because this code behaves as expected, you may be tempted to say that these variables are inherited. That is not how Ruby works. If a subclass uses an instance variable with the same name as a variable used by one of its ancestors, it will overwrite the value of its ancestor's variable.

Composition

Composition and Inheritance are ways to reuse code to get additional functionality. In Inheritance, a new class, which wants to reuse code, inherit an existing class, known as super class. This new class is then known as sub class. On composition, a class, which wants to use the functionality of an existing class, doesn't inherit, instead it holds a reference of that class in a member variable.

Favour composition over inheritance is a one of the popular object oriented design principle, which helps to create flexible and maintainable code. one of the disadvantage of Inheritance is that it breaks encapsulation. If sub class is depending on super class behaviour for its operation, it suddenly becomes fragile. Composition offers better testability of a class than Inheritance. If one class is composed of another class, you can easily create Mock Object representing composed class for sake of testing.

This is a general known rule of thumb: if the relationship is "is-a" - use inheritance, and if the relationship is "has-a" - use composition. But this is not always the case, you may think that a ThickBorderedRectangle is-a Rectangle, which seems reasonable at first sight, and decide to use inheritance. But this situation is better described saying that a Rectangle has-a Border, which may or may not be a ThickBorder. In this case he would better prefer composition. In the same fashion, one may think that a ThickBorder is-a special Border and use inheritance; but it's better to say that a Border has-a width, hence preferring composition.

Using inheritance:One of the strengths of OOP languages is the use of inheritance or subclassing whereby we create our own specialised classes from abstract or parent classes to incorporate more advanced functionality by overriding the methods of the super class it inherits from. an example of inheritance:

```
class Vehicle
def start_engine
# start the engine
end

def stop_engine
#stop the engine
end
end

class Car < Vehicle
def sunday_drive
start_engine
stop_engine
end
end
```

If we look at the Vehicle example before, we see that it works for any type of transport which has an engine. But how do you deal with new types of vehicles which may not have an engine? If we were to continue to use the Vehicle superclass, we would still inherit the start and stop engine methods for vehicles without any engines. Although you could override them to return nil it is still not the best practice.

This is the subtle point of having an inheritance hierarchy – the subclasses are tied to the parent class which means changes made to the parent will be rippled through to the sub-classes.

Using composition: A more rational way would be to break out the engine functionality into a new class of its own and include it within the subclasses that need it such as a Car.

This is known as composition whereby you build up the functionality of a class through other classes. A revised code of the Car class can be as follows:

```
class Engine
def initialize
# set engine properties here etc
end

# other engine methods
end

class Car < Vehicle
def initialize
@engine = Engine.new
end

def sunday_drive
start_engine
stop_engine
end

def start_engine
@engine.start
end

def stop_engine
@engine.stop
end
```

Method visibility : public, private, protected

All class methods can be tagged as public, private or protected to determine which other classes may call them. By default, all your methods in Ruby classes are public - accessible by anyone except the initialize method for any class.

The concept of private, protected and public methods in Ruby is somewhat different than it is for languages like Java. In Java if a method is declared private, it can only be accessed from other methods in the same class. When a method is declared protected it can be accessed by other classes in the same package as well as by subclasses of its class in a different package. When a method is public it is – of course – always visible to everyone. So in essence with Java, these keywords protect the various members from access by classes, depending on where these classes are in the inheritance/package hierarchy.

In Ruby, the inheritance hierarchy or the package/module does not really enter into the equation, it is rather all about which object is the receiver of a particular method call.

Private methods in Ruby are accessible from children. You can't have truly private methods in Ruby; you can't completely hide a method.

Those private methods will be available in the child class just like they are in the parent. Remember, Ruby's only concern is how the method is called, not who's receiving the call.

Public

Public methods can be called by everyone - no access control is enforced. A class's instance methods (these do not belong only to one object; instead, every instance of the class can call them) are public by default; anyone can call them. The initialize method is always private.

Private

Private methods can be called only in the context of the current object; you cannot invoke another object's private methods. Private methods can only be called with implicit receiver. As soon as you specify a receiver, even using 'self' then your call will be rejected.

```ruby
class A
def public_method
private_method
end

def other_public_method
self.private_method
end

private
def private_method
"I'm private"
end
end
```

```
A.new.public_method
=> "I'm private"

A.other.public_method
```

```
=> NoMethodError: private method `private_method' called for
#<A:0x007fc40297e730>
```

```
A.new.other_public_method
=> NoMethodError: private method `private_method' called for
#<A:0x101538a20>
```

Protected

Protected methods can be called implicitly or explicitly, as long as the receiver is 'self' or of the same class as self. This is useful when you need to compare two objects on private attributes.

```
class ClassAccess
def m1 # this method is public
end
protected
def m2 # this method is protected
end
private
def m3 # this method is private
end
end
```

```
>ca = ClassAccess.new
>ca.m1
=> nil
```

```
ca.m2
>NoMethodError: protected method `m2' called for
#<ClassAccess:0x00000102048668>
```

```
ca.m3
>NoMethodError: private method `m3' called for
#<ClassAccess:0x00000102048668>
```

Another example: Private methods cannot be called with an explicit receiver. They can be called only in the defining class and by direct descendents within that same object. So what is an explicit receiver?

```
class Foo
private
def name
"Who is calling me? #{<span>self.class</span>}"
end
end

class Bar < Foo
def call_parent_method_name
# implicit receiver
puts name
# explicit receiver
puts self.name rescue puts 'NoMethodError'
# explicit receiver
puts Foo.new.name rescue puts 'NoMethodError'
end
end

Bar.new.call_parent_method_name
```

Output:

```
Who is calling me? Bar
NoMethodError
NoMethodError
```

The problem is that any access to a private method from outside the object context where it was defined, such as the two last calls made by an explicit receiver, will put Ruby complaining about that. By changing the private access of "name" method to a protected access, all the calls will output successfully.

Another example: Protected methods are similar to private methods and can only be called within the class in which they're defined. Protected methods are slightly different from private methods because they can be called with an explicit receiver, but only when the explicit receiver equals self. The following example highlights this subtle difference:

```
class A
def aaa
self.bbb
end

private
def bbb
'bbb'
end
end

# raises an exception because an explicit receiver is used

A.new.aaa
```

Output:

```
=> NoMethodError: private method 'bbb' called
```

Another example:

```
class A
def aaa
self.bbb
end

protected
def bbb
'bbb'
end
end

# doesn't raise an exception because the explicit receiver is self
A.new.aaa
```

Output:

```
'bbb'
An exception is raised when A#bbb is called with an explicit
receiver other than self, similar to private
A.new.bbb
# => NoMethodError: protected method `bbb' called
```

The send() method can be used to easily bypass private and protected methods and call them with explicit receivers. The public_send() method is similar to dot notation and will raise an exception if a private method is called.

```
class House
private
def something
'something'
end
end

h = House.new
h.send(:something) # => "something"
h.public_send(:something) # => NoMethodError: private method
`something' called
```

Design patterns

Design patterns are, by principle, well-thought out solutions to programming problems. It is a template that has to be implemented in the correct situation. It is not language-specific either. A good design pattern should be implementable in most—if not all—languages, depending on the capabilities of the language. The famous book, Design Patterns: Elements of Reusable Object-Oriented Software, make the design pattern concept popular. There are tens of patterns used, some of the more popular are MVC, singleton, factory. for example:

Singleton

The singleton pattern defines a class that can only have one instance of itself and provides global access to that one instance, which means it can be accessed in all parts of your system. The rationale behind this pattern is that there may be only one unique object of a class in your application space, for instance a logger and it does not make sense to instantiate new instances of that class every time you need access to it. Ruby has a built-in Singleton module in the standard library which allows you to create a singleton from a given class just by including it:

```
require 'singleton'
```

```
class MyClass
attr_accessor :data
include Singleton
end

a = MyClass.instance
b = MyClass.instance

#both a and b point to the same object

a.data=123
p b.data #also prints out 123
```

Modules

Modules are a way of grouping together some methods variables and classes, but a module is not really a class. You can't instantiate a Module, and thus it does not have self, there's no form of hierarchy of inheritance for modules, they are standalone.

To use modules with classes, you have to specify that you want the functionality of a particular module to be added to the functionality of a class, or of a specific object by "mixing" it in. Modules are a good place to collect all of your constants in a central location. Typically you use modules to define common methods that could be included in other class definitions.

But modules in Ruby could also be used just to group methods into some namespace. So your example in Ruby would be (module is named as Module1 as Module is standard Ruby constant):

```
# module1.rb
module Module1
def self.helloworld(name)
puts "Hello, #{name}"
end
end
# main.rb
require "./module1"
Module1.helloworld("Jim")
```

If a module is defined in a separate file, then it is required to include that file using require statement before embedding module in a class.

Mixins

If a class mixes in a module, that module's instance methods become available as if they had been defined in the class. They get mixed in. Ruby does not support multiple inheritance directly but Ruby Modules have another good use, they pretty much eliminate the need for multiple inheritance, providing a facility called a **mixin**. Example:

```
module A
def a1
puts 'a1 is called'
end
end

module B
def b1
puts 'b1 is called'
end
end

class Test
include A
include B
def display
puts 'Modules are included'
end
end

object=Test.new
object.display
object.a1
object.b1

Output:
Modules are included
a1 is called
b1 is called
```

Module A consists of the method a1. Module B consists of the method b1. The class Test includes both modules A and B. The class Sample can access all four methods, namely, a1, a2, b1, and b2. Therefore, you can see that the class Test inherits from both the modules. Thus, you can say the class Test shows multiple inheritance or a mixin.

Threads

Every time you execute Ruby, Rails or IRB, you are creating a process. The memory space where a given application is executed is called a process. Within this process the thing that is really executing is the thread. The key difference is that processes are fully isolated from each other, threads share (heap) memory with other threads running in the same application. That's why it is more economical to have threads than processes in terms of memory. Threads can directly communicate with other threads of the process.

Note: This gem http://rubydoc.info/gems/thread/0.1.4/frames, adds various extensions to the thread library.

Your operating system starts every process with a "main" thread. Ruby allows you to create as many additional threads as you want by calling Thread.new with a block of code to be executed. Once the block of code has finished executing, the thread is considered dead. If the main thread exits, the process dies:

```
t1 = Thread.new do
i = 0
1_000_000.times do
i += 1
end
end

t2 = Thread.new do
j = 0
1_000_000.times do
j += 1
end
end
t1.join
t2.join
```

Above we have two threads independently counting up to one million, while the main thread waits for them to finish by calling join on each thread. These two threads will execute concurrently ("operating or occurring at the same time") with your process's main thread.

You could have synchronisation issues if you share variables, Threads have such a terrible reputation because locks are very painful to use in practice. Store this file as:threading.rb:

```
i = 0
t1 = Thread.new do
1_000_000.times do
i += 1
end
end
t2 = Thread.new do
1_000_000.times do
i += 1
end
end
t1.join
t2.join
puts i
```

You'd expect the result to print "2000000", right? One of the features of threads is that they are controlled by the operating system; the operating system can decide to stop Thread 1 and start executing Thread 2 at any point in time. This means that the operating system can stop your thread after it has read the value of 'i' into a register.

```
> ruby threading.rb
1330864
```

You make sure only one thread modifies a variable at a time use a Mutex. Mutex is short for "mutual exclusion" as in "only one thread can be executing this code at a time"

```
@mutex = Mutex.new
@mutex.synchronize do
i += 1
end
```

Only one thread can be in the synchronize block at a time, we won't have any problems with race conditions; the Mutex effectively makes the increment atomic (an atomic operation must be performed entirely or not performed at all).

MRI is not particularly suited to high concurrency applications - threads running in parallel; JRuby is a better choice. Other languages like Clojure or Erlang were designed with concurrency as a language feature right from the start. The Clojure language mandates transactional memory for all variable changes. Scala and Erlang offer Actors. Using plain old threads and locks is akin to writing in assembly language: there are better ways now.

Multi-threading is not a usual reason to choose Ruby, there are other languages better suited for this.

Even though we have native threads since Ruby 1.9, only one thread will be executing at any given time, even if we have multiple cores in our processor. This is because of the GIL (Global Interpreter Lock) or GVL (Global VM Lock) that MRI Ruby (JRuby and Rubinius do not have a GIL, and, as such, have "real" threads) uses.

Global Interpreter Lock is a mechanism used in computer language interpreters to synchronize the execution of threads so that only one thread can execute at a time. An interpreter which uses GIL will always allow exactly one thread to execute at a time, even if run on a Multi-core processor This prevents other threads from being executed if one thread is already being executed by Ruby. Use of a Global Interpreter Lock in a language effectively limits the amount of parallelism reachable through concurrency of a single interpreter process with multiple threads. The reasons for employing such a lock include:

- increased speed of single-threaded programs (no necessity to acquire or release locks on all data structures separately).
- easy integration of C libraries that usually are not thread-safe.
- ease of implementation (having a single GIL is much simpler to implement than a lock free interpreter or one using fine grained locks).

config.threadsafe! what does it do?

The Rails framework was originally designed to process one request at a time. The framework is gradually moving away from this design towards a thread safe implementation that allows for concurrent processing of requests in a single Ruby process. Rails 4 is now config.threadsafe, until Rails 4, the core framework didn't enable concurrent request handling by default. And even in Rails 4, concurrent request handling is multiplexed on a single CPU core, leaving Rails unable to take advantage of the parallelism of modern architectures. Let's take a look at the threadsafe! method:

```
def threadsafe!
  @preload_frameworks = true
  @cache_classes = true
  @dependency_loading = false
  @allow_concurrency = true
  self
end
```

Calling this method sets four options in our app configuration.

- preload_frameworks - load up the Rails framework up before any threads are ready to handle requests.
- cache_classes - Remember when you're doing "TDD" in your application? You modify a controller, then reload the page to "test" it and see that things changed? Ya, that's what this option controls. In production, we know that classes aren't going to be modified on the fly, so doing the work to figure out whether or not to reload classes is just wasting resources, so it makes sense to never reload class definitions.
- dependency_loading - Disabling this option in production because code loading is not threadsafe, and we expect to have all code loaded before any threads can handle requests.
- allow_concurrency - This option controls whether or not the Rack::Lock middleware is used in your stack. Rack::Lock wraps a mutex around your request. The idea being that if you have code that is not threadsafe, this mutex will prevent multiple threads from executing your controller code at the same time. When threadsafe! is set, this middleware is removed, and controller code can be executed in parallel.

Threaded Alternatives to MRI

JRuby does allow for parallel processing of requests across CPU's, but some gems often (unfortunately) still make the simplifying assumption that there's only ever a single request in the Rails process, and thus they are not safe for use in a concurrent environment.

If you are running a production server which allows for concurrency, such as Puma, you must ensure all your code is thread safe. This includes all gem dependencies of your application. You should do an investigation of every gem included in your project to see if it is thread safe. Not all Ruby code is threadsafe and it can be difficult to determine if your code and all of the libraries you are using can be run across multiple threads. Once all gems have been evaluated, the next step should be to look into your own project code. Go through your application and look for any shared code, such as:

```
Class Variables
Constants
Global Variables
```

If you run a web server such as Unicorn, even if your application is set to be thread safe, all requests will still run in isolation. Each worker process only runs a single thread at a time.

Fibers

Fibers are lightweight concurrency elements that are much lighter than threads. Basically they are a means of creating code blocks that can be paused and resumed, much like threads. The main difference is that they are never preempted and that the scheduling must be done by the programmer and not the VM. When a fiber is created it will not run automatically. Rather it must be be explicitly asked to run using the Fiber#resume method.

```
fiber = Fiber.new do |first|
second = Fiber.yield first + 2
end
>puts fiber.resume 10
12
>puts fiber.resume 14
16
```

Background jobs

The delegation of long running, computationally expensive and high latency jobs to a background (asynchronously) worker queue is a common pattern used to create scalable web applications. Isolated longer running jobs can be handled by a separate worker pool that can scale independently. To process background jobs, for example to send customer emails once a day, it is best to outsource the job to a dedicated tool such as Sidekiq or Resque. This gives more flexibility than starting internal threads. Sidekiq is better than Resque for performance and the GUI monitoring panel but requires thread-safety of your code and all dependencies. A gem such as foreman, http://ddollar.github.io/foreman/, can start the background processes.

How Resque jobs work with Redis

Resque's real power comes with Redis NoSQL key-value store. Resque uses Redis to store it's job queues. Redis is installed as it's own server. Resque leans on the Redis list datatype, with each queue name as a key, and a list as the value. Jobs are enqueued (the

Redis RPUSH command to push onto the right side of the list) on the list, and workers dequeue a job (LPOP to pop off the left side of the list) to process it.

As these operations are atomic, queuers and workers do not have to worry about locking and synchronizing access. Data structures are not nested in Redis, and each element of the list (or set, hash, etc.) must be a string.

Redis does not use SQL to inspect its data, instead having its own command set to read and process the keys. It provides a command-line interface, redis-cli, to interactively view and manipulate the dataset.

Resque stores a job queue in a redis list named "resque:queue:name", and each element is the list is a hash serialized as a JSON string. Redis also has its own management structures, including a "failed" job list.

Redis-cli is the command line interface to talk with Redis. Some commands are:

```
$ redis-cli
redis> keys *
1) "resque:stat:processed" # <= Number of jobss successfully processed
2) "resque:failed" # <= This is the failed job list (not a queue)
3) "resque:queue:myqueue" # <= This is your work queue!
4) "resque:queues" # <= The "Set" of work queues
5) "resque:stat:failed" # <= The number of failed jobs
6) "resque:workers" # <= Set of workers
7) "resque:worker:host.example.com:79163:myqueue:started" # <= Count of jobs processed by worker
8) "resque:processed:host.example.com:79163:myqueue:started" # <= Timestamp of worker start
redis> get resque:stat:processed # <= Returns the count of processed jobs
"9"
redis> smembers resque:queues # <= Prints the members of the set of queues
1) "myqueue"
redis> smembers resque:workers # <= Prints the set of workers
1) "host.example.com:79163:myqueue"
```

Designed to work with Ruby on Rails, Resque jobs are submitted and processed like the following boilerplate:

```
class MyModel
@queue = :myqueue # <= jobs will be placed in this queue name
# call to queue processing in Resque until later
def defer(*args)
Resque.enqueue(MyModel, self.id, *args)
End
```

```
# Resque calls this method with the additional arguments. Must be named
#process
def self.process(id,*args)
model = MyModel.find(id)
#Do something here, raise an exception to send job to failure list
raise "Oh Noes!" if failed?
end
end
```

This does not serialise an object to the queue, instead it saved the (ActiveRecord) model name and record id which is re-instantiated from the database later. The additional arguments are saved in an array to call later. To keep the operation light, do not pass a lot of data to the job. Instead pass references to other records, files, etc.

Each job in Resque is a hash serialized as a JSON string (remember data structures can not be nested in Redis) of the format:

```
{"class":"MyModel", "args":[123, "arg1", "arg2",...]}
```

When the job is popped from the queue, Resque instantiates the ActiveRecord object and calls its process method, passing the additional parameters. Functionally, the worker code behaves something like this (simplified):

```
class, args = Rescue.reserve(queue_name)
model = class.process(*args)
```

Gems

RubyGems is a package manager for the Ruby programming language that provides a standard format for distributing Ruby programs and libraries (in a self-contained format called a "gem"). The gem command is used to build, upload, download, and install Gem packages.

```
gem update —system # Update to the latest Rubygems version
gem list —local # Listing installed gems
gem install mygem # Install a gem called, mygem
```

A gem is a packaged Ruby application or library. Every gem is different, but most follow a basic structure, The gemspec contains your gem's specification by defining several attributes.

```
gem/
|-- lib/
|   |-- gem.rb
|-- test/
|-- README
|-- Rakefile
|-- gem.gemspec
```

Making your own gem is nothing more than packaging your library or application according to the structure stated above.

Ruby code can come build as gems which you can reuse from the community, https://www.ruby-toolbox.com/ is an excellent library of gems, RubyGems.org is the Ruby community's gem hosting service. Many Ruby developers create and publish gems which address specific requirements, solve specific problems.

Whenever you create Rails application it creates a Gemfile and a Gemfile.lock file, you can create these manually for ruby project if you wish. The Gemfile in your profile contains the gems needs for your application, whenever you add new gems to your code you place it here and run

```
>bundle install
```

There is also a Gemfile.lock for each project which contains the gems from the Gemfile but with the exact version from each gem used. You can also specify th exact gem version to be used in your Gemfile, if you do not have good test coverage you could fix your versions used as upgrading a gem may break your application.

It is common for job interviewers to ask to see your projects on github, so its good practice to share your gem code on github, a Java person would not be asked for this, it is expected for Ruby person to be actively sharing with the community.

Package Your Code into Gems and Plugins

When you write code you think is general enough to be reused, think about how you can extract it into a gem suitable for a wider range of purposes. It also forces you to stop and evaluate your approach to the problem. Extracting code from an application can lead to a simpler design.

Remember, that unlike say, Java, which is more enterprise backed and stable, gems are generally written by individuals so when you upgrade to a major version of Rails these gems may not be updated anymore, forcing you to replace it totally or debug it. So be careful in the type and quantity of gems used. A topic we will dicuss later is breaking your large application into smaller services which helps to isolate issues like this.

Manage ruby versions

When you upgrade Ruby Rails, you will be left with several versions on your computer, the rvm or rbenv tool's help to specify which versions you want to use.

As of ruby 2.0. rvmrc has been deemed deprecated. You can generate two new files that will tell the project which Ruby version to use along with which gemset to use so you don't have to switch between different versions of Ruby for different projects. To accomplish this, use the command below for example:

```
rvm --create --ruby-version use ruby-2.0.0-p247@myapp
```

This will create a. ruby-version file that contains "ruby-2.0.0-p247" and a. ruby-gemset file that contains "myapp".

People have compared rvm versus rbenv to Rails[robust] versus Sinatra [lightweight].

The UNIX philosophy encourages an approach to software in which small, sharp tools are designed and used to address discrete needs. By this standard, RVM simply does too much. It is responsible not only for changing Ruby versions, but for installing rubies and managing gemsets. A gemset is a separate gem directory, so the gems in one gemset don't conflict with the gems in another gemset. Breaking these responsibilities apart and selecting a tool for each job is a good alternative to using RVM. Along with rbenv, thoughtbot [people behind many good tools https://github.com/thoughtbot] using Bundler to manage gems (replacing gemsets) and ruby-build to install rubies.

Development Tools

For writing code a text editor such as the free Mac textedit, or commercial editors such as sublime or TextMate are good enough to develop with, Sublime has lots of plugins, https://sublime.wbond.net/, to use for Ruby. A more advanced tool is Rubymine from Jet-brains [they also do a javascript IDE called Webstorm], which allows setting breakpoints, stepping through the code, and deployment. I use Rubymine to generate a database schema design from the existing rails code [I have not yet found a good tool for generating rails code directly from a schema as you can in Java].

Another tool for generating a model and controller UML class diagram is https://github.com/preston/railroady.

Rails Overview

Of all the Ruby Frameworks to make it easier to write a Web application, Ruby on Rails is the most popular and comprehensive feature set. Alternatives are:

- Rack, http://rack.github.io/, a minimal, modular, which wraps HTTP requests in the simplest way possible.
- Sinatra is another minimal framework, some people use Padrino framework on top of Sinatra.

Rails adds extra language syntax to Ruby, for example #blank? is a method provided by Rails and is not available in Ruby. Active Support is the Ruby on Rails component responsible for providing Ruby language extensions, utilities, and other transversal stuff.

Reference: http://guides.rubyonrails.org/active_support_core_extensions.html

The best way to get started is to create a Rails application, It is good at this stage to install a database, sqlite3 is the default. PostgreSQL is an open source leader, personally I prefer it to Mysql as I view it as more open source since Oracle purchased Mysql [or even it's equivalent open source alternative MariaDB].

Mysql's advantage is better Amazon Web Services (AWS) support - read replicas and it is slightly cheaper. Heroku has PostgreSQL by default and support read replica, on AWS PostgreSQL performance is slightly better than Mysql.

Environments

Rails ships with a default configuration for the three most common environments that all applications need: test, development, and production. test is for running automated tests, development when you develop the code, and production when you deploy your application. Each has a corresponding configuration file:

- config/environments/development.rb
- config/environments/production.rb

- config/environments/test.rb

In development mode Rails will reloads all app classes and turn any caching off to allow a faster development cycle. This is how the app runs on a development workstation.

In production mode all caching is turned on, often pointing to a memcached server. This is how the app runs on the live server.

The test mode is used in the tests, we have a special throw away database used only for test, wiped out between test runs.

That's a great start, and for smaller apps, probably enough too. But for larger projects, for example at Basecamp they have another three:

- **Beta:** For testing feature branches on real production data. they often run feature branches on one of our five beta servers for weeks at the time to evaluate them while placing the finishing touches. By running the beta environment against the production database, they get to use the feature as part of the daily use of Basecamp. That's the only reliable way to determine if something is genuinely useful in the long term, not just cool in the short term.
- **Staging:** This environment runs virtually identical to production, but on a backup of the production database. This is where they test features that require database migrations and time those migrations against real data sizes, so they know how to roll them out once ready to go.
- **Rollout:** When a feature is ready to go live, we first launch it to 10% of all Basecamp accounts in the rollout environment. This will catch any issues with production data from other accounts than our own without subjecting the whole customer base to a bug.

These environments all get a file in confg/environments and they're all based off the production defaults.

To run six environments like we do, you can't just rely on Rails.env.production?, checks scattered all over your code base and plugins. It's a terrible anti-pattern, https://github.com/dhh/custom_configuration/ allows you to do configuration points, It simply exposes config.x and allows you to set any key for a namespace and then any key/value pair within that. Now you can set your configuration point in the main environment configuration files and pull that data off inside your application code.

Rails 4.2 Introduced this x namespace for defining custom configuration options:

```
# config/environments/production.rb
```

```
config.x.payment_processing.schedule = :daily
config.x.payment_processing.retries = 3
config.x.super_debugger = true
```

These options are then available through the configuration object:

```
Rails.configuration.x.payment_processing.schedule # => :daily
Rails.configuration.x.payment_processing.retries # => 3
Rails.configuration.x.super_debugger # => true
```

Create a new Rails application

To create a new Rails project:

```
rails new dating —database=postgresql
```

In your config/database.yml add your database username/password:

```
development:
adapter: postgresql
encoding: unicode
database: dating_development
pool: 5
user: postgres
password: '123456'
host: localhost
```

run this command to start your application:

```
>rails server
```

Likewise for test and production, use the same username and password for the test and production databases also, you can change the production later, or as many people do is to use an environment variable for the production user/password and not to check your database.yml into your version control for security. There will be three copies of your database created for development [dating_development],test [dating_test] and production [dating_production] by default.

It is best just to study the directory and files created, Ruby Rails is a convention based framework, or opinionated, where the directories created have a standard layout.The advantage of that is that the configuration etc. is in a standard directory, compared to say Java where there is no standard.

Rails server

Ruby code can be exposed to the World-Wide-Web through one of the many available web servers. While each one of them come with unique qualities and offer different possibilities, there is one thing in common these servers share: a way (an interface) to talk with your application called Rack.

The default Rails server for a new project is WEBrick, but it is not used for production due to its poor performance under load. The most popular production Rails servers are discussed next, it is interesting AWS opsworks only has Apache2/Passenger or Nginx/Unicorn as default.

Rack

Rack is a minimal interface between web-servers that support Ruby, and Ruby frameworks. It's purpose is to act as a common interface, so that a web-server simply implements Rack and can now support any Ruby web framework that also supports Rack, and vice-versa. Many Ruby web frameworks, including Rails and Sinatra, are built on top of Rack.

Rack middleware gem, https://github.com/rack/rack, implementing the Rack specification, for receiving and transmitting HTTP requests/reponses.

Phusion passenger

Passenger is a mature, feature rich product. It eliminates the traditional middleman server set up architecture by direct integration within Apache and NGINX (front-facing) web servers. Passenger provides the ability to work with multiple applications hosted on the same server. Its open-source version has a multi-process single-threaded operation mode, whilst the Enterprise version can be configured to work either single-threaded or multi-threaded.

For enterprise users, Passenger provides some further features such as concurrency and multithreading.

Passenger is best used in situations where its unique spawning method can really shine. Passenger has the ability to kill off workers that don't have enough traffic to justify their existence (so, zero traffic) to conserve memory, and dynamically respawn them as needed. the problem with this method for large, dedicated applications is that, during periods of low traffic (during the night, for example), workers will be killed off, and then when traffic picks up in the morning, requests will hang inside Passenger while it tries to launch new worker processes in memory. There is a significant benefit for machines with multiple applications that have low to moderate traffic, Passenger 4 has multi-threaded in the paid for the Enterprise version. In short, Passenger can be great for digital agencies looking to host multiple applications on medium-sized virtual machines. Google cloud offer Passenger as their Rails server

https://developers.google.com/cloud/ruby/.

Unicorn

Unicorn is a mature web application server. Unicorn's master process spawns workers, as per your requirements, to serve the requests. Unicorn works use the operating system for load balancing. All workers run within a given isolated address space, serving one request at a time.

While Unicorn is the recommended default web server for Ruby apps running on Heroku, it may not be the best choice for your particular combination of application and workload. In particular, if your application receives requests with large body payloads from slow clients, you may be better off using a different web server. An example would be a an app that receives images uploaded by users from mobile phones that are not on wifi, 4G or other fast networks.

Unlike Passenger (even the enterprise version), Unicorn is capable of a zero downtime deploy. Unicorn is best used in situations with one specific application on a host, as it will spawn several workers as configured and maintain them at all times. Memory consumption could be a problem if you launch more workers than you have memory to reasonably support.

Unicorn's best use case is with a single, dedicated application running at all times behind a reverse proxy (nginx) and load balancer (haproxy or ELB on Engine Yard) that stick to a regular, request/response application flow cycle. It generally processes requests very fast and has a highly stable architecture. unlike Thin or Puma, Unicorn is not multi-threaded.

Puma, Thin or Rainbows! are alternative web servers that may work better under load generated by slow clients.

Puma

Puma's primary strength is that it's a truly concurrent application server. unlike Thin and Unicorn, Puma will open a new thread for each incoming request. This means that blocking actions that aren't necessarily heavy on CPU usage should not be a problem for Puma.

Puma is a fully threaded application server and like Unicorn it can run several workers pulling requests off of a centralised unix socket, or it can bind a worker to a port. Puma doesn't maintain a master process like Unicorn, however. Puma uses threads, in addition to worker processes, to make more use of available CPU. You can only utilize threads in Puma if your entire code-base is thread safe. Otherwise, you can still use Puma, but must only scale out through worker processes.

However, when discussing threading, we must constantly be aware of Ruby's Global VM Lock (GVL). This is a limitation (possibly a feature?) of the language interpreter that ensures that even when launching new threads, except in specific cases, Ruby will only execute one Ruby code instruction at a time per process. MRI can still hand off async instructions to underlying C-based drivers, for example, but as for executing actual Ruby code, the GVL ensures that only one instruction is processed at a time per each Ruby process. For this reason, Puma will run best under JRuby or Rubinius.

On MRI, there is a Global Interpreter Lock (GIL) that ensures only one thread can be run at any time. IO operations such as database calls, interacting with the file system, or making external HTTP calls will not lock the GIL. Most Rails applications heavily use IO, so adding additional threads will allow Puma to process multiple threads, gaining you more throughput. JRuby and Rubinius also benefit from using Puma. These Ruby implementations do not have a GIL and will run all threads in parallel regardless of what is happening in them.

Puma is best suited to single applications running on a host, just like Thin and Unicorn. However, because it's multi-threaded, if you run a Ruby implementation without an internal GVL (JRuby/Rubinius), you can theoretically run a single Puma process on your machine instead of one worker per core, as you generally have to for the other application servers mentioned here. This is because Puma can request a new thread from the operating system for each incoming request, drop execution of that thread while waiting on external events (disk I/O, database driver access, network I/O, etc.), pick up other threads while this is going on, and then pick up execution of the other thread after the "wait" event is finished.

Under MRI, because of the GVL, Puma can't quite shine as well as it would under a non-GVL-addled interpreter. However, even still, there are several cases where Puma may be a good fit. If you have an application that executes multiple external requests to databases, APIs, and disk I/O, Puma may provide a performance boost.

Rainbow app server is similar to Puma.

Puma can allow multiple slow clients to connect without requiring a worker to be blocked on the request transaction. Because of this, Puma handles slow clients gracefully. Heroku recommends Puma for use in scenarios where you expect slow clients.

Thin

Thin is an Event / Machine based application server, Thin is capable of handling long running requests. It's similar to Unicorn in that it launches multiple workers and listens to a socket, but different in that it has no master controlling process and has one specific socket per worker process. Applications that can benefit from an event architecture - for example, a long-polling application - may benefit significantly from Thin.

Version control

It is good practice to start using version control in a project, even a small one in order to recover from any mistakes made or lost code, and to share your work. GIT and SVN are popular choices, SVN was more popular but hosting services such as github has made GIT more popular. Git makes creating temporary code branches and merging it back into the main code base easy.

For Facebook their internal dependencies are very complex. But instead of building a new system from scratch, they decided to take an existing one and make it scale. They concluded that Git's internals would be difficult to work with for an ambitious scaling project. Instead, they chose to improve Mercurial.

Git

Git is a distributed version control system. This means there's no central server, even when working in a group you don't continually need to check in your changes until you want the other team members to know about it. When working in a group Git can push your changes to a "remote", so and you can pull changes made by others from it.

you can run git locally on your computer, to share with other users the most popular remote cloud servers are Github and Bitbucket, I like Bitbucket because private projects are free to host. Both also provide a Wiki for your code documentation. Google cloud offers free Git repositories when you use Google cloud hosting.

You need to install Git, most people prefer the console Git commands rather than graphical tools. Sourcetree from Atlassian is a good GUI tool or https://mac.github.com/. there is also a build in GUI tool with git call 'gitk'.

List of basic git commands:

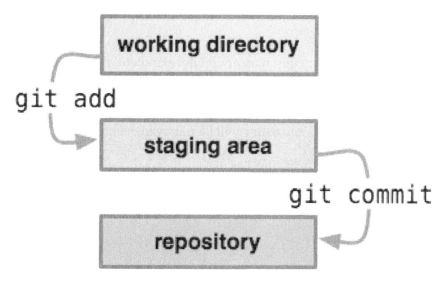

To create a new git repository.

```
git init.
```

The Git add command moves changes from the working directory to the staging area.

```
git add .
```

The Git commit takes the staged snapshot and commits it to the project history

```
git commit -m 'first time committing'
```

it is recommended to create tags for software releases.

```
git tag 1.0.0
```

Strategy for software branches

You could imple just have one version of your code, which is small if you are working along, but on longer projects you need to control how many add new feaures, versions in different stages of QA etc. There is a popular strategy called gitflow, and some command line Git extensions to make implementing this strategy easier at: https://github.com/nvie/gitflow

Next to the two core main branches: master and development, the development process uses a variety of supporting branches to aid parallel development between team members, ease tracking of features, prepare for production releases and to assist in quickly fixing live production problems. Unlike the main branches, these branches always have a limited life time, since they will be removed eventually.

The different types of branches we may use are:

- Feature branches
- Release branches
- Hotfix branches

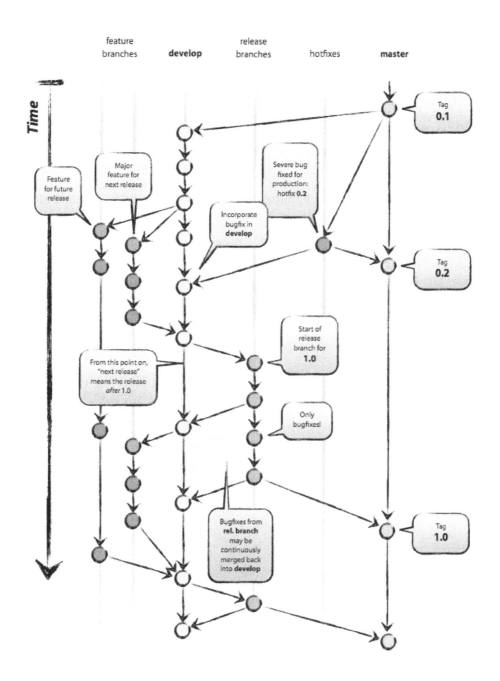

Testing

You could ship you code without any automated tests, as many startups do in a rush to market, but eventually it will hide home that it takes longer and longer to test each new release and a lot of manual test time is needed. As soon as you prove your minimum viable product I recommend to invest time in having automated test coverage for all your new features.

You could either have a separate application containing your tests or alternatively have your tests in the same application as your main code – I would recommend this second way.

The popular testing libraires are rspec for Test Driven Development [TDD] and cucumber for Behavious Driven Development [BDD] but both are normally used together.

Rspec

The default unit test framework with Rails is called MiniTest but rspec is still a more popular choice that we will be using. Add rspec to your dating app, to Gemfile add

```
group :development, :test do
gem 'rspec-rails'
end
```

run:

```
bundle install
rails generate rspec:install
```

This adds spec/spec_helper.rb and. rspec files that are used for configuration.

The files generated by the installation are:

```
create  .rspec
create  spec
create  spec/spec_helper.rb
```

Cucumber

Cucumber is a popular choice framework for doing Behaviour Driven Development integration tests. Add the gem to your project's Gemfile as follows:

```
group :test do
gem 'cucumber-rails', :require => false
# database_cleaner is not required, but highly recommended
gem 'database_cleaner'
end
```

run:

```
bundle install
rails generate cucumber:install
```

Add boiler plate code for our dating app

we shall describe html5boilerplate and Twitter Bootstrap later but we shall include then now so as to have them installed in the dating application.

Html5 boilerplate

HTML5 Boilerplate is a set of CSS3/HTML5 code snippets collecting best practices and making a good project starting point. to install html5boilerplate, you can do this manually or use an existing gem https://github.com/khelben/rails-boilerplate.

to Gemfile add:

```
gem "rails-boilerplate"
```

run:

```
rails g boilerplate:install
```

output:

```
conflict app/views/layouts/application.html.erb
Overwrite app/views/layouts/application.html.erb? (enter "h" for help) [Ynaqdh] Y
force app/views/layouts/application.html.erb
```

```
insert  app/assets/stylesheets/application.css
insert  app/assets/javascripts/application.js
insert  config/environments/production.rb
conflict  public/robots.txt
create  public/crossdomain.xml
create  public/humans.txt
conflict  public/favicon.ico
force  public/favicon.ico
create  public/apple-touch-icon-114x114-precomposed.png
create  public/apple-touch-icon-57x57-precomposed.png
create  public/apple-touch-icon-72x72-precomposed.png
create  public/apple-touch-icon-precomposed.png
create  public/apple-touch-icon.png
```

There are several gems which do similar such as:

- https://github.com/russfrisch/h5bp-rails, or download it manually
- http://html5boilerplate.com/ and read the doc/usage.md to see how to copy over the files manually.
- https://github.com/sporkd/html5-rails which creates header/footer files with media queries (add gem 'compass-rails' to get it working)

There is also a mobile only html5boilerplate, http://html5boilerplate.com/mobile/, if you just want to write a mobile only site, we will discuss the pros/cons of this later but for now I recommend the regular htm5boilerplate code.

Add Twitter Bootstrap

This is to make our site responsive with a grid layout.

to Gemfile add: gem 'bootstrap-sass'

run:

```
bundle install
```

To prove it works, create a file

```
rails g controller testpage index
```

to app/view/index.html.erb add:

```
<h1>Testpage#index</h1>
<p>Find me in app/views/testpage/index.html.erb</p>
<div class="row">
<div class="col-md-6 col-lg-3">
<div class="visible-lg text-success">Large Devices!</div>
<div class="visible-md text-warning">Medium Devices!</div>
<div class="visible-xs visible-sm text-danger">
Extra Small and Small Devices</div>
</div>
<div class="col-md-6 col-lg-3">
<div class="visible-lg text-success">Large Devices!</div>
<div class="visible-md text-warning">Medium Devices!</div>
<div class="visible-xs visible-sm text-danger">
Extra Small and Small Devices</div>
</div>
<div class="col-md-6 col-lg-3">
<div class="visible-lg text-success">Large Devices!</div>
<div class="visible-md text-warning">Medium Devices!</div>
<div class="visible-xs visible-sm text-danger">
Extra Small and Small Devices</div>
</div>
<div class="col-md-6 col-lg-3">
<div class="visible-lg text-success">Large Devices!</div>
<div class="visible-md text-warning">Medium Devices!</div>
<div class="visible-xs visible-sm text-danger">
Extra Small and Small Devices</div>
</div>
</div>
```

Twitter recommend: Import Bootstrap into a Sass file (for example, `application.css.scss`) to get all of Bootstrap's styles, mixins and variables.

They recommend against using `//= require` directives, since none of your other stylesheets will be able to access the Bootstrap mixins or variables.

rename app/assets/stylesheets/application.css as application/css.scss

and add:

```
@import "bootstrap";
```

in your browser enter: http://localhost:3000/testpage/index

Resize the browser and check the display order changes as you reduce the screen.

MVC

Rails architecture is based around Model View Controller (MVC) design, which basically means one 'view' file displays the HTML, which view page to display is controlled by the 'controller' file which decides the logic for example if a HTML form is submitted it goes to the controller to decide what to do with it. The model contains calls to the database to store, for example, the form data entered.

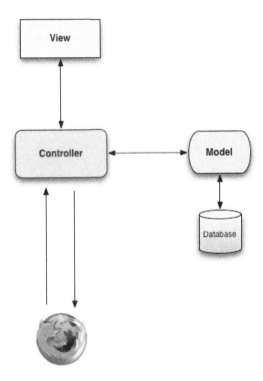

Before discussing MVC in detail it is good at this stage to generate a total working basic MVC application for example for a user to submit his details and view all other users.

Rails has a generate scaffold command to generate a view, controller and model but I find it more flexible to create the view and controller together and the the model separately as the model will normally be changing more often or a controller may refer to several differ-ent models. To see all generate command options that we can use enter 'rails generate', or 'rails g'.

Now its time to get back to creating the dating app. This shall be the home page as shown in this balsamiq mockup, 12 column grid with spacings between each grid column. 12 columns is the default bootstrap layout, with a gutter (margin) between each column. This gutter is standard in grid design to allow spacing between components. We will improve the layout later.

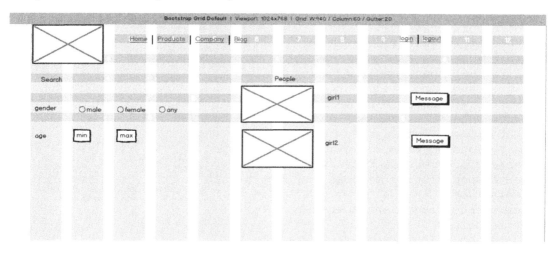

The naming convention of controllers in Rails favours pluralisation of the last word in the controller's name, for example SiteAdminsController is preferable to SiteAdminController or SitesAdminsController.

For the very first page in a project I like to use scaffolding, get the initial model and development flow going and see if there are any new syntax changes made by any new Rails upgrade, after that then for each controller, view and model I create each manually without the scaffolding in order to have full control as for example some pages such as 'edit' action may not be needed and you might use a different model with the controller.

Let's create the code for each dating member, to generate the view pages and controller for the member, and have all default actions:

```
rails generate scaffold Member first_name:string last_name:string description:text
```

```
invoke  active_record
create    db/migrate/20140928135845_create_members.rb
create    app/models/member.rb
invoke    rspec
create      spec/models/member_spec.rb
```

```
      invoke  resource_route
       route    resources :members
      invoke  scaffold_controller
      create    app/controllers/members_controller.rb
      invoke  erb
      create    app/views/members
      create    app/views/members/index.html.erb
      create    app/views/members/edit.html.erb
      create    app/views/members/show.html.erb
      create    app/views/members/new.html.erb
      create    app/views/members/_form.html.erb
      invoke  rspec
      create    spec/controllers/members_controller_spec.rb
      create    spec/views/members/edit.html.erb_spec.rb
      create    spec/views/members/index.html.erb_spec.rb
      create    spec/views/members/new.html.erb_spec.rb
      create    spec/views/members/show.html.erb_spec.rb
      create    spec/routing/members_routing_spec.rb
      invoke    rspec
      create      spec/requests/members_spec.rb
      invoke  helper
      create    app/helpers/members_helper.rb
      invoke  rspec
      create    spec/helpers/members_helper_spec.rb
      invoke  jbuilder
      create    app/views/members/index.json.jbuilder
      create    app/views/members/show.json.jbuilder
      invoke  assets
      invoke    coffee
      create      app/assets/javascripts/members.js.coffee
      invoke    scss
      create      app/assets/stylesheets/members.css.scss
      invoke  scss
      create    app/assets/stylesheets/scaffolds.css.scss
```

To create the models in the database, run:

```
rake db:migrate
```

```
== CreateMembers: migrating
======================================================
-- create_table(:members)
   -> 0.1368s
== CreateMembers: migrated (0.1369s)
=========================================
```

Now run Rails by entering 'rails server', or 'rails s' this runs the app in development mode by default. Click 'New member' and create a member. To test in the browser enter:

```
http://localhost:3000/members
```

To examine what is in the database you could use postgreSQL pgAdmin and enter SQL statements, alternatively in the Rails console enter:

```
rails console
Member.find(:all)
```

Alternatively you could use:

```
rails dbconsole
```

This drops you into whichever command line interface you would use with the the specific database.

Routes/config

The routes file maps the HTML URL to a controller. Rails follows a RESTful URL mapping to a controller action, REST stands for Representational State Transfer, uses the HTTP methods GET, POST, PUT, PATCH and DELETE to execute different operations.

Reference: http://guides.rubyonrails.org/routing.html

This line in routes.rb creates the RESTful routes for all the member actions.

```
resources :members
```

To view the routes created by the application so far, enter:

```
Rake routes
```

```
Prefix Verb URI Pattern Controller#Action
members GET /members(.:format) members#index
POST /members(.:format) members#create
new_member GET /members/new(.:format) members#new
edit_member GET /members/:id/edit(.:format) members#edit
member GET /members/:id(.:format) members#show
PATCH /members/:id(.:format) members#update
```

```
PUT     /members/:id(.:format)  members#update
DELETE  /members/:id(.:format)  members#destroy
```

For example in a view page:

```
<%= link_to 'Show', @member %> |
<%= link_to 'Back', members_path %>
```

Model

The model uses ActiveRecord Object Relational Model (ORM), to store/read the data in a database. Using activerecord is straight forward, for example to create and save a new record:

```
Person.create first_name: "Jane", last_name: "Smith"
```

To find all records:

```
Person.all, or Person.find_by_first_name "John"
```

Reference: http://guides.rubyonrails.org/active_record_querying.html

Scope

Scoping allows you to specify commonly used queries which can be referenced as method calls on the models. If we wish for a scope to be applied across all queries to the model we can use the default_scope method within the model itself. scope is a set of constraints on database interactions (such as a condition, limit, or offset) that are chainable and reusable. As a result, I can call MyModel.my_scope.another_scope.

For example to add this query to all queries automatically so we do not have to specify it each time:

```
class Client < ActiveRecord::Base
default_scope { where("removed_at IS NULL") }
end
```

When queries are executed on this model to the SQL database, the SQL query [converted from the rails code] will now look something like this:

```
SELECT * FROM clients WHERE removed_at IS NULL
```

Lambda in activerecord

You can pass a lambda to a scope which will be executed at runtime, not at the initialisation time.

```
scope :published, lambda { where('published_at < = ?', Time.now) }
```

This would then allow us to use Post.published.all

Strong parameters

In Rails 3 the model was responsible for checking that the model fields from say a web form are present such as a members name must be entered into the form, but in Rails 4, strong parameters were introduced. The basic idea behind Strong Parameters is to move mass-assignment protection out of the model and into the controller where it belongs. It provides an interface for protecting attributes from end-user assignment. This makes Action Controller parameters forbidden to be used in Active Model mass assignment until the parameters have been whitelisted.

For example: The Rails way of creating a 'member' is often done by sending parameters from a form view page and creating/updating the object in the controller. This way we don't need to set value of each attribute. The format it arrives into the controller would be say:

```
params[:member] = {:name => 'Foo',:email => 'foo@example.com'}
```

And you then create a new member object based on these parameters:

```
@member = Member.new(params[:member])
```

But there is a security problem with this mass-assignment of parameters which saves us the need to assign values to each attribute of the model, but it can create problems. Since we aren't restricting which attributes can be set nor are we checking the values of these attributes, a malicious hacker could assign any value to any attribute. For example, they could set the value of admin true, making himself a super user:

```
http://www.example.com/user/signup?user[name]=ow3ned&user[admin]=1
```

Rails has solutions to prevent this:

Rails 3 has a class method, attr_protected, that is used to specify attributes that can not be part of mass-assignment:

```
class User < ActiveRecord::Base
attr_protected :admin
end
```

Now the admin value is not accessible for mass-assignment. Attackers can not update this value in URL or through a form.

But now mass-assignment Protection is going to be done in a new way in Rails 4. mass-assignment protection moves into the controller, in our dating app [this code is created by the scaffolding]:

```
def create
Person.create(person_params)
end
# Never trust parameters from the internet,
# only allow the white list through.
def member_params
params.require(:member).permit(:first_name, :last_name,
:description)
end
```

ORM Design patterns

To better understand the active record design pattern some alternatives will be discussed.

There are two main design patterns of object persistence:

Active Record — Objects manage their own persistence. ActiveRecord violates of the Single Responsibility Principle - combining business logic and persistence logic in the same class. The Single Responsibility Principle is important because it allows us to make modifications to code without changing every single thing that that particular piece of code works with.

Data Mapper — Object persistence is managed by a separate mapper class, you end up with more objects to manage.

ActiveRecord uses the active record design pattern, while hibernate ORM in Java uses the data mapper design pattern. The active record design pattern can be used in any programming language. This pattern allows us to retrieve and manipulate data as objects, not as static rows of data, it makes objects intelligent. The objects know how how to create and read rows etc., there is no need to write raw sql. For example:

```
user = User.new
user.first_name='bob'
user.save
```

Alternative SQL frameworks

While activerecord is the most popular ORM, there are other frameworks:

ORM Adapter https://github.com/ianwhite/orm_adapter

Provides a single point of entry for popular ruby ORMs. Its target audience is gem authors who want to support more than one ORM.

Sequel http://sequel.jeremyevans.net/

Sequel provides thread safety, connection pooling and a concise DSL for constructing SQL queries and table schemas.

DataMapper https://github.com/datamapper/dm-core

The idea behind the Data Mapper pattern is that the objects don't know anything about persistence or even the classes/objects that map them to the database. This helps with writting unit tests.

Methods on ActiveRecord classes are intended to operate over the entire collection of objects breaking the Single Responsibility Principle - a domain object should only have a single responsibility, i.e. its own business logic.

A disadvantage of the data mapper is you end up with more objects to manage, which makes the calling code a little more complex and slightly harder to follow. Using a data mapper though does lead to cleaner, easier to test, easier to maintain code, and allows for greater extensibility - at the cost of slightly increased complexity.

Nosql database

Other database types such as Nosql are also supported ei example mongoDB which is a document database (for semi structured data such as JSON or XML), I prefer the mongoid framework over the other popular mongomapper framework. Nosql is a bit of a misleader, there is for example no schema in the database, but you need to reconstruct it to objects in your code if you wish to treat the data as objects.

Google cloud supports it: https://cloud.google.com/solutions/mongodb/

For large amounts of noSQL data, Cassandra is a preferred choise which Google cloud support: https://cloud.google.com/solutions/cassandra/

Schema

A database schema is like the floor plans of a house, it shows the relationship between the different tables. ArgoUml, http://argouml.tigris.org/, is a good free tool to draw relationship, may tools exist for Java to auto-generate hibernate code from the schema but I have not found a good tool in Rails to do this.

Activerecord (Rails less than 4.2) does not create foreign keys for your databases, this can help with integrity at the expense of performance (your database has to work to verify relationships). If data is very important such as in financial applications it would be useful to use foreign keys.

The Active Record design pattern claims that intelligence belongs in your models, not in the database. As such, features such as triggers or foreign key constraints, which push some of that intelligence back into the database, are not heavily used. The foreigner gem, https://github.com/matthuhiggins/foreigner, adds foreign key helpers to migrations and correctly dumps foreign keys to schema.rb.

Rails 4.2 migration DSL now supports adding and removing foreign keys. For example:

```
# add a foreign key to `articles.author_id`
# referencing `authors.id`
add_foreign_key :articles, :authors
```

A use of foreign key is for example if someone tries to save a Child with a parent_id of 5, but there's no Parent with id 5, then the database itself (not Rails) will reject the record if there's a foreign key constraint linking children.parent_id and parents.id. However, if your project grows to have code that also accesses these tables from other languages such as node.js/Java, they will not have the benefit of rails enforcing the relations if no foreign keys exist. These foreign key constraints are baked into the SQL tables themselves, so can protect non-rails code.

This will be the schema we will be using for the dating app:

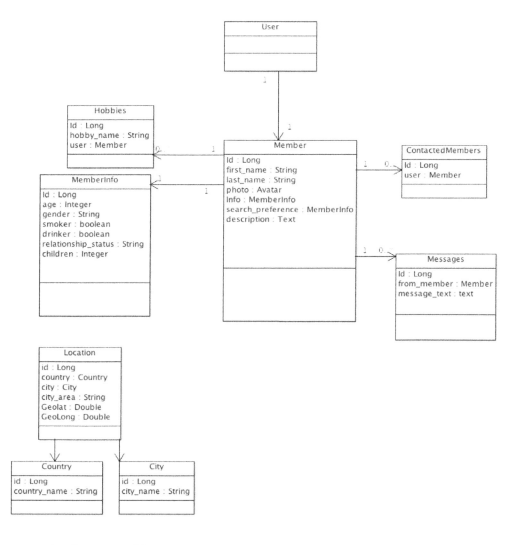

Some good reference guides are:

- http://guides.rubyonrails.org/active_record_basics.html
- http://guides.rubyonrails.org/active_record_querying.html
- http://guides.rubyonrails.org/association_basics.html
- http://guides.rubyonrails.org/association_basics.html#polymorphic-associations

Generate Model

To create the model a useful command is:

```
rails generate model field(s)
```

For example to create a model [table] called 'ad' with fields called, name and description:

```
rails generate model ad name:string description:text
```

The field type is normally one of the migrations native types, which is one of the following:

```
:primary_key, :string, :text, :integer, :float, :decimal,
:datetime, :timestamp, :time, :date, :binary, :boolean
```

Useful rake db commands

The default build tool rake is a simple ruby build program with capabilities similar to make. Rake, has several useful database commands, such as, rake db:migrate.

When you add new database fields, the best way rather than modify the database directly is to create a migrations file and run rake db:migrate. After awhile all these old migrations mount up so best to delete them and use a db/schema.rb file, this schema file documents the final current state of the database schema.

In Rails, we use what are called migration scripts to setup the tables in the database. When the migration command is executed, it will look in db/migrate/ for any Ruby files and execute them starting with the oldest (the database stores the last executed migration so only newer migration s will be executed). You could use 'rake db:create' to create a database and then run 'rake db:migrate' to add your changes.

Reference: http://guides.rubyonrails.org/migrations.html

db/schema.rb

Migration files are not the authoritative source for your database schema. That role falls to db/schema.rb which Active Record generates by examining the database, which is not designed to be edited, they just represent the current state of the database.

There is no need (and it is error prone) to deploy a new instance of an app by replaying the entire migration history. It is much simpler and faster to just load into the database a description of the current schema.

Schema files are also useful if you want a quick look at what attributes an Active Record object has. This information is not in the model's code and is frequently spread across several migrations, but the information is nicely summed up in the schema file. Because schema dumps are the authoritative source for your database schema, it is strongly recommended that you check them into source control.

How migrations relate to schema.rb

A schema starts off with nothing in it, and each migration modifies it, to add or remove tables, columns, or entries. Active Record will also update your db/schema.rb file to match the up-to-date structure of your database.

```
rake db:migrate # Updating the database with any migrations created
```

Running the 'rake db:migrate' task also automatically invokes the db:schema:dump task, which will update your db/schema.rb file to match the structure of your database:

```
rake db:schema:dump # Create db/schema.rb file
rake db:schema:load # Load schema.rb file into the database
```

Creating the Database, the database should be created when you first create a Rails project or after rake db:drop is run:

```
rake db:create
```

Note: By default running rake db:migrate will run in the development environment. To run migrations against another environment you can specify it using the RAILS_ENV environment variable while running the command, likewise for other commands. For example to run migrations against the test environment you could run:

```
rake db:migrate RAILS_ENV=test
```

Setting up seed data

Often, we have default data that we want to have in our application that is tedious to manually enter each time. The seeds command exists to automate this process. In the seed file, db/seeds.rb you may find admin users, default blog categories, and etc.. With the file db/seeds.rb, Rails have given us a way of feeding default values easily and quickly to a fresh installation. but you can simply use the following file, db/seeds.rb containing for example:

```
Country.create(name: 'Germany', population: 81831000)
Country.create(name: 'France', population: 65447374)
Country.create(name: 'Belgium', population: 10839905)
Country.create(name: 'Netherlands', population: 16680000)
```

You then populate it with data via rake db:seed. You should add seed data to the database after new seed data is added to db/seed.rb or after creating a new database with"

```
rake db:create
```

Dropping the Database

Sometimes, we want to delete all of the data and tables so that we can start from fresh such as when you want a clean slate, that is what this command automates. This will delete the entire database, which holds the tables. Consequently, any data that was in the tables will also be deleted with:

```
rake db:drop
```

Rolling Back a Migration

When this command is run, it will look at the last migration created and undo it with:

```
rake db:rollback
```

If for example you need to rollback a production deployment to fix a bug, you could try to reload a previous schema.rb or if you need to roll back say ten migrations:

```
rake db:rollback STEP=10
```

How can i use all these commands together

While developing an application, you will find that your run series of commands in sequence often. Here is an order of commands that you could use everyday:

```
rake db:drop
```

```
rake db:create
rake db:migrate
rake db:seed
```

alternatively you can call: rake db:setup

The rake db:setup task will create the database, load the schema and initialise it with the seed data.

```
rake db:reset
```

The rake db:reset task will drop the database and set it up again. This is functionally equivalent to rake db:drop db:setup. this is not the same as running all the migrations. It will only use the contents of the current schema.rb file.

```
RAILS_ENV=test rake db:create
```

This will create the database in your test database. You will normally run the rake commands for test and development at the same time during development.

```
rake db:test:prepare
```

rake db:test:prepare will look at your db/schema.rb file to determine if any migrations that exist in your project that have not been run. Assuming there are no outstanding migrations, it will then empty the database and reload it based on the contents of the db/schema.rb file.

One common busy-task which occupies Rails developers during development is keeping the test database migrated inline with the development database. This involves running rake db:test:prepare every time you want to run tests after you've run a migration.

Note: since Rails 4.1, it deprecated rake db:test:* tasks as the test database is now automatically maintained. In Rails 4.1 there's a "magical" line which can be added to your test or spec_helper.

```
ActiveRecord::Migration.maintain_test_schema! if
defined?(ActiveRecord::Migration)
```

This line of code effectively runs the rake db:test:prepare code before your test run so you can be certain that you're testing against the most recent database schema.

Summary

```
rake db:create creates the database for the current
env
rake db:create:all creates the databases for all envs
rake db:drop drops the database for the current env
rake db:drop:all drops the databases for all envs
rake db:migrate runs migrations for the current env
that have not run yet

rake db:migrate:up runs one specific migration
rake db:migrate:down rolls back one specific migration
rake db:migrate:status shows current migration status
rake db:rollback rolls back the last migration
rake db:forward advances the current schema version
to the next one

rake db:seed (only) runs the db/seed.rb file
rake db:schema:load loads the schema into the current
env's database
rake db:schema:dump dumps the current env's schema
rake db:setup runs db:schema:load, db:seed
rake db:reset runs db:drop db:setup

rake db:migrate:reset runs db:drop db:create db:migrate
rake db:migrate:redo runs (db:migrate:down db:migrate:up) or
(db:rollback rake
db:migrate:migrate) depending on the
specified migration
```

Concerns

Concerns provides you with a simple way to organise your Controllers and Models and split them into smaller chunks of logic, so let's say we have a Post model which is getting a bit lengthy, and not very nice to look at. With the Concerns, we can split it up into nice little chunks. Because we have lots of validations, let's start by pulling them out and placing them within a concern file.

```
class Post < ActiveRecord::Base
include Commentable
end
```

Now, we can replace everything we moved out of our Post model with one single line of code:

```
module Commentable
extend ActiveSupport::Concern
included do
has_many :comments, as: :parent
scope :commented, -> { joins(:comments).
group('posts.id').
having('COUNT(comments.id) > 0') }
end
end
```

Continuous deployment for databases

Contiuous deployment of software gets complicated when for example different features make changes to a database, also if you use for example many read replica databases with several application servers –it can get complicated. Continuous Deployment step by step. It does not have to be all or nothing. It can be:

- automatic deployment only for builds without database migrations, manual for the rest.
- automatic deployment only for build without db migrations or with non-destructive migrations, manual for the rest.
- automatic deployment for all builds, but those with destructive migration will temporarily disable the app and will be only allowed to be executed during selected time window.
- Prefer ADD's over ALTER's - non breaking expansion.

Many database refactorings, such as adding a column, can be done without having to update all the code that accesses the system. If code uses the new schema without being aware of it, the column will just go unused. Many changes, however don't have this property. We call these **destructive changes,** an example of which is making an existing nullable column not null. For destructive changes you need a good strategy. For example let's say you are replacing the Member model by two models as you add more data fields: Member and MemberInfo, run your migrations, some steps could be:

1. Add new version to schema
2. Write to both versions
3. Backfill historical data
4. Read from new version
5. Cut off writes to old version

View

Action View and Action Controller are the two major components of **Action Pack.** In Rails, web requests are handled by Action Pack, which splits the work into a controller part (performing the logic) and a view part (rendering a template). Typically, Action Controller will be concerned with communicating with the database and performing CRUD actions where necessary. Action View is then responsible for compiling the response.

Reference: http://guides.rubyonrails.org/action_view_overview.html

The view displays the information to a member, embed ruby code in an. erb page, for example to display a string in a view page,

```
<%= @member.first_name %>
```

To debug the data sent from a controller, in your view add: <%= debug @member%>

Partials

Partial templates - usually just called "partials" - are a way for breaking the rendering process into more manageable chunks. They can make the view easier to read. With a partial, you can move the code for rendering a particular piece of a response to its own file to make the file more readable and for reuse. You can also pass local variables into partials.

reference: http://guides.rubyonrails.org/layouts_and_rendering.html#using-partials

To render a partial as part of a view, you use the render method within the view:

in app/views/members/new.html.erb

```erb
<%= render 'form' %>
```

That code will pull in the partial from app/views/members/_form.html.erb. A partial can use its own layout file, just as a view can use a layout. For example, you might call a partial like this:

```erb
<%= render partial: "link_area", layout: "graybar" %>
```

This would look for a partial named _link_area.html.erb and render it using the layout file: _graybar.html.erb.

In the generated dating app code, index.html.erb, to display all members:

```erb
<% @members.each do |member| %>
<tr>
<td><%= member.first_name %></td>
<td><%= member.last_name %></td>
<td><%= member.description %></td>
<td><%= link_to 'Show', member %></td>
<td><%= link_to 'Edit', edit_member_path(member) %></td>
<td><%= link_to 'Destroy', member, method: :delete, data: { confirm: 'Are you sure?' } %></td>
</tr>
<% end %>
```

This could be replaced with

```erb
<% @members.each do |member| %>
<%= render partial: "show_member", locals: {member: member} %>
<% end %>
```

This would look for a partial named _show_member.html.erb and render it using the layout _show_member.html.erb. Note that layouts for partials follow the same leading underscore naming as regular partials, and are placed in the same folder with the partial that they belong to (not in the master layouts folder).

create a new file: app/views/members/_show_member.html.erb

```erb
<tr>
```

```
<td><%= member.first_name %></td>
<td><%= member.last_name %></td>
<td><%= member.description %></td>
<td><%= link_to 'Show', member %></td>
<td><%= link_to 'Edit', edit_member_path(member) %></td>
<td><%= link_to 'Destroy', member, method: :delete,
data: { confirm: 'Are you sure?' } %></td>
</tr>
```

Note: To make entering the fields mandatory to the model/member.rb add:

```
validates :first_name,:last_name,:description,
:presence => true,
:uniqueness => { :case_sensitive => true }
```

View render

To render the response to an action in the controller, for example:

```
class MembersController < ApplicationController
def index
@members = Member.all
end
end
```

We don't have an explicit render at the end of the index action in accordance with "convention over configuration" principle. The rule is that if you do not explicitly render something at the end of a controller action, Rails will automatically look for the action_name.html.erb template in the controller's view path and render it. So in this case, Rails will render the app/views/members/index.html.erb file.

Reference: http://guides.rubyonrails.org/layouts_and_rendering.html

If you want to render the view that corresponds to a different template within the same controller, you can use render with the name of the view, for example:

```
def update
@book = Book.find(params[:id])
if @book.update(params[:book])
redirect_to(@book)
else
render "edit"
end
end
```

If you prefer, you can use a symbol instead of a string to specify the action to render:

```
render :edit
```

if you want to render a template from an entirely different controller from the one that contains the action code, If you want to be explicit, you can use the :template option, for example:

```
render template: "products/show"
```

Redirect response

Another way to handle returning responses to an HTTP request is with redirect_to. As you've seen, render tells Rails which view (or other asset) to use in constructing a response. The redirect_to method does something completely different: it tells the browser to send a new request for a different URL. For example, you could redirect from where ever you are in your code to the index of member photos in your application with this:

```
redirect_to photos_url
```

In destroy the redirect is used:

```
def destroy
@member.destroy
respond_to do |format|
format.html { redirect_to members_url }
format.json { head :no_content }
end
end
```

Why use redirect or render

With the code in this form, there will likely be a problem if the @book variable is nil. Remember, a render :action doesn't run any code in the target view, so nothing will set up the @books variable that the index view will probably require. One way to fix this is to redirect instead of rendering:

```
def show
@book = Book.find_by(id: params[:id])
if @book.nil?
redirect_to action: :index
```

```
end
end
```

With this code, the browser will make a fresh request for the index page, the code in the index controller method will run, and all will be well.

JSON support

JSON is a JavaScript data format used by many Ajax libraries and Single Page Applications. The popular choice for building JSON responses in Rails is with:

- https://github.com/rails/jbuilder
- A more advanced gem is: https://github.com/nesquena/rabl, To better help build your JSON to your needs.

This JSON syntax defines an employees object, with an array of 3 employee records (objects):

```
{"employees":[
{"firstName":"John", "lastName":"Doe"},
{"firstName":"Anna", "lastName":"Smith"},
{"firstName":"Peter", "lastName":"Jones"}
]}
```

The less popular alternative would be to use XML, which are more popular in the enterprise type of applications such as an interface to a Telco billing system:

```
<employees>
<employee>
<firstName>John</firstName> <lastName>Doe</lastName>
</employee>
<employee>
<firstName>Anna</firstName> <lastName>Smith</lastName>
</employee>
<employee>
<firstName>Peter</firstName> <lastName>Jones</lastName>
</employee>
</employees>
```

For example to support HTML and JSON requests:

```
def create
@user = User.new(user_params)
respond_to do |format|
```

```
if @user.save

  cformat.html { redirect_to @user, notice:
  'User was successfully created.' }
  format.json { render action: 'show',
  status: :created, location: @user }
else
  format.html { render action: 'new' }
  format.json { render json: @user.errors,
  status: :unprocessable_entity }
end
end
end
```

if you wanted just to support JSON for the index action, instead of HTML:

```
def show
end
```

change to:

```
def show
  render json: @member
end
```

Layout

When Rails renders a view as a response, it does so by combining the view with the current layout. To find the current layout, Rails first looks for a file in app/views/layouts with the same base name as the controller. For example, rendering actions from the PhotosController class will use app/views/layouts/photos.html.erb (or app/views/layouts/photos.builder). If there is no such controller-specific layout, Rails will use app/views/layouts/application.html.erb.

Note: A Use gem for generating layout files for Zurb or Bootstrap which also adds viewport, navigation links and flash messages plus simpleCSS classes for styling is:

https://github.com/RailsApps/rails_layout

You can override the default layout conventions in your controllers by using the layout declaration. For example:

```
class ProductsController < ApplicationController
```

```
layout "inventory"
#...
end
```

Now lets add a header/footer for our dating app, in app/views/layouts/application.html.erb, change from:

```
<!DOCTYPE html>
<html>
<head>
<title>Dating App</title>
<%= stylesheet_link_tag "application", media: "all",
"data-turbolinks-track" => true %>
<%= javascript_include_tag "application",
"data-turbolinks-track" => true %>
<%= csrf_meta_tags %>
</head>
<body>
<%= yield %>

</body>
</html>
```

Instead of having to, for example code for the HTML header/footer into each page you can use a layout shown below, and also insert notice messages which we will discuss layer.

```
<!DOCTYPE html>
<html>
<head>
<title>Dating app</title>
<%= stylesheet_link_tag "application", media: "all",
"data-turbolinks-track" => true %>
<%= javascript_include_tag "application",
"data-turbolinks-track" => true %>
<%= csrf_meta_tags %>
</head>
<body>

<%= render "layouts/header" %>

<% if notice %>
<p class="alert alert-notice"><%= notice %></p>
<% end %>
<% if alert %>
```

```
<p class="alert alert-error"><%= alert %></p>
<% end %>

<%= yield %>

<%= render "layouts/footer" %>
</body>
</html>
```

Add the new files to the project:

```
app/views/layouts/_header.html.erb
app/views/layouts/_footer.html.erb
```

in _header.html.erb, you could customise the CSS yourself, for example:

```
<header id="banner" class="body">
<nav><ul>
<li><%= link_to( image_tag("dating_logo.png",
:alt => "dating site") )%></li>
<li>    </li>
<li class="active"><a href="#">search</a></li>
<li><a href="#">inbox</a></li>
<li><a href="#">logout</a></li>
</ul></nav>
</header>
</br>
```

To app/assets/css/application.css add:

```
nav {
background-color:#2C5463;
height:40px;
}

nav ul {
font-family: Arial, Verdana;
font-size: 20px;
margin: 0;
padding: 0;
list-style: none;
}


nav ul li {
display: block;
```

```css
position: relative;
float: left;
}

nav li ul {
display: none;
}

nav ul li a {
display: block;
text-decoration: none;
padding: 7px 15px 3px 15px;
background: #2C5463;
color: #ffffff;
margin-left: 1px;
white-space: nowrap;
height:30px; /* Width and height of top-level nav items */
width:90px;
text-align:center;
}

nav ul li a:hover {
background: #617F8A;
}

nav li:hover ul {
display: block;
position: absolute;
height:30px;
}

nav li:hover li {
float: none;
font-size: 11px;
}

nav li:hover a {
background: #3A464F;
height:30px; /* Height of lower-level nav items is shorter than main level */
}


nav li:hover li a:hover {
background: #95A9B1;
```

```
}
nav ul li ul li a {
text-align:left; /* Top-level items are centered, but nested
list items are left-aligned */
}
```

I put this code down to show you alternatively what could be done with Bootstrap to reduce the code you have to write without the need to write this custom CSS, in _header.html.erb:

```
<div class="navbar navbar-default" role="navigation">
<div class="container-fluid">
<div class="navbar-header">
<button type="button" class="navbar-toggle" data-toggle="collapse"
data-target=".navbar-collapse">
<span class="sr-only">Toggle navigation</span>
<span class="icon-bar"></span>
<span class="icon-bar"></span>
<span class="icon-bar"></span>
</button>

<%= link_to( image_tag("dating_logo.png", :alt => "dating site"),
:class=> "navbar-brand")%>
</div>
<div class="navbar-collapse collapse">
<ul class="nav navbar-nav">
<li><%= link_to "search",{controller: "users",
action: "index"} %></li>
<li><%= link_to "inbox", {controller: "messages", action: "index"}
%></li>
</ul>

<ul class="nav navbar-nav navbar-right">
<li class="active"><a href="../navbar-static-top/">Inbox</a></li>
<li><a href="../navbar-fixed-top/">Logout</a></li>
</ul>
</div><!--/.nav-collapse -->
</div><!--/.container-fluid -->
</div>
```

This also collapses the menu when you reduce the browser size simulating a smaller device screen. To get the collapse working you need to copy the bootstrap/javascript files into assets/javascript, and to app/assets/javascripts/application.js, add:

```
//= require bootstrap/transition
```

- bootstrap-sass.gemspec
- bower.json
- CHANGELOG.md
- composer.json
- CONTRIBUTING.md
- Gemfile
- 📁 lib
- LICENSE
- Rakefile
- README.md
- 📁 tasks
- 📁 templates
  - ▶ 📁 project
- 📁 test
- 📁 vendor
  - ▼ 📁 assets
    - ▶ 📁 fonts
    - ▼ 📁 javascripts
      - ▶ 📁 bootstrap
      - bootstrap.js
    - ▶ 📁 stylesheets

Helpers

In app/helper directory, you can put code to make your views cleaner to read and maintain, for example:

```
module ApplicationHelper
# Return a title on a per-page basis.
def title
base_title = "Ruby on Rails Tutorial Sample App"
if @title.nil?
base_title
else
"#{base_title} | #{@title}"
end
end
end
```

Then in your _header.html.erb, note that there is now no @ sign in front of title here. you could have

```
<title><%= title %></title>
```

Rails view helpers

Rails provides methods for generating HTML that links views to assets such as images, javascript, stylesheets,

```
<%= image_tag "home.gif", alt: "Home" %>
<%= favicon_link_tag 'myicon.ico' %>
<%= javascript_include_tag "xmlhr" %>
<%= stylesheet_link_tag "style" %>
```

Form helper

Form markup can quickly become tedious to write and maintain because of form control field naming and their numerous attributes. Rails provides view helpers for generating form markup.

Reference: http://guides.rubyonrails.org/form_helpers.html

For example in app/views/users/_form.html.erb:

```
<%= form_for(@user) do |f| %>
<% if @user.errors.any? %>
```

```erb
<div id="error_explanation">
<h2><%= pluralize(@user.errors.count, "error") %> 
prohibited this user from being saved:</h2>
<ul>
<% @user.errors.full_messages.each do |msg| %>
<li><%= msg %></li>
<% end %>
</ul>
</div>
<% end %>
<div class="field">
<%= f.label :name %><br>
<%= f.text_field :name %>
</div>
<div class="field">
<%= f.label :hobbies %><br>
<%= f.text_field :hobbies %>
</div>
<div class="actions">
<%= f.submit %>
</div>
<% end %>
```

There are popular gems for giving more flexibility with forms such as https://github.com/plataformatec/simple_form, and https://github.com/justinfrench/formtastic, especially when a form contains nested models.

form_tag versus form_for

form_for is a bit easier to use for creating forms for a model object because it figures out which URL to use and which HTTP method to use depending on whether the object is a new record or a saved record:

```erb
<% form_for(@user) do |f| %>
```

And from then on you can add fields using the 'f' variable you just defined, like f.text_field or f.select. The other difference is that the way you declare the fields themselves changes. text_field becomes text_field_tag, select becomes select_tag and so on. The reason is that text_field is meant, just like form_for, to interact with a defined object model.

When defining a form_tag you can't just pass it an object and let rails figure out what needs to happen. It is good when you done have say a model than fits into your form, giving you more flexibility.

```
<% form_tag(create_user_path, :method=>'post',
:multipart => true) do %>
```

form_tag simply creates a form. form_for creates a form for a model object, it is a more advanced tool. They are not interchangeable and you should use the one that is appropriate for a given case.

Add side column for searching for members

The **content_for** method allows you to insert content into a named yield block in your lay-out, basically you can pass code to the layout and the yield will place the code into the section.

Let's add a sidebar to the dating page for list members as this is the main page of this application. To do this in a layout friendly way, we will use the content_for helper method to define the sidebar:

```
<style type="text/css">
#sidebar { float: left; width: 40%; }
#content { float: right; width: 60%; }
</style>
```

We could put this in it's own file (in the public/stylesheets directory), but for the purposes of this demonstration, it works just as well in the head of the document.

Create a new layout file app/views/layouts/list_members.html.erb containing:

```
<!DOCTYPE html>
<html>
<head>
<title>dating</title>
<%= stylesheet_link_tag "application", media: "all",
"data-turbolinks-track" => true %>
<%= javascript_include_tag "application",
"data-turbolinks-track" => true %>
<%= csrf_meta_tags %>
<style type="text/css">
```

```erb
#wrap {
width:100%;
margin:0 auto;
}
#sidebar {
float:left;
width:25%;
background-color: Aqua;
}
#content{
float:right;
width:75%;
}
</style>
</head>
<body>
<%= render "layouts/header" %>
<% if notice %>
<p class="alert alert-notice"><%= notice %></p>
<% end %>
<% if alert %>
<p class="alert alert-error"><%= alert %></p>
<% end %>
<div id="wrap">
<div id="sidebar" >
<%= yield :sidebar %>
</div>
<div id="content">
<%= yield :content %>
</div>
</div>
<%= render "layouts/footer" %>
</body>
</html>
```

This defines two new div's for the content and sidebar portions of the document. The first call to yield renders the content portion of a view (everything apart from regions defined by calls to content_for). The second call to yield passes the name of our content region as a symbol. When yield is called with a symbol, it renders the associated content region. In our case yield :sidebar causes the server to render the content that we defined for the :sidebar region at that point in the layout. In members_controller.rb change:

```
def index
  @members = Member.all
end
```

To:

```
def index
  @members = Member.all
  render layout: "list_members"
end
```

Now in app/views/members/index.html.erb, we need to have the layout sections, we will fill in the sections later:

```
<% content_for :sidebar do %>
<% end %>
<% content_for :content do %>
#place the current contents of index.html.erb inside here
<% end %>
```

Template engines

ERB (Embedded RuBy, a. html.erb file) isn't beautiful, but some alternatives allow much of the power of ERB while improving on the aesthetics. ERB is good if you have a web designer that will work on plain HTML and does not know a templating script such as Haml, http://haml.info. or slim, http://slim-lang.com/, this way the designer can write HTML and you can embed ruby logic with the proper tags.

Example output:

ERB:

```
<h1> Just simple erb template</h1>
<p>there is no ruby code or smth else, just text</p>
```

Haml:

```
%h1 Just simple erb template
%p there is no ruby code or smth else, just text
```

Slim:

```
h1 Just simple erb template
p there is no ruby code or smth else, just text
```

Liquid, https://github.com/Shopify/liquid, was extracted from Shopify and powers their shop building efforts, has some useful filter tags.

If you'd like to avoid logic in your views to make the code easier to read and maintain, have a look at something like Mustache, https://github.com/mustache/mustache. It uses a template style that emphasises a more strict separation of logic from presentation. Compiling templates such as handlebars, http://handlebarsjs.com/, can give performance improvements,

Performance

It is worth considering performance if you decided to use a template engine and do some tests. Erubis, http://www.kuwata-lab.com/erubis/, claim they are almost three times faster than ERB.

-ERB

```
<h1> Just simple erb template</h1>
<p>there is no ruby code or something else, just text</p>
<% 100.times do %>
<%= rand(1000) %>
<% end %>
```

-Haml

```
%h1 Just simple erb template
%p there is no ruby code or something else, just text
- 100.times do
= rand(1000)
```

-Slim

I think we can call it light-weight Haml. Same idea, but more effective.

```
h1 Just simple erb template
p there is no ruby code or something else, just text
```

```
- 100.times do
= rand(1000)
```

Against 100 requests and average value:

Haml - 0.00026751000000000005
Slim - 0.00014951999999999994
ERB - 0.00012785999999999993

These results are relative. Here ERB gave better result than Slim. But Haml is slow. These are just an indication that its worth prototyping an engine before deciding on it, and the main thing also to see if you enjoy writing in the template syntax.

Later we will talk about generating a mobile native app with phonegap, it would be worth testing the template compile time on the iOS/android before deciding if to use a template engine.

Some people prefer to use a template engine as an alternative to ERB such as haml, Erubis, Slim, Liquid, Mustache although it reduces the code size I think it can make the code harder to read and for a learning curve for new team members. For example with Haml, if all you get in the end is pretty whitespace and automatically closed tags I can just use HTML Tidy, I found it very frustrating having to make sure it is indented correctly, having to use http://html2haml.heroku.com/ to convert and just swapping one language for another.

Controller

After routing has determined which controller to use for a request, your controller is responsible for making sense of the request and producing the appropriate output. A controller is a Ruby class which inherits from ApplicationController and has methods just like any other class. So it is a normal class with in instantiated and has session variables. The members URL requests map to actions [methods] inside a controller.In practice it is good to have only standard naming actions such as new/create and not to make up names.

Reference: http://guides.rubyonrails.org/action_controller_overview.html

For example in the file: app/controllers/members_controller.rb:

```ruby
class MembersController < ApplicationController
before_action :set_member, only: [:show, :edit,
:update, :destroy]

private
# Use callbacks to share common setup or constraints
# between actions.
def set_member
@member = Member.find(params[:id])
end

# Never trust parameters from the scary internet,
# only allow the white list through.
def member_params
params.require(:member).permit(:first_name, :last_name,
:description, :avatar, member_info_attributes:
[:smoker, :gender, :relationship_status,
:age, :drinker] )
end
end
```

Session

Cookies are key-value data pairs that are stored in the user's browser until they reach their specified expiration date. With each new request to your server, the browser will send along all the cookies and you can access them in your controllers and views like a normal hash.

"Sessions" are the idea that your user's state is somehow preserved when he/she clicks from one page to the next. HTTP is stateless. Think about how websites keep track of how a user is logged in when the page reloads. HTTP requests are stateless so how can you tell that a given request actually came from that particular user who is logged in? This is why cookies are important -- they allow you to keep track of your user from one request to another until the cookie expires. To identify a user's session information, Rails stores a special secure and tamper-proof cookie on the user's browser that contains their entire session hash.

Why would you need both cookies and sessions? They are similar but not the same. session is an entire hash that gets put in the secure session cookie that expires when the user closes the browser. If you look in your developer tools, the "expiration" of that cookie is "session". Each value in the cookies hash gets stored as an individual cookie.

All session stores use a cookie to store a unique ID for each session (you must use a cookie, Rails will not allow you to pass the session ID in the URL as this is less secure).

So cookies and sessions are sort of like temporary free database tables for you to use that are unique to a given user and will last until you either manually delete them, they have reached their expiration date, or the session is ended (depending what you specified).

session and cookies aren't really hashes, Rails just pretends they are so it's easy for you to work with them.

You are size-limited in terms of how much you can store inside a session hash or browser cookie (~4kb) Sessions can hold any kind of data object (with some limitations). The session is only available in the controller and the view and can use one of a number of different storage mechanisms such as cookie in the users browser or on the server in the Rails cache or database.

An example of how to store and delete cookie values.

```ruby
class CommentsController < ApplicationController
def new
# Auto-fill the commenter's name if it has been
# stored in a cookie
@comment = Comment.new(author: cookies[:commenter_name])
end

def create
@comment = Comment.new(params[:comment])
if @comment.save
flash[:notice] = "Thanks for your comment!"
if params[:remember_name]
# Remember the commenter's name.
cookies[:commenter_name] = @comment.author
else
# Delete cookie for the commenter's name cookie, if any.
cookies.delete(:commenter_name)
end
redirect_to @comment.article
else
render action: "new"
end
end
end
```

Likewise if you use session data: session[:current_user_id] = user.id

Note: that while for session values you set the key to nil, to delete a cookie value you should use cookies.delete(:key).

Session security

The session cookie is signed and encrypted (encryption is new in Rails 4) when you use the default browser store.

The three cookie storage types that are available to you:

- ActionDispatch::Sessions::CookieStore (default)
- ActionDispatch::Sessions::CacheStore
- ActionDispatch::Sessions::MemCacheStore

It's important to note that the last two stores will save the session id to the cookie unencrypted and unsigned.

It is interesting that the single page application framework Meteor uses HTML5 local storage for session tokens for extra security making Meteor apps immune to CSRF attacks.

https://www.meteor.com/blog/2014/03/14/session-cookies

Form parameters

To extract parameters entered into the form, app/views/members/_form.html.erb

There are two kinds of form parameter ways of sending their parameters possible in a web application:

- The first are parameters that are sent as part of the URL, called query string parameters. The query string is everything after "?" in the URL.
- The second type of parameter is usually referred to as POST data. This information usually comes from an HTML form which has been filled in by the user. It's called POST data because it can only be sent as part of an HTTP POST request.

Rails does not make any distinction between query string parameters and POST parameters, and both are available in the 'params' hash in your controller. For an example of a HTML form [Rails form], and view:

```
<form accept-charset="UTF-8" action="/clients" method="post">
<input type="text" name="client[name]" value="Acme" />
<input type="text" name="client[phone]" value="12345" />
<input type="text" name="client[address][postcode]"
value="12345" />
<input type="text" name="client[address][city]"
value="Carrot City" />
</form>
```

When this form is submitted, the value of params[:client] will be

```
{ "name" => "Acme", "phone" => "12345", "address" => { "postcode"
=> "12345", "city" => "Carrot City" } }.
```

Note the nested hash in params[:client][:address].

you can extract form parameters using say,

```
@member = Member.new(member_params)

def member_params
params.require(:member).permit(:first_name,
:last_name, :description)
end
```

Fat Model, Skinny Controller

A common term is, "Fat Model, Skinny Controller". The "skinny" controller is simply a light interface between the view and model. For example a complex query should be a method in the model rather than the controller calling several queries and doing logic on them. That any non response related logic should go in the model, ideally in a nice, testable method. Meanwhile, the "skinny" controller is simply a nice interface between the view and model. By moving any logic that isn't about the response to the model not only have you promoted reuse where possible but you've also made it possible to test your code outside of the context of a request.

Filters

Filters are methods that are run before, after or "around" a controller action. Filters are inherited, so if you set a filter on ApplicationController, it will be run on every controller in your application.

Reference: http://guides.rubyonrails.org/action_controller_overview.html#the-flash

"Before" filters may halt the request cycle. A common "before" filter is one which requires that a user is logged in for an action to be run. You can define the filter method this way:

```
class ApplicationController < ActionController::Base
before_action :require_login

private
def require_login
unless logged_in?
flash[:error] = "log in to access this section"
redirect_to new_login_url # halts request cycle
end
end
end
```

Ajax

Ajax is an acronym for Asynchronous JavaScript and XML. When you type a URL into your browser's address bar and hit 'Go,' the browser makes a request to the server. It parses the response, then fetches all associated assets, like JavaScript files, stylesheets and images. It then assembles the page. If you click a link, it does the same process: fetch the page, fetch the assets, put it all together, showing you the results. Ajax is used to update a web page without having to refresh the page using Javascript. If someone has Javascript disabled then it will not work, but studies have shown less than a few percentage of people do this (progressive enhancement will be discussed later).

JavaScript can make requests to the server, and parse the response. It also has the ability to update information on the page. Combining these two powers, JavaScript can make a web page that can update just parts of itself, without needing to get the full page data from the server. This is a powerful technique that we call Ajax.

reference: http://edgeguides.rubyonrails.org/working_with_javascript_in_rails.html

In the dating app lets use Ajax for delete members

For example in the index page, for the delete member button, instead of a page refresh make the delete update the member list using javascript.

In the destroy action, add 'format.js' containing:

```
def destroy
@user.destroy
respond_to do |format|
format.html { redirect_to users_url }
format.json { head :no_content }
format.js
end
end
```

in app/views/members/_show_members.html.erb change:

```
<td><%= link_to 'Destroy', member, method: :delete,
data: { confirm: 'Are you sure?' } %></td>
```

to

```
<td><%= link_to 'Destroy', member, method: :delete,
data: { confirm: 'Are you sure?' }, :remote => true %></td>
```

Create a new file app/views/members/destroy.js.erb containing query javascript:

```
$('#<%= dom_id @member%>').fadeOut();
```

This makes deleting a member use Ajax.

Exceptions

Errors occur in software, and it is a MUST DO practice to handle them, for example such as not being able to write to a database. The easiest way to catch these is to add a handler in the controller. Even just redirecting the user to an error page or displaying a flash error is better than a user being displayed some error code. For example to catch all exemptions in a controller.

```
class ApplicationController < ActionController::Base
# Rescue general exception
rescue_from Exception, :with => :serious_problem
def serious_problem(e)
redirect_to error_serious_path , :flash =>
{ :error => "Serious error " + e.message }
end
end
```

https://github.com/smartinez87/exception_notification is a useful gem, or there are exception cloud services such as https://airbrake.io/ that receive your exceptions allowing you to filter for messages etc. No exception should be caused unless there is a real problem, do not for example create a exception for a user who did not enter an extra parameter otherwise you cannot determine real issues in your code from the trivial stuff.

The following figure shows the Ruby exception hierarchy:

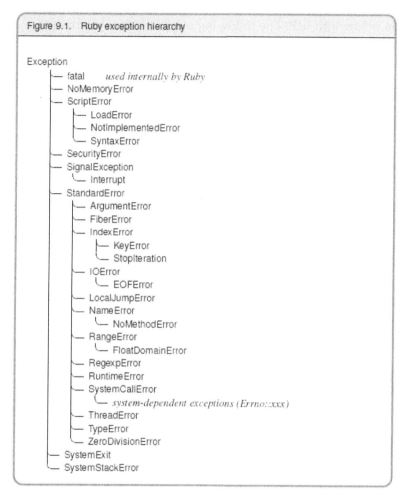

The chart shows that most of the subclasses extend a class known as StandardError. These are the "normal" exceptions that typical Ruby programs try to handle. The other exceptions represent lower-level, more serious, or less recoverable conditions, and normal Ruby programs do not typically attempt to handle them.

Example of forcing an exception to happen

Paste the code below into IRB. The following method raises an exception whenever it's called by calling 'raise'. Its second message will never be printed:

```
def raise_exception
puts 'I am before the raise.'
raise 'An error has occured'
puts 'I am after the raise'
end
raise_exception
```

The output is:

```
I am before the raise.
RuntimeError: An error has occured
from (irb):3:in `raise_exception'
```

By default, 'raise' creates an exception of the RuntimeError class. To raise an exception of a specific class, you can pass in the class name as an argument to raise. For example create a file called inverse.rb:

```
def inverse(x)
raise ArgumentError, 'Argument is not numeric' unless x.is_a?
Numeric
1.0 / x
end
puts inverse(2)
puts inverse('not a number')
```

run: ruby inverse.rb

output:

```
0.5
ArgumentError: Argument is not numeric
from (irb):8:in `inverse'
```

Handling an Exception

To do exception handling in order to capture the problem so we can then decide what to do with this problem, we enclose the code that could raise an exception in a begin-end block and use one or more rescue clauses to tell Ruby the types of exceptions we want to handle. You can stack rescue clauses in a begin/rescue block. Exceptions not handled by one rescue clause will trickle down to the next. If you need the guarantee that some processing is done at the end of a block of code, regardless of whether an exception was raised then the **ensure** clause can be used. ensure goes after the last rescue clause and contains a chunk of code that will always be executed as the block terminates. The ensure block will always run. For example:

```
begin
# something which might raise an exception
rescue SomeExceptionClass => some_variable
# code that deals with some exception
rescue SomeOtherException => some_other_variable
# code that deals with some other exception
else
# code that runs only if *no* exception was raised
ensure
# ensure that this code always runs, no matter what
end
```

To illustrates this:

```
def raise_and_rescue
begin
puts 'I am before the raise.'
raise 'An error has occured.'
puts 'I am after the raise.'
rescue
puts 'I am rescued.'
end

puts 'I am after the begin block.'
end
```

The output is:

```
I am before the raise.
I am rescued.
I am after the begin block.
```

Observe that the code interrupted by the exception never gets run. Once the exception is handled, execution continues immediately after the begin block that spawned it. If you write a rescue clause with no parameter list, the parameter defaults to StandardError. Each rescue clause can specify multiple exceptions to catch.

If you want to determine the exception cause, you can map the Exception object to a variable within the rescue clause. The Exception class defines two methods that return details about the exception. The **message** method returns a string that may provide human-readable details about what went wrong. The other important method is **backtrace**. This method returns an array of strings that represent the call stack at the point that the exception was raised:

```
begin
raise 'A test exception.'
rescue Exception => e
puts e.message
puts e.backtrace.inspect
end
```

The output is:

```
A test exception.
```

Improper error messages can provide critical information about an application which may aid an attacker in exploiting the application, also they look ugly. The most common problem occurs when detailed internal error messages such as stack traces, database dumps, and error codes are displayed to the user. Security analysts view logging and error handling as potential areas of risk. It is recommended that production applications should not use, for example the 'puts e.backtrace.inspect' call unless it is being directly committed into a log that is not viewable to the end user.

Which exceptions to catch

Exception is the root of the exception class hierarchy in Ruby. Everything from signal handling to memory errors will raise a subclass of Exception. Here's the full list of exceptions from ruby-core that we'll inadvertently rescue when rescuing Exception.

```
SystemStackError
NoMemoryError
SecurityError
ScriptError
NotImplementedError
LoadError
Gem::LoadError
SyntaxError
SignalException
Interrupt
SystemExit
```

```
Gem::SystemExitException
```

Do you really want to rescue a NoMemoryError and send an email saying the job failed?

rescue => e is shorthand for rescue StandardError => e and is almost certainly the broadest type of Exception that we want to rescue. In almost every circumstance, we can replace rescue Exception => e with rescue => e and be better off for it.

The only time when that's not a good idea is for code that's doing some kind of exception logging/reporting/management. In those rare cases, it's possible we'll want to rescue non-StandardErrors — but we still need to think pretty hard about what happens after we've rescued them.

Some typical code is:

```
def upload_to_app
#... do something...
rescue => e
flash[:error] = "The upload has an error"
end
```

However, there's a major gotcha with this code: we're still rescuing many exceptions we're not aware of. The typical standard errors are:

```
StandardError
FiberError
ThreadError
IndexError
StopIteration
KeyError
Math::DomainError
LocalJumpError
IOError
EOFError
EncodingError
Encoding::ConverterNotFoundError
Encoding::InvalidByteSequenceError
Encoding::UndefinedConversionError
Encoding::CompatibilityError
RegexpError
SystemCallError
RangeError
FloatDomainError
ZeroDivisionError
RuntimeError
```

```
Gem::Exception
NameError
NoMethodError
ArgumentError
Gem::Requirement::BadRequirementError
TypeError
```

If we wrapped the entire process in a rescue => e (which is rescuing StandardError) the NoMethodError is going to be swallowed and our graceful error handling code is going to be run instead. When we run our well written tests, they'll fail, as in Test Driven development where the tests are written first. But rather than raising a straight-forward NoMethodError, it'll look like there was an gracefully handled connectivity problem. If we want to catch connectivity problems in an API integration, our code will be qualified to rescue from a long list of Net related exceptions.

Custom exceptions

You could write a custom exception to make the code cleaner. for example write a CustomException module:

```
module CustomException
#example on how to call it:
#raise SeriousError
#for a serious error log it
class SeriousError < StandardError
attr_accessor :exception, :request
def initialize(exception, request=nil)
@exception = exception
@request = request
end

# Log error information to the console
# msg is optional custom message to show
def logging(msg=nil)
Rails.logger.error 'reason = ' +
(msg.present? ? msg : @exception.message)
end
end
```

then use it in the controller, to raise the custom exceptions:

```
class ApplicationController < ActionController::Base
include CustomException
```

Logs

All errors or messages that can help you find a problem should be written to a log file [or preferable to an output stream and not stored on the server] and also errors maybe to a database or sent in an email. We will discuss best practices for deployment later.

Reference: http://guides.rubyonrails.org/debugging_rails_applications.html

Rails makes use of the ActiveSupport::Logger class to write log information. by default, you can replace this with the more powerful log4r (based on log4j from Java)

The available log levels are: :debug, :info, :warn, :error, :fatal, and :unknown, in this order of importance. For example in your code add: logger.debug 'new member joined'

You could for example use logger.debug and turn on your log configuration for development print all debug messages but for production do not print debug messages by raising the log level.

'warn' in ruby 2.0 now works just like puts, taking multiple arguments, or an array, and outputting them, but on stderr rather than stdout. For example:

```
warn "foo", "bar"
```

Syslog

Syslog is a way for scalable servers to send event messages to a logging server in production – usually known as a Syslog server. As a de facto standard for computer message logging, syslog has been around many years. Fundamentally, every Linux and Unix variant delivers some level of syslog message logging as a default. Like any other logging capability, syslog must be enabled to work and the user needs to decide what to do with the data being logged. The choice of destination can be as simple as log files or you can use database logging. Splunk is a popular tool for collecting logs. For cloud based servers logging such as AWS cloud trail you do not need to be aware of syslog details. Since Ruby 2 it is easy to switch between logging to a file descriptor and to syslog:

```
if ENV["RACK_ENV"] == "production"
require "syslog"
logger = Syslog::Logger.new("my_app")
else
require "logger"
logger = Logger.new(STDOUT)
end
logger.debug("about to do stuff")
begin
do_stuff
rescue => e
logger.error(e.message)
end
logger.info("stuff done")
```

Print debugging

For console debugging we have 'p' and 'puts'. What's the Difference? 'p' will give you some more information because it runs the #inspect method on the object while #puts runs the #to_s method. #inspect is meant to be informative where #puts is better formatted output The difference may not be readily apparent while you're only working with simple objects like strings and arrays, but you'll notice it when you start creating your own objects and you want to see what's inside (without typing out puts my_object.inspect).

Garbage collection

Garbage Collection (GC) is a feature to automatically detect and free the memory which has become unnecessary. such as when created objects are no longer needed. With garbage collection, the worry, When should I have to free() some objects memory, has become unnecessary.

The garbage collector in Ruby 2.1 implements a form of generational garbage collection, with Ruby calling their implementation RGenGC (Restricted Generational Garbage Collection). This replaces the "Mark & Sweep" implementation used in previous versions of Ruby. At any point in time we can get a snapshot of the current situation with GC.stat:

```
GC.stat
```

```
=> {:count=>25,
:heap_used=>263,
:heap_length=>406,
:heap_increment=>143,
:heap_live_slot=>106806,
:heap_free_slot=>398,
:heap_final_slot=>0,
:heap_swept_slot=>25258,
:heap_eden_page_length=>263,
:heap_tomb_page_length=>0,
:total_allocated_object=>620998,
:total_freed_object=>514192,
:malloc_increase=>1572992,
:malloc_limit=>16777216,
:minor_gc_count=>21,
:major_gc_count=>4,
:remembered_shady_object=>1233,
:remembered_shady_object_limit=>1694,
:old_object=>65229,
:old_object_limit=>93260,
:oldmalloc_increase=>2298872,
:oldmalloc_limit=>16777216}
```

We can tune our settings,

```
RUBY_GC_MALLOC_LIMIT: (default: 16MB)
RUBY_GC_MALLOC_LIMIT_MAX: (default: 32MB)
RUBY_GC_MALLOC_LIMIT_GROWTH_FACTOR: (default: 1.4x)
```

With the popular cloud monitoring service tool called, newrelic, you can monitor it. You could stress test you app and monitor for example the number of connections in the queue versus the garbage collection settings used.

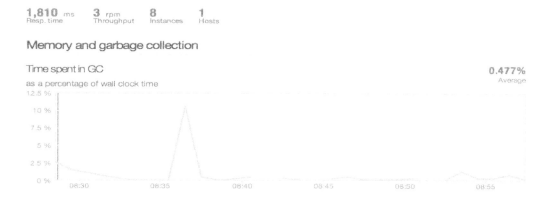

Memory Leaks

Some useful tools to help find memory leaks are:

- https://github.com/noahd1/oink
- http://valgrind.org/

Heroku will, thankfully, automatically reset your server once your memory leak exceeds a limit.

Flash

Flash is a way to pass messages from the controller to the view to inform the user of some even such as invalid form field. The flash is a special part of the session which is cleared with each request. This means that values stored there will only be available in the next request, which is useful for passing error messages etc..

Reference: http://guides.rubyonrails.org/action_controller_overview.html#the-flash

Let's use logging out as an example. The controller can send a message which will be displayed to the user on the next request:

```
class LoginsController < ApplicationController
def destroy
session[:current_user_id] = nil
flash[:notice] = "You have successfully logged out."
redirect_to root_url
end
end
```

Note that it is also possible to assign a flash message as part of the redirection. You can assign :notice, :alert or the general purpose :flash:

```
redirect_to root_url, notice: "You have successfully logged out."
redirect_to root_url, alert: "You're stuck here!"
redirect_to root_url, flash: { referral_code: 1234 }
```

To display the flash message in a view, This way, if an action sets a notice or an alert message, the layout will display it automatically:

```
<html>
<!-- <head/> -->
<body>
<% flash.each do |name, msg| -%>
<%= content_tag :div, msg, class: name %>
<% end -%>

<!-- more content -->
</body>
</html>
```

Custom flash types

As of Rails 4, developers will have the ability to register their own flash types by using the new ActionController::Flash.add_flash_types macro style method.

Here is an example of setting an error flash type in Rails 3:

```
# app/controllers/users_controller.rb
class UsersController < ApplicationController
def create
. . .
flash[:error] = "An error message for the user"
redirect_to home_path
end
end

# app/views/home/index
<%= flash[:error] %>
```

Here is the same example as above, using Rails 4:

```
# app/controllers/application_controller.rb
class ApplicationController
. . .
add_flash_types :error, :success
end
# app/controllers/users_controller.rb
class UsersController < ApplicationController
def create
...
```

```
redirect_to @user, success: "User created!"
  end
end
# app/views/home/index
<%= success %>
```

Asset pipeline

The Rails asset pipeline provides a framework to concatenate and minify or compress Javascript and CSS assets. It also adds the ability to write these assets in other languages and pre-processors such as CoffeeScript, Sass and ERB. The first feature of the pipeline is to concatenate assets, which can reduce the number of requests that a browser makes to render a web page. Web browsers are limited in the number of requests that they can make in parallel, so fewer requests can mean faster loading for your application.

Reference: http://guides.rubyonrails.org/asset_pipeline.html

Making the asset pipeline a core feature of Rails means that all developers can benefit from the power of having their assets pre-processed, compressed and minified by one central library, Sprockets. The asset pipeline is enabled by default.

In development mode, or if the asset pipeline is disabled, when these files are requested they are processed by the processors provided by the coffee-script and sass gems and then sent back to the browser as JavaScript and CSS respectively. When asset pipelining is enabled, these files are preprocessed and placed in the public/assets directory for serving by either the Rails app or web server.

The asset pipeline is technically no longer a core feature of Rails 4, it has been extracted out of the framework into the sprockets-rails gem. Sprockets concatenates all JavaScript files into one master. js file and all CSS files into one master. css file. In production, Rails inserts an MD5 fingerprint into each filename so that the file is cached by the web browser. You can invalidate the cache by altering this fingerprint, which happens automatically whenever you change the file contents.

The second feature of the asset pipeline is asset minification/compression. For CSS files, this is done by removing whitespace and comments. For JavaScript, more complex processes can be applied. You can choose from a set of built in options or specify your own.

The third feature of the asset pipeline is it allows coding assets via a higher-level language, with pre-compilation down to the actual assets. Supported languages include Sass for CSS, CoffeeScript for JavaScript, and ERB for both by default. for example:

The asset pipeline automatically evaluates ERB. This means if you add an erb extension to a CSS asset (for example, application.css.erb), then helpers like asset_path are available in your CSS rules:

```
.class { background-image: url(<%= asset_path 'image.png' %>) }
```

In development mode, assets are served as separate files in the order they are specified in the manifest file. In production during the pre-compilation phase an MD5 is generated from the contents of the compiled files, and inserted into the filenames as they are written to the public directory and will be served as static assets by your web server. These fingerprinted names are used by the Rails helpers in place of the manifest name.

For example this:

```
<%= javascript_include_tag "application" %>
<%= stylesheet_link_tag "application" %>
```

generates something like this:

```
<script src="/assets/application-908e25f4bf641868d8683022a5b62f54.js"></script>
<link href="/assets/application-4dd5b109ee3439da54f5bdfd78a80473.css" media="screen" rel="stylesheet" />
```

Rails comes bundled with a rake task to compile the asset manifests and other files in the pipeline. Compiled assets are written to the location specified in config.assets.prefix. By default, this is the /assets directory.

The rake task is:

```
RAILS_ENV=production bundle exec rake assets:precompile
```

Capistrano (a production deployment tool) includes a recipe to handle this in deployment. Add the following line to Capfile:

```
load 'deploy/assets'
```

Turbolinks

Turbolinks uses Ajax to speed up page rendering, makes following links in your web application faster. Turbolinks will improve your page load significantly if your pages share JavaScript and CSS styling. Instead of letting the browser recompile the JavaScript and CSS between each page change, it keeps the current page instance alive and replaces only the body and the header title. The more CSS and JavaScript you have, the bigger the benefit of not throwing away the browser instance and recompiling all of it for every page. With Turbolinks pages will change without a full reload. By default, all internal HTML links will be funnelled through Turbolinks. Rails 4 comes with Turbolinks enabled by default.

reference:
http://guides.rubyonrails.org/working_with_javascript_in_rails.html#turbolinks

If you have a lot of existing JavaScript that binds elements on jQuery.ready(), you can pull the jquery.turbolinks library into your project that will trigger ready() when Turbolinks triggers the the page:load event.

If you are using the turbolinks gem, which is included by default in Rails 4, then include the 'data-turbolinks-track' option which causes turbolinks to check if an asset has been updated and if so loads it into the page:

```
<%= stylesheet_link_tag "application", media: "all", "data-turbolinks-track" => true %>
<%= javascript_include_tag "application", "data-turbolinks-track" => true %>
```

You can check if everything is working by opening the chrome developer tools in your browser and opening the Network tab. You should see that turbolink.js is handling the requests when you click on a link in the dating site. On all requests made by a browser that supports pushState will be handled by turbolinks.

A project to check if turbo link helps your speed boost is https://github.com/steveklabnik/turbolinks_test to run benchmarks for different situations. His results are with 100 pages:

```
$ rspec
```

```
user              system      total         real
no turbolinks     1.640000    0.190000      2.140000 ( 15.652763)
with turbolinks   1.120000    0.090000      1.210000 (  7.776116)
```

Transition Cache, added in v2.2.0 of turbolinks, makes loading cached pages instantaneous. Once a user has visited a page, returning later to the page results in an instant load. To enable Transition Cache, include the following in your Javascript:

`Turbolinks.enableTransitionCache();`

Disadvantages:

Javascript does not have a way to directly erase an object once it was created. Engine automatically destroys all instances that are not referenced from anywhere. In theory even with Turbolinks, as soon as we drop the page out and load the next one we are supposed to detach the application. Dereferenced application gets collected and our RAM is free again, but Turbolinks save DOM. And DOM has bindings, and bindings reference you application. They are stored for a reason. As soon as you go back – it restores your DOM. Therefore restoring your application parts. So big parts of your application survive at page reload. Therefore in practice there's a HUGE chance that Turbolinks will boost RAM usage alot. So it is worth to demo it's use before using it.

PJAX

another alternative to turbolinks is https://github.com/defunkt/jquery-pjax or https://github.com/eval/rack-pjax whereby you can optimise only some specific parts of you page if you like. Pjax works by grabbing HTML from your server via Ajax and replacing the content of a container on your page with the ajax'd HTML. Turbolinks claim that it is the successor to Pjax that seamlessly works out of box. There is a Rails gem called pjax_rails.

Internationalisation

Ruby uses a default utf-8 encoding to give better support for foreign characters. If you think your site will have more than one foreign language it is good to get this library in as soon as possible in order to have the hooks for using the different language string files in place. you need to do is maintain a YAML file of translations, using I18n is useful for more than just rolling your app out to more locales. When it comes time to rename something in your interface, having a single place to look for the string in question in order to replace it across the whole application is much quicker than scouring your code for every occurrence.

Reference: http://guides.rubyonrails.org/i18n.html

Rake Task

While much of your application is built to (swiftly) respond to a web request, there are many scenarios where you would like to access and run pieces of your application outside of that request/response cycle. You may want to run maintenance tasks, periodic calculations, or reporting in your production environment. The rake gem is Ruby's most widely accepted solution for performing these types of tasks.

Rails uses a task management tool called rake with capabilities similar to 'make'. It allows you to specify tasks and describe dependencies, all the task are written in Ruby. We already used it above with activerecord. You can view your most common application's rake tasks by entering:

```
rake -T
```

Bundle exec

You may have to use, bundle exec rake. bundle exec is a bundle command to execute a script in the context of the current bundle. The Bundler tool maintains a consistent environment for ruby applications. It tracks an application's code and the rubygems it needs to run, so that an application will always have the exact gems (and versions) that it needs to run.

To list all the gems within the global gem set enter:

```
gem list
```

If you have multiple versions of some executable (which is used to run other files) like rake, rspec etc. in your gemset, it could throw error due to conflict. For example:

```
gem list | grep rake
rake (10.3.2, 10.3.1, 10.2.2, 10.1.1, 10.1.0)
```

A solution is to prefix 'bundle exec' to run your executable. It will run the version associated with your gem file, thus removing the conflict. Running any executable without bundle exec will have Rubygems fetching the latest version of the gem installed in your system. By adding the bundle exec prefix instead will have the executable running in the context of your Gemfile.lock, which means that will be run using the version defined in the gem file.

Alternatively remove the gem causing the conflict. If you do not want to prefix 'bundle exec' with your executable command like rake respec etc, remove the conflicting gem:

```
gem uninstall rake -v 10.0.3
```

Note: It is good practice to run all the executable commands with bundle exec prefix, which will ensure that your command will always work.

Example custom rake task

You can write your own rake tasks. Rails will automatically pick up tasks in lib/tasks. Any files named with the. rake extension will get picked up when you do rake -T.

The most simple way to define a Rake task is to write the following Ruby code and save as 'rakefile', An example, create a file called enter.rake in lib/tasks:

```
desc 'Ring the bell'
task :ring do
puts "Bell is ringing."
end
desc 'Enter home'
task :enter => :ring do
puts "Entering home!"
end

>rake enter
Entering home!
>rake ring
Bell is ringing.
```

The description tag, 'desc' will not only serve you as an inline comment, it will also appear on the list of available tasks. Let's print the descriptions:

```
$ rake -T
rake enter # Enter home
rake ring  # Ring the bell
```

You can get access to your models, and in fact, your whole environment by making tasks dependent on the environment task. This lets you do things like run:

```
rake RAILS_ENV=staging db:migrate
```

Scheduling rake tasks

Cron is a unix utility for scheduling and executing commands.To utilise cron, you create a crontab file to enter the commands to be executed with:

```
crontab -e
```

You can use cron to schedule rake tasks. To list your exisiting cron entries use 'crontab -l'. The timing of a cron job follows a standard format that, while is a little intimidating at first. In fact, it's very much like a time based regex in the following pattern:

minute hour day month weekday

An example is:

```
15 * * * *
```

Run on the 15th minute of every hour of the day, every day of the month, every month of the year, every day of the week. Let's say you wanted to run the account email expiration task every night at 12:15 on your production server, you might have something like this:

```
15 * * * * cd /data/my_app/current && /usr/bin/rake RAILS_ENV=production accounts:email_expiring
```

Rails Rakefile

When you create any new rails project, you will find a file called Rakefile in your project root directory. Rake finds these tasks by reading the Rakefile. In our dating application, the Rakefile will look like this:

```
require File.expand_path('../config/application', __FILE__)
Dating::Application.load_tasks
```

You should add your own rake tasks in the lib/tasks. This is possible thanks to the load_tasks call made to your application object. Say, for example, that we're going to create a file: lib/tasks/myrailsapp.rake.

It's a good practice to wrap your tasks into a namespace to make sure they don't collide with tasks from Rails or other libraries. In the Rakefile, you'd create a namespace like this:

```
namespace :myrailsapp do
task purge_audits: :environment do
puts "Purging old audits..."
Audit.purge
end
end
```

It starts with the task method which takes a hash parameter. The key, here :purge_audits, will be the name of the task. When your task depends on :environment, it will load your entire Rails application. If your task doesn't actually need Rails, don't depend on :environment and you can greatly increase startup time and decrease memory usage.

Generate task

If you want to write your own rake task you have 2 ways to do it. Write it from scratch or just use this rake generator:

```
rails g task my_namespace my_task1 my_task2
output>create lib/tasks/my_namespace.rake
```

It will generate scaffold for our new rake task: lib/tasks/my_namespace.rake

```
namespace :my_namespace do
desc "TODO"
task :my_task1 => :environment do
end
desc "TODO"
task :my_task2 => :environment do
end
end
```

Let's make sure these rake tasks exist and we are able to use them:

```
$ rake -T | grep my_namespace
rake my_namespace:my_task1 # TODO
rake my_namespace:my_task2 # TODO
```

TESTING : UNIT, RSPEC, CUCUMBER

One of Rails main selling point is having tests being a core part of the framework. Rails by default uses the MiniTest library for unit tests, many people like myself prefer to use Rspec, and use Shoulda for the result (assertions) checking with mocha for the stubbing/mocking code that is not written yet or you want to test in isolation.

Reference: http://guides.rubyonrails.org/testing.html

Testing Levels

There are generally four recognised levels of tests: unit testing, integration testing, system testing, and acceptance testing.

Unit testing, also known as component testing, refers to tests that verify the functionality of a specific section of code, usually at the function level. In an object-oriented environment, this is usually at the class level.It is performed by the software developer or engineer during the development. Unit testing is all about testing small sections of code (normally a single method, but a unit is a flexible beast) and testing it in isolation. Unit testing has to do with testing each method, for example check a model can be created. You can test each layer, Model, View, Controller, but some people are in favour of just testing say the model and View layers as the view will test the controller.

Integration testing is any type of software testing that seeks to verify the interfaces between components against a software design. Integration tests are from a users perfective such as clicking on form buttons and checking the responsive generated. The process of combining and testing multiple components together. You don't have to use Cucumber for integration tests, you could create Rspec integration tests. It is a preference as some people like/hate user story testing with Cucumber, personally I like Cucumber as it captures business requirements.

System testing, or end-to-end testing, tests a completely integrated system to verify that it meets its requirements. For example, a system test might involve testing a logon interface, then creating and editing an entry, plus sending or printing results, followed by summary processing or deletion (or archiving) of entries, then logoff. The testing carried out to analyze the behavior of the whole system according to the requirement specification is known as system testing.

At last the system is delivered to the user for Acceptance testing. acceptance testing is a test conducted to determine if the requirements of a specification or contract are met.

Blackbox, white box, grey box

System tests and acceptance tests can be classified into white, black or grey box testing.

QA Software testing methods are traditionally divided into white- and black-box testing. These two approaches are used to describe the point of view that a test engineer takes when designing test cases.

White-box testing tests internal structures or workings of a program, as opposed to the functionality exposed to the end-user. In white-box testing an internal perspective of the system, as well as programming skills, are used to design test cases. The tester chooses inputs to exercise paths through the code and determine the appropriate outputs.

While white-box testing can be applied at the unit, integration and system levels of the software testing process, it is usually done at the unit level. It can test paths within a unit, paths between units during integration, and between subsystems during a system-level test. Though this method of test design can uncover many errors or problems, it might not detect unimplemented parts of the specification or missing requirements.

Black-box testing treats the software as a "black box", examining functionality without any knowledge of internal implementation. The testers are only aware of what the software is supposed to do, not how it does it.[

Grey-box testing involves having knowledge of internal data structures and algorithms for purposes of designing tests, while executing those tests at the user, or black-box level. The tester is not required to have full access to the software's source code.

Software testing methodologies

The current trend to to write tests before you write the code called Test Driven Development (TDD), this is not everyones taste, in my option as long as the final test coverage is high it will be a well tested product, but it is worth doing TDD for a few days to see if it makes you more productive, less bugs and enjoyable. People have lost job interviews by not beginning their interview coding task as TDD.

No tests

Many people do not write any tests. The problem is when you change the code and it is harder to see if your changes will break other parts of the code.

Write tests after you write the code

This is the traditional way of software design, implement your functionality then write unit tests afterwards - mainly because your boss wants test coverage.

TDD

Test driven development is all about writing the tests before you write the code. This does add a large overhead, but when do you think it is cheaper than to find/fix a bug. Much less sending it to the testing team, waiting a week for them to run a set of tests against it and then having to be pulled of a different user story to try to work out what I was thinking a week ago.

1. Write a test - test the bit of functionality you want (but doesn't exist yet)
2. Write the littlest bit of code - fill in enough to make the test you just wrote pass
3. Repeat - go back to step 1 until you have all the functionality you want

The philosophy of TDD is that you want 100% (ideally) test coverage. Logically, if you want to write tests, you have the option to write them before or after you actually code the functionality. The advantages of doing it before you code are:

- You actually test your tests, since they should fail (when you write them) then pass (when you write your code)
- You guarantee that you have a lot of test coverage at all times.
- When you go to refactor you know you have lots of test coverage to ensure you don't do something stupid (this is the biggest advantage I see, since lots of times you're working on old code that you've forgotten the details about).
- Some people say that it helps them clearly define what they're about to do, so they can actually fill in the code faster. Even if it takes longer, it does seem

advantageous to build in the test coverage when you go back to that code and refactor/change/optimise it later.

Fixtures

Fixtures is a fancy word for sample data. Fixtures allow you to populate your testing database with predefined data before your tests run, either unit or integration tests. Fixtures are database independent written in YAML. There is one file per model.

Reference: http://guides.rubyonrails.org/testing.html#the-low-down-on-fixtures

for example:

```
member1:
name: paul
last_name: smith
```

then in your tests you can use,

```
members(:member1)
```

You'll find fixtures under your test/fixtures directory. When you run 'rails generate model' to create a new model, then fixture stubs will be automatically created and placed in this directory. The testing environment will automatically load the all fixtures into the database before each test. Loading involves three steps:

1. Remove any existing data from the table corresponding to the fixture.
2. Load the fixture data into the table.
3. Dump the fixture data into a variable in case you want to access it directly.

Alternative to Rails fixtures

Many people prefer to use factory_girl gem for test fixtures. FactoryGirl replaces fixtures in tests. Other gems people use instead of test fixtures are Machinist and Fabrication. But Factory girl would still be the most popular, Some think Machinist is faster.

Useful rake commands for running tests

```
RAILS_ENV=test rake db:drop #drop the test database
RAILS_ENV=test rake db:create #create test database
RAILS_ENV=test rake db:migrate
RAILS_ENV=test rake db:seed
RAILS_ENV=test db:schema:load #creates tables and columns
within the database following schema.rb
RAILS_ENV=test db:setup #does db:create, db:schema:load, db:seed
RAILS_ENV=test db:reset #does db:drop, db:setup
RAILS_ENV=test db:test:prepare #depreciated
```

Integration tests

Automated Integration testing is the phase in software testing in which individual software modules are combined and tested as a group. Traditionally It occurs after unit testing and before validation testing. In TDD you write your integration tests before the unit tests.

Popular gems for testing web pages are selenium-webdriver, capybara or webrat, my favourite is capybara - this is a layer on top of selenium.

For integration tests capybara can be used to extract HTML page elements, for example to fill in a form and press submit. you can use selenium to interact with a real browser or headless browser (browser without a graphical user interface) to use as a simulated browser for performance reasons. Capybara helps you test web applications by simulating how a real user would interact with your app. It is agnostic about the driver running your tests and comes with Rack::Test and Selenium support built in.

I have seen code break regularly on different browsers due to javascript/CSS issues so being able to test multiple browsers automatically is a goal to aim for. An interesting tool for cross browser testing is Selenium grid, which is used to allow the tests to run on different browsers across different servers. Selenium Grid solves the scalability problem by coordinating many Selenium web driver instances, allowing you to run multiple tests in parallel on different machines.

For automated test speed then a headless browser such as PhantomJS is popular, also for example to test IE browser on linux has limitations. Microsoft have test Virtual Machines of Internet Explorer at www.modern.ie

To test multiple browsers in the cloud good options are with saucelabs, and browserstack.com.

Cucumber

The Cucumber library is a great framework to document your stories and implement the steps from this, Gherkin is the language used to for this. Cucumber lets software development teams describe how software should behave in plain text. The text is written in a business-readable domain-specific language and serves as documentation, automated tests and development aid - all rolled into one format.

Every. feature file conventionally consists of a single feature. A feature usually contains a list of scenarios.

Every scenario consists of a list of steps, which must start with one of the keywords: Given, When, Then, But or And. Cucumber treats them all the same, but you shouldn't. Here is an example:

```
Feature: Serve coffee
Coffee should not be served until paid for
Coffee should not be served until the button has been pressed
If there is no coffee left then money should be refunded

Scenario: Buy last coffee
Given there are 1 coffees left in the machine
And I have deposited 1$
When I press the coffee button
Then I should be served a coffee
```

Step definitions

For each step Cucumber will look for a matching step definition. A step definition is written in Ruby. Each step definition consists of a keyword, a string or regular expression, and a block. Example:

```
# features/step_definitions/coffee_steps.rb
Then "I should be served coffee" do
  @machine.dispensed_drink.should == "coffee"
end
```

Cucumber will also report the total test coverage percentage. For TDD over 90% test coverage would be a goal, but in reality 60% test coverage would be good enough for most people, it usually drops as the project gets older with more code added, something which service orientated architecture is good at by reducing the size of any one large application so we can 'start fresh'. In practice I use model tests and cucumber integration tests. It is important to monitor your integration test times as it can easily creep up to an hour or more if there are lots of tests. Tests can be run in parallel such as with: https://github.com/grosser/parallel_tests

Number of QA people

What is the ideal number of QA testers per developers? This can be debated, larger well funded projects can have an equal number of QA and developers, while a ratio of 3 developers to one QA person for medium size projects may do depending on the testing strategy/automation - how technical is the QA person with developing the Cucumber steps for example, or reviewing the code produced etc.. Google have Software Engineers in Test roles to advise on testing strategy for the developers.

Native Mobile device testing

Testing native mobile front ends have their challenges in that swipe, touches need to be supported. For native apps [just for reference]:

- iOS uses instrument Automation [you can record tests with it also],.
- Android uses uiAutomator for unit tests, or Robotium for integration tests [there is also a paid for robotium test recorder].

Two popular tools to write once and test across multiple devices are

- Appium [https://saucelabs.com/appium]
- Calaba [http://calaba.sh/]

I feel appium has access to more device capabilities such as tap. Saucelabs using appium is a cloud service used to test multiple devices. These frameworks could also be used for testing mobile web sites.

Rather than develop two different tests, you could use a common testing script such as Appium to test. pro's/cons to both, if you are familiar with android/eclipse and ios/xcode I would recommend going native in order to access all functionality. Appium is a good solutino if say both iOS/Android apps are in sync with the same features.

Test Javascript

We will discuss single page applications in Javascript later, two popular testing frameworks are Mocha with Chai or Jasmine. I prefer Jasmine as it is self contained.

Continuous integration

When you release new code changes, it is standard practice now to have a tool for running all your tests [unit/integration], that typically hooks into your version control and detects when new code is released or do it periodically.

Popular tools are http://hudson-ci.org/, http://jenkins-ci.org/, http://www.jetbrains.com/teamcity/, https://www.atlassian.com/software/bamboo (the Bamboo rails plugin will not work for their cloud service) or a cloud services like https://codeship.io/features or https://travis-ci.com/. I like Teamcity but lately starting to use codeship.io more. Codeship creates a new Virtual Machine for each test run including creating a database for your tests: https://codeship.io/documentation/databases/postgresql/.

Newer continuous integration cloud services such as codeship.io allows you to run your tests against multiple browsers, and also for example to connect to saucelabs [uses appium] for better access to different browser versions for testing.

Remember that continuous delivery != continuous deployment. Continuous delivery just means that every change to your code is proven to be deployable at any time.

Code metrics

It is useful to run regular analysis of your code, to get the stats on your code.

```
rake stats
```

```
+----------------+-------+-------+---------+---------+-----+-------+
| Name           | Lines |  LOC  | Classes | Methods | M/C | LOC/M |
+----------------+-------+-------+---------+---------+-----+-------+
| Controllers    |  176  |  149  |   10    |   18    |  1  |   6   |
| Helpers        |   38  |   35  |    0    |    4    |  0  |   6   |
| Models         |  183  |  147  |    5    |   20    |  4  |   5   |
| Libraries      |    0  |    0  |    0    |    0    |  0  |   0   |
| Integration tests|  0  |    0  |    0    |    0    |  0  |   0   |
| Functional tests|855  |  686  |    9    |    3    |  0  |  226  |
| Unit tests     |  684  |  568  |    7    |    0    |  0  |   0   |
+----------------+-------+-------+---------+---------+-----+-------+
| Total          | 1936  | 1585  |   31    |   45    |  1  |  33   |
+----------------+-------+-------+---------+---------+-----+-------+
  Code LOC: 331     Test LOC: 1254     Code to Test Ratio: 1:3.8
```

Other useful gems are 'flog', 'metric_fu', and rcov.

System tests

Part of final system tests may involve manual tests, rather than use an excel/document to record these tests some useful test management tools are tarantula www.testiatarantula.com/ (free). Commercial ones are HP quality center, IBM rational Quality manager.

Mobile debug tools

Some useful debugging tools are:

1. Chrome developer

You can enable remote debugging from Chrome to your android device. In your browser enter this URL and Select – Discover USB devices, next go to the web page you want to debug and select this page and enter as the URL:

chrome://inspect/#devices

Reference: https://developer.chrome.com/devtools/docs/remote-debugging

It has a mobile emulation feature to simulate a mobile device also supports touch emulation. Open developer console in chrome, and press 'esc', emulator tab appears. You can change the viewport, pixel ratio and also use touch commands.

Reference: https://developers.google.com/chrome-developer-tools/docs/mobile-emulation

2. Safari - Safari has a good web inspector develop option. Use Apple's Safari web browser for testing your iOS ready website by simulating an HTTP request from Safari on the iPad, iPhone. Enable developer mode (under preferences), you can then simulate different devices by changing the user agent.

You can also enable remote web inspector to debug mobile web pages on your iOS device from your desktop safari. On your device, head to Settings > Safari > Advanced You'll find the Web Inspector toggle there.

Once enabled, you'll need to physically connect your iPhone or iPad to your Mac, this is Mac only at this point. In Safari's Preferences panel under Advanced, check the Show Develop menu in the menu bar checkbox. Select the Develop menu, and your iDevice should be a menu option. You should now be able to inspect DOM elements, modify CSS on the fly, and run Javascript commands.

Note: this procedure will also enable remote debugging of your PhoneGap (Cordova) and other UIWebView based projects.

3. Firebug is a great debug tool to use with Firefox:

Reference: http://getfirebug.com/

For responsive design overview the Firefox Responsive_Design_View plugin is very useful.

https://developer.mozilla.org/en-US/docs/Tools/Responsive_Design_View

4. Opera dragonfly has remote debugging which allows you to connect to the Opera browser on your device and to start debugging:

Reference: http://www.opera.com/dragonfly/

5. Useful tool for tweaking css and javascript http://tin.cr

6. Weinre is a debugger for web pages, like FireBug (for FireFox) and Web Inspector (for WebKit-based browsers), except it's designed to work remotely, and in particular, to allow you debug web pages on a mobile device such as a phone, maybe not so useful now with easy of chrome/safari remote debugging.

Caching

To get high performance with as little resources as possible, the trick is not to hit the backend database as this is generally the slowest component with physical moving parts etc.. It can get complicated with no many powerful caching mechanisms provided.

HTTP caching occurs when the browser stores local copies of web resources for faster retrieval the next time the resource is required. As your application serves resources it can attach cache headers to the response specifying the desired cache behaviour. For instance, once CSS stylesheets from your application are downloaded by the browser there's no need to download them again during the user's session. When an item is fully cached, the browser may choose to not contact the server at all and simply use its own cached copy. An Rails app using HTTP cache headers is able to control this caching behaviour.

To start testing caching you'll want to ensure that config.action_controller.perform_caching is set to true, if you're running in development mode as it is only turned on in production mode normally.

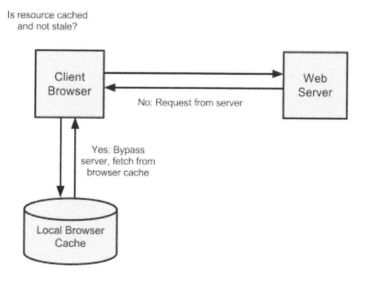

With Single Page Applications you will not benefit from the Rails view caching which is worth taking into account in deciding your technology stack.

Out of the box, Rails provides a simple HTTP caching configuration for static pages and assets. While your application benefits from this setup, specifying cache headers for all requests, even dynamic ones, can give you an order of magnitude improvement in response times.

Some challenges I have seen is for example in displaying content based on a users location, in which case there is an argument for making the landing (and content) pages more generic to all users so it can be cached. Rails has great built in caching features.

Reference: http://edgeguides.rubyonrails.org/caching_with_rails.html

Asset Pipeline Cache

Rails added HTTP cache headers to prevent refetching identical assets across requests. Requests for assets come with multiple HTTP headers defining how that asset should be stored locally such as cache-control, and etag.

Setting the cache headers for maximum performance remains your responsibility as an application developer.

HTTP cache headers

There are two primary cache headers: Cache-Control and Expires.

Cache-Control header

The Cache-Control header is the most important header to set as it effectively 'switches on' caching in the browser. With this header in place, and set with a value that enables caching, the browser will cache the file for as long as specified. Without this header the browser will re-request the file on each subsequent request. The value of the Cache-Control header is a composite one, For example:

```
Request Header:
Cache-Control:max-age=0
```

Or:

```
Response Header:
Cache-Control:max-age=0, private, must-revalidate
```

Note: private resources are bypassed by intermediate proxies and can only be cached by the end-client. Public resources can be cached not only by the end-user's browser but also by any intermediate proxies that may be serving many other users as well.

By default, Cache-Control is set to private for all requests. However, some cache settings can overwrite the default behaviour making it advisable to explicitly specify private resources:

```
expires_in(1000.seconds, public: false)
```

Public responses don't contain sensitive data and can be stored by intermediate proxy caches. Use public: true in caching methods to identify public resources.

```
expires_in(3.minutes, public: true)
```

Max-age cache

The max-age value sets a timespan for how long to cache the resource (in seconds). Max-age=0 means do not cache. A max-age value prevents the resource from being requested by the client for the specified interval. This serves as a course-grained approach to caching and is useful for content that changes infrequently.

The cache-control expires field simply sets a date from which the cached resource should no longer be considered valid. From this date forward the browser will request a fresh copy of the resource. Until then, the browsers local cached copy will be used. If both Expires and max-age are set max-age will take precedence.

Rails provides two controller methods to specify time-based caching of resources via the Expires HTTP header – **expires_in** and **expires_now**. The Cache-Control header's max-age value is configured using the expires_in controller method (used in the show action of the sample app):

```
def show
@member = Member.find(params[:id])
expires_in 3.minutes, :public => true #180seconds
#...
end
```

When a request is made for a member resource the Cache-Control header will be set appropriately. When used in conjunction with Rack::Cache requests for these resources hit the controller only once in the specified interval.

You can force expiration of a resource using the **expires_now** controller method. This will set the Cache-Control header to no-cache and prevent caching by the browser or any intermediate caches:

```
def show
@member = Member.find(params[:id])
expires_now if params[:id] == '1'
#...
end
```

expires_now will only be executed on requests that invoke the controller action. Resources with headers previously set via expires_in will not immediately request for an updated resource until the expiration period has passed.

HTTP Header Time Based Cache

Last modified

To enable conditional requests the application specifies the last modified time of a resource via the Last-Modified response header. The **stale?** controller method gets the appropriate ETag and Last-Modified-Since headers and determines if the current request is stale (needs to be fully processed) or is fresh (the web client can use its cached content):

```
def show
@member = Member.find(params[:id])
#...
if stale?(etag: @member, last_modified: @member.updated_at)
respond_to do |format|
format.html # show.html.erb
format.json { render json: @member }
end
end
end
```

Nesting respond_to within the stale? block ensures that view rendering, often the most-expensive part of any request, only executes when necessary. When view processing is avoided with HTTP caching fewer database calls are required, resulting in significant additional gains. If content is not stale subsequent requests skip view rendering and return a 304 Not modified avoiding the most expensive part of the request.

Fresh_when

While the stale? method returned a boolean value, letting you execute different paths depending on the freshness of the request, **fresh_when** just sets the ETag and Last-Modified-Since response headers and, if the request is fresh, also sets the 304 Not Modified response status.

This example will automatically send back a :not_modified if the request is fresh, and will render the default template (member.*) if it's stale:

```
def show
@member = Member.find(params[:id])
fresh_when last_modified: @member.published_at.utc,
```

```
etag: @member
end
```

HTTP Header Content Based Cache

ETag

The HTTP ETag (or Entity Tag) works in a similar way to the Last-Modified header except it's value is a digest of the resources contents (for instance, an MD5 hash). This allows the server to identify if the cached contents of the resource are different to the most recent version. While this approach is transparent to the application it still requires the application to fully process the request to hash the response body. The only savings are the cost of sending the full response over the network back to the end client since an empty response with the 304 Not Modified response status is sent instead, which makes sense for a slow bandwidth mobile connection.

This tag is useful when for when the last modified date is difficult to determine. As with the If-Modified-Since header, if the current version has the same ETag value, indicating its value is the same as the browser's cached copy, then an HTTP status of 304 is returned.

For example:

```
Request Header
Cache-Control:max-age=0
If-None-Match:"095e9cc3da076284913e7dec2ef11e3a"
Response Header
Cache-Control:max-age=0, private, must-revalidate
Connection:Keep-Alive
Date:Sun, 20 Sep 2014 11:58:45 GMT
Etag:"095e9cc3da076284913e7dec2ef11e3a"
```

On subsequent browser requests the If-None-Match request header is sent with the ETag value of the last requested version of the resource. if the current version has the same ETag value, indicating its value is the same as the browser's cached copy, then an HTTP status of 304 is returned.

Rails 4 etags

One of the new features in Rails 4 is the ability to suffix controller-wide information to ETags. At the controller class level, you can set data by passing a block to the new etag macro style method. The etag method can be called multiple times, with each subsequent call suffixing the information to the response's ETag for easy client-side caching.

```
class PhotoController < ApplicationController
etag { current_user.try :id }
def show
@photo = Photo.find(params[:id])
fresh_when(@photo)
end
end
```

By using etag to include the id of the current user, we are ensuring that only that authenticated user will be able to generate the same ETag. This technique will prevent cached authorised pages from being accessible to other users.

If an Active Record model is passed into fresh_when, the response's ETag is set to the model's cache_key plus the current user id. The fresh_when method calls ActiveSupport::Cache.expand_cache_key behind the scenes. If we were using an array of items, instead of a single model, the ETag would include the cache_key of each item of the array and the current user id, all concatenated into a single unique identifier.

In the above example, we passed a single Active Record model to the fresh_when method. The code is equivalent to:

```
fresh_when(etag: @photo, last_modified: @photo.try(:updated_at))
```

Rack::ETag provides support for conditional requests (the browser can ask the server if it has an updated copy of the resource.) by automatically assigning an ETag header and Cache-Control: private on all responses.

Rack::Cache

A good way to speed up delivery of your assets such as images files is to use say a CDN such as amazon cloud front with S3. If you are using a CDN, then adding Rack::Cache will not speed up delivery of assets, If you do not wish to use a CDN, Rack::Cache is an good way to speed up asset delivery which we will discuss now.

Rack::Cache is a Rack middleware that enables HTTP caching on your application and allows an application to serve assets from a storage backend without requiring work from the main Rails application.

Reverse-proxy caches, such as Rack::Cache, stand between web clients (browsers) and your application and transparently cache publicly cacheable resources. In production mode, all your pages with public cache headers will be stored in Rack::Cache acting as a middle-man proxy. As a result, your Rails stack will be bypassed on these requests for cached resources. By default Rack::Cache will use in-memory storage. In highly distributed environments a shared cache resource such as memcached should be used (use the gems, dalli, rack-cache) and in production.rb add config.cache_store = :dalli_store.

Additionally, specify how long an item should stay cached by setting the Cache-Control headers. Without a Cache-Control header static files will not be stored by Rack::Cache.

To production.rb add:

```
config.static_cache_control = "public, max-age=3600"
```

Note: You could also cache static content with nginx or apache in front of the Rails app.

View Page Fragment caching

Dynamic web applications usually build pages with a variety of components not all of which have the same caching characteristics. In order to address such a dynamically created page where different parts of the page need to be cached and expired differently, Rails provides a mechanism called Fragment Caching.

Fragment Caching allows a fragment of view logic to be wrapped in a cache block and served out of the cache store when the next request comes in. Then you could easily cache the partial for each individual member with fragment caching. Rails will automatically generate a cache key if you pass it an ActiveRecord object:

```
<% cache do %>
All available members:
<% Member.all.each do |p| %>
<%= link_to p.name, product_url(p) %>
<% end %>
<% end %>
```

To expire this cache in the controller you could call the expire_fragment method.

A fragment caching strategy is to cache widgets or other discrete portions of pages that do not need to be refreshed from your live datastore for each new page load. If for example the front page of your website listed top selling products, you could cache this fragment. Let's assume that you want to refresh the information every hour:

```
<% cache("top_products", :expires_in => 1.hour) do %>
<div id="topSellingProducts">
<% @recent_product =
Product.order("units_sold DESC").limit(20) %>
<%= render :partial => "product",
:collection => @recent_products %>
</div>
<% end %>
```

Trying to expire fragments correctly is hard to get right when you originally write the code, but becomes impossible once you start adding more content to your pages, and reusing fragments across pages.

If you are using a memcache store for your Rails cache store, and your really should be, then you have the option of expiring fragments by time. Here is an example:

```
<% cache @post, :expire_in => 2.hours %>
<%= render @post %>
<% end %>
```

If you want to avoid expiring the fragment manually, whenever an action updates a product, you can define a helper method:

module ProductsHelper

```
def cache_key_for_products
count = Product.count
max_updated_at =
Product.maximum(:updated_at).try(:utc).try(:to_s, :number)
"products/all-#{count}-#{max_updated_at}"
end
end
```

This method generates a cache key that depends on all products and can be used in the view:

```erb
<% cache(cache_key_for_products) do %>
All available products:
<% end %>
```

Sweepers

Calling an expire method inside a controller action is a bad idea. Rails provides another mechanism for this expiration process: Sweepers. Sweepers are responsible for expiring caches. They observe models and execute callbacks as defined in the sweeper.

For example:

```ruby
class BlogSweeper < ActionController::Caching::Sweeper
observe Blog
def after_update(blog)
expire_action(:controller => :blogs, :action => :index)
end
def after_create(blog)
expire_action(:controller => :blogs, :action => :index)
end
end
```

But we need to call this sweeper in our controller for this call cache_sweeper method in the controller:

```ruby
class BlogController < ApplicationController
cache_sweeper :blog_sweeper, :only => [:index]
end
```

Cache digests

For views the cache digests generates a MD5 checksum of the file on the cache key. If anything in the file changes, the cache key changes and it fetches everything again.

```erb
<% cache @user do %>
...
<% end %>
```

This will generate a key like

```
# views/users/1-201222172130/1a79a4d60de6718e8e5b326e338ae533
```

Cache digests are a better way to handle fragment caching. It's based on a Russian Doll scheme, meaning, when you have nested cached fragments and the nested content changes, only expire the cache for that content reusing the rest of the cache. It's called "russian doll caching" because it nests multiple fragments, alluding to the traditional Russian nesting dolls.

Reference: https://github.com/rails/cache_digests

For example using a blog example:

```ruby
class User < ActiveRecord::Base
has_many :blogs
end

# Blog model
class Blog < ActiveRecord::Base
has_many :comments
belongs_to :user, :touch => true
end

#comment model
class Comment < ActiveRecord::Base
belongs_to :blog, :touch => true
end
```

We are using the **touch** option here so if we update a comment, the blog will get a new updated_at value.

Here is the 'users/show.html.erb', showing user's detail with their blog and comments:

```erb
<%cache @user do%>
<div> Name:<%= @user.name %></div>
<div> Email:<%= @user.email %></div>
<%= render @user.blogs%>
<%end%>
<!-- 'blogs/blog.html.erb' -->
<%cache blog do%>
<div><%= blog.title %></div>
<div><%= blog.desc %></div>
<%= render blog.comments%>
<%end%>
<!-- 'comments/comment.html.erb' -->
<%cache comment do%>
<%= comment.value %>
<%end%>
```

You can see that we cache the comments inside the blog and the blog inside the user. In an example where we have a single user with 2 blog posts and 1 comment, the cache keys look like:

```
views/users/1-20130118063610
views/blogs/1-20130118063600
```

It is a combination of view path, object id, and timestamp of the last time it was updated. This combination ensures a cache will always be expired if a model is updated. If we add a new blog or edit a blog it will expire the cache of user along with blog cache. Because we have used the touch option in our blog model.

Likewise, if we add or edit a comment, everything expires. However, if we change any thing in the view itself, such as a new style, reloading the page will not reflect the change as our cache keys are not expired. We can mitigate this by keeping a version of the cache keys and changing that version as needed:

```erb
<%cache ['v1', @user] do%>
<div>Name:<%= @user.name %></div>
<div>Email:<%= @user.email %></div>
<%= render @user.blogs%>
<%end%>
<!-- 'blogs/blog.html.erb' -->
<%cache ['v2',blog] do%>
<div><%= blog.title%></div>
<div><%= blog.desc %></div>
<%= render blog.comments%>
<%end%>
<!-- 'comments/comment.html.erb' -->
<%cache ['v3',comment] do%>
<%= comment.value %>
<%end%>
```

Every time we modify our view, we need to update the version of the cache key. Now we have more problems:

- We need to remember the version number of the template.
- Parent template versions should be changed if child template is modified.
- If the same partial is used in different views, then it hard to maintain versions.

In Rails 4, **cache_digests** have been added to maintain nested fragment caching. With Cache Digests, we actually don't need to worry about expiring caching and versioning when we have nested fragment caching. The cache key for users/show is suffixed with an MD5 of the template itself and all its dependencies. If we change anything in any view(users/show, _blog or _comment) and restart the server, it will automatically expire the cache key and recompute a new cache key.

To check the dependencies of a view, the cache_digests gem provides two rake tasks:

```
rake cache_digests:dependencies TEMPLATE=users/show
```

and

```
rake cache_digests:nested_dependencies TEMPLATE=users/show
```

Note: every time a blog is rendered, Rails reads the fragment from the cache. If you have, say, 20 blogs, then you will make 20 calls to the cache to retrieve the cached fragment for that blog. This is very inefficient, worth looking at the gem multi_fetch_fragments to improve this.

If your site is localised, then you must make sure to include the user's current locale in all of the fragment cache keys in your templates, such as:

```
<% cache [@posts, @user.locale.to_s ] do %>
<%= render :partial => 'post/posts.html.erb',
:collection => @posts,
:cache => Proc.new{ |post| [ post, @user.locale.to_s ] } %>
<% end %>
```

The basic usage of Rails fragment caching is actually hard to get correct, but once you do it correctly, you can get great performance for your view rendering.

Action cache

If your pages requires authentication or other before/after filters, the content can still be cached using Rails built-in action caching. Action caching uses (and requires) a Memcache add-on. In order to use page and action caching, you will need to add actionpack-page_caching and actionpack-action_caching to your Gemfile.

Simply add caches_action :<action_name> to your controller to turn on caching for specific actions. If your layout contains dynamic elements (such as your user's name or email address in the header), you can render the layout dynamically while still caching the action's contents. Use the :layout => false flag to accomplish this. Finally, you can use the expire_action command to remove the action from you cache when new data is written.

```
class MembersController < ActionController
before_filter :authenticate
caches_action :index
caches_action :show, :layout => false
def index
@members = Member.all
end
def show
@member = Member.find(params[:id])
end
def create
expire_action :action => :index
end
end
```

Model cache

Query caching is a Rails feature that caches the result set returned by each query so that if Rails encounters the same query again in the same method, it will use the cached result set as opposed to running the query against the database again. For example:

```
class ProductsController < ApplicationController
def index
# Run a find query
@products = Product.all
. . .
# Run the same query again
@products = Product.all
end
end
```

Low level caching

Low-level caching entails using the Rails.cache object directly to cache any information. Use it to store any data that is costly to retrieve and that can afford to be somewhat out-of-date. Database queries or API calls are common uses for this.

The most efficient way to implement low-level caching is using the Rails.cache.fetch method. It will read a value from the cache if it available; otherwise it will execute a block passed to it and return the result:

```
>> Rails.cache.fetch('answer')
==> "nil"
>> Rails.cache.fetch('answer') {1 + 1}
==> 2
Rails.cache.fetch('answer')
==> 2
```

You can configure Rails to use an external memory store for the cache such as memcached.

External cache

Memcached, Redis, Riak are good external key/value caches to use for storing data, they can also be shared between Rails app server if required. By using something like memcached or redis you can have all of your server processes accessing the same cache and you can have a much bigger cache meaning that cached information becomes stale a lot less frequently. You can write once to the cache and all server processes benefit and you can clear once and all processes know it is cleared.

Memcached is a very fast in-memory object caching system that can make Rails run much faster with very few changes. Also memcache-like stores remove oldest keys first when it's running out of space. The Dalli Ruby Gem is very powerful and takes care of spreading keys across a cluster of memcached servers, which distributes the load and increases your memcached capacity. To use it add to Gemfile:

```
gem install dalli
```

To config/environments/production.rb add:

```
config.cache_store = :dalli_store
```

Next, we will tell ActionController to perform caching. Add this line to the same file:

```
config.action_controller.perform_caching = true
```

For example: If you have a very expensive operation or object that you must create each time, you can store and retrieve it in Memcached. Let's say your action looks like this:

```
def slow_action
slow_object = create_slow_object
end
```

We can store the result in memcached by changing the action like this:

```
def slow_action
slow_object = Rails.cache.fetch(:slow_object) do
create_slow_object
end
end
```

Rails will ask Memcached for the object with a key of 'slow_object'; if it doesn't find that object, it will execute the block given and write the object back into it.

HTML5/CSS3 Overview

HTML5 is the newest hyper text markup language for websites from the World Wide Web Consortium (W3C), official it is still in development. HTML5 works with CSS3. Many of the features it comes with have been created with the consideration that users should be able to run heavy content on mobile devices. HTML5 is the default used by Rails. Not all devices support modern HTML5 and JavaScript features equally.

html5test.com/results/desktop.html shows which browsers are HTML5 compatible. You may need for example to decide not to support older browsers such as IE 6, 7 or even 8, and if you plan to support them to use a library such as html5shim. For example angularjs does not support IE 8 or lower.

<!DOCTYPE html> is the web page header replacing the previous cumbersome HTML 4 syntax and CSS2. For smartphones supporting only HTML5 is a safe bet.

HTML5 features

Some new HTML5 features are:

- Web Workers: Certain web applications use heavy scripts to perform functions. Web Workers use separate background threads for processing and it does not effect the performance of a web page.
- Video: You can embed video without third-party proprietary plug-ins or codec. Video becomes as easy as embedding an image.
- Canvas: This feature allows a web developer to render graphics on the fly. As with video, there is no need for a plug in.
- Web notifications : The web notification permits the user to show the notifications for given events and on user interactions irrespective of the tab it is focusing on. Browser notifications are similar to desktop notifications.

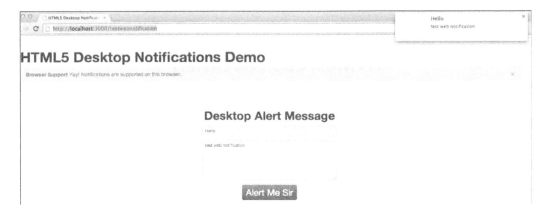

- Application caches: It's becoming increasingly important for web-based applications to be accessible offline. HTML5 provides offline capabilities. Using the cache interface gives your application offline browsing - users can navigate your full site when they're offline. You need to write a cache manifest file which is a simple text file that lists the resources the browser should cache for offline access. The manifest attribute should be included on every page of your web application that you want cached. A rails gem to help with static assets is https://github.com/wycats/rack-offline. For example:

```
<html manifest="example.appcache">
CACHE MANIFEST
index.html
stylesheet.css
images/logo.png
scripts/main.js
http://cdn.example.com/scripts/main.js
</html>
```

- Geolocation: Best known for use on mobile devices but also on desktop browsers now. Rather than having to use a service such as freegeoip to translate your IP to longitude/latitude you can use the javascript navigator.geolocation API.
- Local web storage : It is a simple client side database that allows the users to persist data in the form of key/value pairs. It can store up to 10MB of data per domain. Unlike cookies, the data stored are not included with every HTTP request. Older browsers may not support this http://caniuse.com/#search=sessionstorage.

- New form controls, like calendar, date, time, email, URL, search. but for example the date select field can render different on different browsers and you may still want to use jquery UI to keep it consistent.

Modernizr

Modernizr is a JavaScript library that helps us to detect the browser support for HTML5 and CSS3 features:

```
<script type="text/javascript" src="modernizr.min.js"></script>
if (Modernizr.localstorage) {
//use localStorage object to store data
localStorage.setItem('bgcolor', favcolour);
} else {
alert('Cannot store user preferences as your browser do not support local storage');
}
```

alternatively without this library,

```
if ('localStorage' in window && window['localStorage'] !== null) {
//use localStorage object to store data
localStorage.setItem('bgcolour', favcolour);
} else {
alert('Cannot store user preferences as your browser do not support local storage');
}
```

When we set or remove data from the web storage, a storage event will be fired on the window object. We can add listeners to the event and handle the storage changes if required.

We can check whether the data is stored in local storage by using the developer tools that comes with the browsers. For instance, in Chrome, right click on the browser and select Inspect Element. Select Resources tab and then click on the local storage item. We can see the user selected data stored in the form of key/value pairs.

HTML5 Structure

HTML 5 introduces a whole set of new elements that make it much easier to structure pages. Most HTML 4 pages include a variety of common structures, such as headers, footers and columns and today, it is fairly common to mark them up using div elements, giving each a descriptive id or class.HTML5 introduced:

- <article> – this tag defines an article, a user comment or a post, so an independent item of content.
- <aside> – the aside tag marks content aside from the page content, which for example could be a lateral sidebar.
- <header>, <footer> – you won't need to manually name ID's for headers and footers, as now you have a predefined tag for them.
- <nav> – the navigation can now be placed in the markup in between the nav tags, which will automatically make your lists act like navigation.
- <section> – this is another important new syntax, as it can define any kind of sections in your document. It works pretty much like a div which separates different sections.
- <audio>, <video> – these two mark sound or video content, which will now be easier to run by devices.
- <canvas> – the canvas tag is quite exciting, as it allows drawing graphics via scripting (mostly JavaScript, but some others can be employed as well)

What is important to remember is that the new HTML5 tags do not always work as the ones before. For example, the header and footer tags will not only mark the start and the end of a page, but also the start and the end of each section you have. This means that these two tags are likely to be used more than once in the whole page.

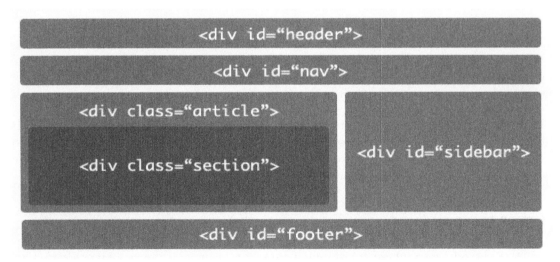

Diagram illustrates a typical two-column layout marked up using divs with id and class attributes. It contains a header, footer, and horizontal navigation bar below the header. The main content contains an article and sidebar on the right.

The use of div elements is largely because current versions of HTML 4 lack the necessary semantics for describing these parts more specifically. HTML 5 addresses this issue by introducing new elements for representing each of these different sections.

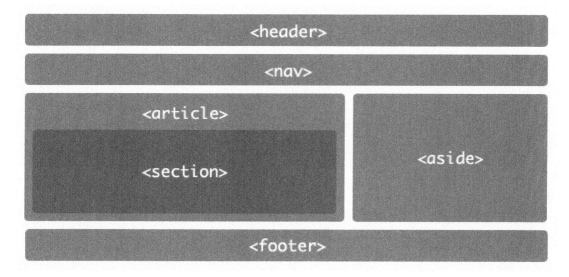

The div elements can be replaced with the new elements: header, nav, section, article, aside, and footer. The markup for that document could look like the following:

```
<body>
<header>...</header>
<nav>...</nav>
<article>
<section>
...
</section>
</article>
<aside>...</aside>
<footer>...</footer>
</body>
```

XHTML

XHTML Mobile Profile was designed for mobile phone web sites, specifically for feature phones which were previous technology to the newer smartphones. For example one contract I had with a major telecoms operator was to support older phones in the market.

```
<?xml version="1.0" encoding="UTF-8"?>
<!DOCTYPE html PUBLIC "-//WAPFORUM//DTD XHTML Mobile 1.2//EN"
"http://www.openmobilealliance.org/tech/DTD/xhtml-mobile12.dtd">
<html xml:lang="en">
<head>
<title>Hello world</title>
</head>
<body>
<p>Hello <a href="http://example.org/">world</a>.</p>
</body>
</html>
```

Feature phones, smartphones

Mobiles can be classified into smartphone or feature phone categories.

Smartphones: Phones with browsers that are capable of rendering normal desktop pages, at least to some extent. This category includes recent mobile browsers that can render HTML5, and covers a diversity of devices, such as Android-based phones and iPhones.

Feature phones: Phones with browsers without the capability to render normal desktop webpages. This includes browsers for cHTML (iMode), WML, WAP, and the like.

In general, there is no need to serve any markup other than plain HTML5 if you wish to only support smartphones. The only exception is certain markets around the world in which feature phones, rather than smart devices, are dominant. In these cases, you need enough flexibility to handle these devices by serving a particular markup such as XHTML MP. You could say depending on the device detected, force the content type in any controller function or using an after filter

```
response.content_type = "application/xhtml+xml"
```

CSS3

CSS3 is the latest standard for CSS. CSS3 is completely backwards-compatible with earlier versions of CSS. CSS3 offers great features such as transitions that used to take a lot of code in CSS2 to produce, and it normally used with HTML5. Some of the most important CSS3 features are:

- Selectors
- Rounded Corners
- CSS Animations and Transitions
- Border Image
- Box and Text Shadow
- Backgrounds and Borders
- Gradient
- 2D/3D Transformations
- RGBA: Color, Now with Opacity
- Transform (Element Rotation)
- Multicolumn Layout

Web Fonts

What we need to do is add the fonts directory within the assets directory so that we can resource these files in our CSS or Sass files using proper Rails conventions and the asset pipeline. The problem is, simply adding a fonts directory isn't picked up by the pipeline.

Open your project's config file, located at config/application.rb and add the following line within your Application class:

```
config.assets.paths << Rails.root.join("app", "assets", "fonts")
```

Media Queries

The media queries might well be the most important addition to CSS3. What it does is simple: it allows certain conditions to be applied to different stylesheets based on device properties, making websites fluid and fit all kinds of screen sizes. Media queries allow developers to tailor to different resolutions without having to change or remove content.

Reference: http://www.w3.org/TR/css3-mediaqueries/

Let's say we want to target iPhones, Android, and such devices which typically have a maximum screen resolution of 480px horizontal:

```
@media screen and (max-width:480px) {
#search_section {
width: 60%;
background-color:red;
}
}
```

http://mqtest.io/ is a tool to see which media queries your browser responds to, For example an android phone:

CSS3 positioning

An important but difficult concept to understand for layouts is the float, fixed, absolute, relative and overlapping layout. Float left, right, none, inherit are hard to understand but its the core of CSS3 layouts.

Reference example: http://www.w3schools.com/css/css_positioning.asp

Flexbox

An interesting new CSS3 which will allow you to build a responsive grid is the CSS3 flexbox property. The new flex layout allows elements within a container to be arranged in a way fitting to the screen or device that it is being viewed on. Flex items have the ability to either increase in size to fill up unused spaced or decrease in size in order to prevent items within the container from flowing outside of the container.

Reference: http://www.w3.org/TR/css3-flexbox/

Zurb foundation's new SPA grid framework will be based around Flexbox. http://zurb.com/article/1333/foundation-a-new-grid

Dating app boilerplate

We already installed html5 boilerplate in the dating app above. html5boilerplate includes the normaliser library to resort browser settings so your code has a standard which you can control then. Rubymine IDE has boilerplate as a project installation option.

www.initializr.com is a template generator for html5 boilerplate and twitter bootstrap. There is a mobile html5boilerplate if you just want to write a mobile only site. It depends on approach. Use HTML5 boilerplate if you are going to have same mark-up for you mobile and desktop website. but if you are making separate websites for mobile and desktop then go for Mobile html5 Boilerplate.

The use of Twitter Bootstrap library can be used to give good layout and the ability to do responsive design.I think Zurb foundation is more powerful for fluid design but Bootstrap is better at supplied CSS components so you need look work from a visual view. Bootstrap will be used here to get more effects for less CCS3 code.

SASS/LESS

CSS3 Stylesheets are getting larger, more complex, and harder to maintain. This is where a preprocessor can help. Sass lets you use features that don't exist in CSS3 like variables, nesting, mixins, inheritance.

Two popular CSS3 preprocessors are SASS and LESS. SASS/LESS for example allow you to specify a colour as a parameter enabling you to use this in CSS statements.

Rails by default uses SASS. Twitter Bootstrap uses LESS [Bootstrap offer a SASS port on their website now] while Zurb uses SASS.

A negative about SASS [and LESS] is that the resulting file will be larger - once you've introduced to the power of mixins and @extend it's easy to start using them in lots of situations, sometimes where they are not needed, and the result can be needlessly repeated code. But at the end of the day the gains in productivity and code organisation I've experienced by using Sass far outweigh any potential increase in CSS file size.

Reference: http://sass-lang.com/guide

Compass

http://compass-style.org/, a layer on top of SASS, and makes things like creating sprites easier, provides mixins. The advantages of compass are:

- **CSS3.** The Compass CSS3 module provides Sass mixins for CSS3 features, allowing you to target multiple browsers' vendor namespaces using a single syntax.
- **CSS sprites**. Reducing the number of HTTP requests is a key factor of web application performance. The sprite helpers will create CSS sprites from a folder of separate assets, handling all the geometry for sprite layout, allowing you to reference icons by name.
- **Typography.** Compass has it's typography helpers.
- **Plugins and so much more.** There is a growing list of community plugins that make it easier to package styles for use across projects.

http://mhs.github.io/scout-app/ is a tool to develop SASS/Compass outside of Rails.

Mobile Pixels

To give an understanding how the native apps tackle screen size and screen density issues. CSS pixels on the mobile web aren't the same as screen pixels. iOS retina devices introduced the practice of doubling pixel density (e.g. iPhone 3GS vs 4, iPad 2 vs 3). The retina Mobile Safari HTTP user-agent still report the same device-width to avoid breaking the Web. As other devices (e.g. Android) get higher resolution displays, they are doing the same device-width trick.

Your media query can combine combineconditions to only capture mobile retina screens, for example:

```
@media (max-width : 600px), and (-webkit-min-device-pixel-ratio
: 1.5), only screen and (min-device-pixel-ratio : 1.5)
```

iOS

Pixel: At the beginning, coordinates of all drawings are specified in Points are abstract units, they only make sense in this mathematical coordinate space. In the original iPhone, points corresponded perfectly to actual pixels on screen, but this is no longer true.

Rendered Pixels: Point-based drawings are rendered into pixels. This process is known as rasterization. Point coordinates are multiplied by scale factor to get pixel coordinates. Higher scale factors as the screen resolution has increased with newer iPhone models resulted in higher level of detail. Typical scale factors are 1×, 2× and 3×

Physical Pixels: Before the image can be displayed on the screen, it must be downsampled (resized) to lower pixel resolution for the iPhone 6 Plus.

Physical Device: The last step is to show the computed pixels on the physical screen. Every screen has pixels-per-inch (PPI) characteristic. This number tells you how many pixels fit into one inch and thus how large the pixels appear in the real world

A Density-Independent Pixel (DIP) corresponds to one pixel on a non-Retina display. A DIP corresponds to 2 pixels of width or height on a Retina display.

In terms of Device Pixel Ratio, the iPhone 6 follows the same value as the previous Retina devices, using a value of 2. The iphone 6 has 326 PPI. The iPhone 6 Plus, has 401 DPI needs a higher value. Apple has decided to give a shot on a new concept: rendered pixels, emulating a 3x device pixel ratio.

To demonstrate different rendering of pixels on various devices, compare how 1-point wide line is rendered on:

- Original iPhone - without retina display. Scaling factor is 1.
- iPhone 5 - with Retina display, scaling factor is 2.

- iPhone 6 Plus - with Retina display HD. Scaling factor is 3 and the image is afterwards downscaled from rendered 2208 × 1242 pixels to 1920 × 1080 pixels.

The downscaling ratio is 1920 / 2208 = 1080 / 1242 = 20 / 23. That means every 23 pixels from the original render have to be mapped to 20 physical pixels. In other words the image is scaled down to approximately 87% of its original size.

Therefore if you are providing 3x images for some Android devices, for example for the Galaxy S5 the image will be taken also for the iPhone 6 Plus but it will be resized by the browser before rendering it on the screen.

Android screen density

With a more variety of android device screen sizes for simplicity Android groups all actual screen densities into four generalised densities: low, medium, high, and extra high. The quantity of pixels within a physical area of the screen; usually referred to as dpi (dots per inch).

Reference http://developer.android.com/guide/practices/screens_support.html

The density-independent pixel is equivalent to one physical pixel on a 160 dpi screen, which is the baseline density assumed by the system for a "medium" density screen. At runtime, the system transparently handles any scaling of the dp units, as necessary, based on the actual density of the screen in use. The conversion of dp units to screen pixels is simple: px = dp * (dpi / 160). For example, on a 240 dpi screen, 1 dp equals 1.5 physical pixels. You should always use dp units when defining your application's UI, to ensure proper display of your UI on screens with different densities.

JAVASCRIPT OVERVIEW

ECMAScript is the Standardisation that forms the basis of JavaScript. It is becoming popular to put more functionality into Javascript, for example in Ajax functionality and Single Page Applications (SPA). Jquery knowledge is useful to have for Javascript development as most projects use this now, zepto, http://zeptojs.com, is a smaller file size suited to mobile but is not IE compatible.

Note: Chrome/Safari have good options for debugging javascript in developer mode, you can set breakpoints, and step through code.

Progressive enhancement

Graceful degradation is the practice of building your web functionality so that it provides a certain level of user experience in more modern browsers, but it will also degrade gracefully to a lower level of user in experience in older browsers or browser not support a certain feature. This lower level is not as nice to use for your site visitors, but it does still provide them with the basic functionality that they came to your site to use; things do not break for them. This might be viable if your product by definition is so dependent on scripting that it makes more sense to maintain a "basic" version rather than enhancing one.

Progressive enhancement is similar, but it does things the other way round. You start by establishing a basic level of user experience that all browsers will be able to provide when rendering your web site, but you also build in more advanced functionality that will automatically be available to browsers that can use it.

In other words, graceful degradation starts from the status quo of complexity and tries to fix for the lesser experience whereas progressive enhancement starts from a very basic, working example and allows for constant extension for future environments. Degrading gracefully means looking back whereas enhancing progressively means looking forward whilst keeping your feet on firm ground. This is generally a better solution than graceful degradation.

There has recently been a lot of discussion around whether Progressive Enhancement, a cornerstone concept in web development, is still relevant. High-profile websites completely break when JavaScript is disabled.

People used to be more worried that users might disable Javascript and implement progressive enhancement to display all basic page features and detect if Javascript was enabled then to turn on features it if was, similar for older mobile devices which were not fully javascript compliant, but this is not such a concern now, and the trend is not to do progressive enhancement. Generally unless you are doing enterprise applications websites are only concerned with relatively browser versions.

Interestingly in Firefox, as part of an effort to simplify the Firefox options set and protect users, the option to disable JavaScript was removed from the Firefox Options window.

Modernizer

Modernizer, http://modernizr.com/, is a popular library for progressive enhancement, but as browsers are becoming more HTML5 compliant and people are upgrading frequently, the need to support older browsers is less, and people are less in favour of progressive support now. Modernizer focuses not on the type of browser but which features the browser supports.

These feature tests are often coupled with "polyfills", that replace missing browser capabilities with JavaScript substitutes. In the JavaScript world, you will frequently encounters the words shim and polyfill. A shim is a library that brings a new API to an older environment. Thus, a polyfill is a shim for a browser API. You typically check if a browser supports an API and load a polyfill if it doesn't.

Note: for the asset pipeline, put the Modernizr library in your /assets/javascript directory but do not put your polyfill library in the asset pipeline manifest (such as Placeholders.js, Placeholders.js is a JavaScript polyfill for the HTML5 placeholder attribute). If you do, it will load for all browsers thus defeating the whole point, but to compile it like the rest of the assets. To config/application.rb add:

```
config.assets.precompile += ['polyfills/Placeholders.js']
```

There is a gem to use it with rails, https://github.com/tsechingho/modernizr-rails

CoffeeScript

Rails by default supports CoffeeScript, this a syntax to reduce the Javascript line count that you have to write.

Reference: http://js2coffee.org/

```javascript
/**
 * Multiline Documentation
 */

var foobar = function(callback) {
    setTimeout(function() {
        // trigger callback after 1000ms
        callback();
    }, 1000);
};

var foo = {
    key: {
        nestedKey: 'value'
    },
    array: [1],
    nestedArray: [1, 2, ['2a', ['2a-I']]]
}

foobar(function() {
    alert(foo.array);
});
```

```coffeescript
# trigger callback after 1000ms
callback()
return
), 1000
return

foo =
    key:
        nestedKey: "value"

    array: [1]
    nestedArray: [
        1
        2
        [
            "2a"
            ["2a-I"]
        ]
    ]

foobar ->
    alert foo.array
    return
```

Note: To switch to Javascript you only need to remove the. coffee extension. However, you also need to make sure you use '//' for comments instead of '#', or else comment out the gem "coffee-script".

Javascript loaders

The Rails Asset Pipeline was envisioned before JS module solutions were robust and common. Consequently, it comes with it's own way to manage dependencies. In the application.js of any non-trivial app, you will find comments specifying which files to include into this file during deployment.

```
//= require jquery
//= require frameworkjs
//= require app
```

Let's look at what happens when the browser's parser encounters a script element with a valid src attribute. First, a request is sent to the server. Hopefully the server responds and the browser proceeds to download (and cache) the requested file. Once these steps are completed the file still needs to be parsed and evaluated. While these steps are blazing fast on modern desktop computers, they aren't on mobile.

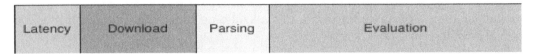

Loading and parsing of a JavaScript file blocks page rendering. This means that your page will not display until each script call in your document head has been loaded and executed. A commonly suggested solution to the problem of startup latency is to load scripts on demand. There are a number of downsides to this approach, however. First of all, the code isn't guaranteed to be delivered: the network or the server can become unavailable in the meantime. Secondly, the speed at which the code is transferred is subject to the network's quality and can thus vary widely. Lastly, the code is delivered asynchronously.

There are articles on **lazy loading** such as Gmail for Mobile HTML5- Reducing Startup Latency, To combine all modules into a single resource, you can write each module into a separate script tag and hide the code inside a comment block (/* */). When the resource first loads, none of the code is parsed since it is commented out. To load a module, find the DOM element for the corresponding script tag, strip out the comment block, and eval() the code. If the web app supports XHTML, this trick is even more elegant as the modules can be hidden inside a CDATA tag instead of a script tag. An added bonus is the ability to lazy load your modules synchronously since there's no longer a need to fetch the modules asynchronously over the network.

Many users may be accessing your site with a slow mobile connection, running on a slow mobile browser. Loading and parsing of a JavaScript file blocks page rendering. This means that your page will not display until each script call in your document head has been loaded and executed.

For example: looking at www.virgin-atlantic.com website with Chrome developer. As the size of Javascript required for a typical site continues to grow, a more comprehensive understanding of how scripts are loaded is needed.

There are some techniques you can use to address this:

1. Combining Scripts like Rails pipeline

If you have four scripts of 20k each, you could combine them into one and have a single call of 80k. If you leave them separate then a modern browser can call all 4 at once, and then parse one by one. Which is fastest? this is difficult to measure, but after experimenting with this, it is best to combine smaller scripts into one larger file.

2. Minify scripts

The minify process will take a script, remove comments and newlines, and rename big variable names in order to make the file size small, such as with:

- http://yui.github.io/yuicompressor/
- https://developers.google.com/closure/compiler/

3.Using a Script Loader

A script loader is a piece of Javascript that manages the loading and parsing of other scripts. it seemed counter-intuitive; in order to make my Javascript faster I am supposed to add yet another script to the mix. This is a misunderstanding. There's a lot of script loaders out there. What you find with asynchronous Javascript is that the page might load quicker on the browser as the scripts are loaded in parallel alongside the rest of the document.

To ensure that our JavaScript is loaded and the application is interactive as soon as possible. To do that, we need to minimise the amount of JavaScript we use: smaller payload over the wire, fewer lines of code to parse, faster to execute. To make sure we only download the JavaScript necessary for the page to work, we needed to get a firm grip on our dependencies.

Using the Rails asset pipeline, does this mean that you can do without JavaScript loaders like AMD? These loaders typically load scripts asynchronously (to bypass the problem of their blocking behaviour) and can also preserve order of execution without requiring sequential download. Serving concatenated JavaScript is still generally the best (and simplest) approach with the asset pipeline. In a lot of cases, waiting for the CSS to finish loading is not as necessary as it may seem. Today there are dozens of Javacript loaders available. The most popular ones are:

require.js

Require.js, the most popular script loader, serves two different purposes, it is an AMD script loader that asynchronously loads your Javascript to improve page load performance, while also providing you there ability to organise your Javascript into self contained modules. It dynamically load modules when that code is required. Each Javascript file represents a module.

RequireJS implements the AMD (asynchronous module definition) specification, which is a method for defining modules which can be loaded. AMD is a system by which you define and require modules asynchronously. Require.js does not explicitly support CSS files. Note: https://github.com/guybedford/require-css is for writing modular CSS dependencies alongside scripts. Not everyone likes AMD, some arguments against it are:

- AMD expects every module to be contained in a separate file.
- AMD requires you to wrap all of your code inside an anonymous function that is passed to the define method:
- AMD has many features, but I think that the extra markup and complex loaders needed to support may outweighs its benefits

When you use RequireJS on a project, the very things that give you an advantage in the development/testing/debugging experience – separate files per module, unminified source, etc. – become weaknesses in a production deployment. At the highest level, r.js (https://github.com/jrburke/r.js/) optimises your RequireJS projects by concatenating and minifying your JavaScript modules and CSS files. The optimiser just becomes an additional step before deployment.

Reference: http://requirejs.org/docs/optimization.html

To use with Rails: which is using requirejs for loading client side while still taking advantage of some of the asset pipeline use https://github.com/jwhitley/requirejs-rails, it used the r.js for production. This also supports Almond.

Almond

It's a bare-bones library made by the author of RequireJS. Some developers like to use the AMD API to code modular JavaScript, but after doing an optimised build, they do not want to include a full AMD loader like RequireJS, since they do not need all that functionality, for example in mobile to reduce the file sizes. By including Almond in the build file, there is no need for RequireJS.

Reference: https://github.com/jrburke/almond

LABjs

It is designed to be an all purpose JavaScript loader that loads scripts efficiently and quickly but unfortunately no future development work expected on this project. Only a JS loader. It pays a lot of attention to some of the intricacies of performance-optimised script loading. Reference: http://labjs.com/

HeadJS

One of the best features of HeadJS is the ability to label your scripts, and run code once certain ones have loaded. For example, let's say you're loading in two scripts, jQuery and Google Analytics, but your code only relies on jQuery, so you want to execute it as soon as jQuery is loaded.

Reference: http://headjs.com/

Curl.js

RequireJS runs in more places than curl.js, but curl.js is a smaller size than requireJS. It is is AMD compliant.

Reference: http://davidwalsh.name/curljs

Yepnode.js

yepnope is designed to be a resource loader that can load in scripts conditionally, based on any statement you can evaluate to either true or false. It's designed for loading in polyfills. It fits perfectly with a feature detection library like Modernizr.

Reference: http://yepnopejs.com/

basket.js

Tests by Google and Bing have shown that there are performance benefits to caching assets in localStorage (especially on mobile) when compared to simply reading and writing from the standard browser cache.

Reference: http://addyosmani.github.io/basket.js/

CREATE THE DATING APPLICATION

For the dating app, first let us enable a member to upload a photo of themselves, code the schema, add login page, and remove unused links such as delete members from the generated scaffold commands earlier. First let's create a profile for the members to create a profile for themselfs.

Upload a photo

We previously created the member's page, now add the ability for a member to upload a photo. Two popular gems for file upload are:

- https://github.com/thoughtbot/paperclip
- https://github.com/carrierwaveuploader/carrierwave

We will use paperclip. To allow image resizing, ImageMagick must be installed [I usually get issues installing this], and Paperclip must have access to it. We will store the uploaded file on the server file system, later we will discuss storing the uploaded photos on amazon S3 cloud server, Heroku recommend uploading to S3 directly if your image size is greater than 4Mb. Large files uploads in single-threaded, non-evented environments (such as Rails) block your application's web dynos and can cause request timeouts. EventMachine, Node.js and JVM-based languages are less susceptible to such issues.

Add to the Gemfile: gem "paperclip"

```
run: bundle install
```

Add the paperclip ability to the current code [a member's photo is called an avatar]:

```
rails generate paperclip member avatar
rake db:migrate
```

```
== AddAttachmentAvatarToMembers: migrating
===================================
-- change_table(:members)
-> 0.0357s
== AddAttachmentAvatarToMembers: migrated (0.0359s)
==========================
```

Add the avatar to the member model file:

```
class Member < ActiveRecord::Base
has_attached_file :avatar
# Validate content type
validates_attachment_content_type :avatar,
:content_type => /\Aimage/
# Validate filename
validates_attachment_file_name :avatar,
:matches => [/png\Z/, /jpe?g\Z/]
end
```

Add the ability to upload a members photo, change app/views/members/_form.html.erb, change:

```
<%= form_for(@member) do |f| %>
```

to:

```
<%= form_for @member, :url => members_path,
:html => { :multipart => true } do |f| %>
```

and add:

```
<div class="field">
<%= f.label :avatar %><br>
<%= f.file_field :avatar %>
</div>
```

Add the image to members_controller.rb:

```
params.require(:member).permit(:first_name, :last_name,
:description, :avatar)
```

Display the member's photo in show.html.erb for displaying one selected member:

```
<p>
<strong>Photo:</strong>
<%= image_tag @member.avatar.url %>
</p>
```

Display a members photo, _show_member.html.erb for displaying all members:

```
<td><%= image_tag member.avatar.url %></td>
```

run the code, 'rails s' to see the photo can be uploaded.

Add the dating schema

A tool I use to see a diagram of the schema from the code is to reconstruct the schema from the code using Rubymine. The schema is shown above in the model section.

Add memberInfo

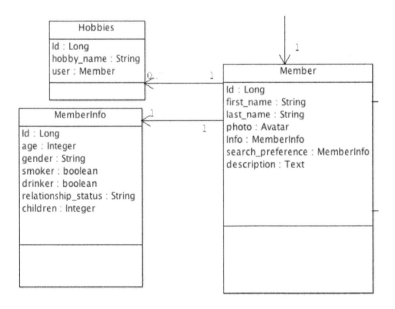

The MemberInfo table stores more member details, a process called de-normalisation, rather than having one very large table ;break it into smaller tables for performance/storage-space, which the member table will reference. The member table will reference another memberinfo table to store the search preferences for each member – rather than create a new preference table specifically.

rails g model MemberInfo age:integer gender:string smoker:boolean drinker:boolean children:integer relationship_status:string

```
invoke  active_record
create    db/migrate/20140904171558_create_member_infos.rb
create    app/models/member_info.rb
invoke  rspec
create    spec/models/member_info_spec.rb
```

Note: this generates this migration file in db/migrate:

```
class CreateMemberInfos < ActiveRecord::Migration
  def change
    create_table :member_infos do |t|
      t.integer :age
      t.string :gender
      t.boolean :smoker
      t.boolean :drinker
      t.integer :children
      t.string :relationship_status
      t.timestamps
    end
  end
end
```

Run:

```
rake db:migrate
==  CreateMemberInfos: migrating ================================================
-- create_table(:member_infos)
   -> 0.0796s
==  CreateMemberInfos: migrated (0.0798s) =======================================
```

The relationship from Member to MemberInfo is a one to one, create a new migration file in order to add this relationship. First step is to change the database so a member references memberInfo, for this, in the postgresql database you need to add a member_id field to the member_infos sql table, there are a few ways to do this, You can either:

1. rails generate migration AddUserRefToMemberInfo member:references

```
invoke  active_record
create    db/migrate/20140910220744_add_user_ref_to_member_info.rb
```

which creates this migration file:

```
class AddUserRefToMemberInfo < ActiveRecord::Migration
def change
add_column :member_infos, :member, :references
end
end
```

or:

2. You can use this syntax which is more in common with the code syntax. belongs_to is actually an alias for references.

rails generate migration AddMemberBelongsToMembersInfo member:belongs_to

```
invoke  active_record
create
db/migrate/20140910220358_add_member_belongs_to_members_info.rb
```

Which creates this migration file:

```
class AddMemberBelongsToMembersInfo < ActiveRecord::Migration
def change
add_column :members_infos, :member, :belongs_to
end
end
```

or:

3. You don't need to add references when you can use an integer id to your referenced class:

```
rails g migration add_member_id_to_MemberInfo member_id:integer
invoke  active_record
create    db/migrate/20140910221732_add_member_id_to_member_info.rb
```

which creates:

```
class AddMemberIdToMemberInfo < ActiveRecord::Migration
def change
add_column :member_infos, :member_id, :integer
end
end
```

To test it worked, to see the current member table fields enter:

```
rails console
Member.column_names
```

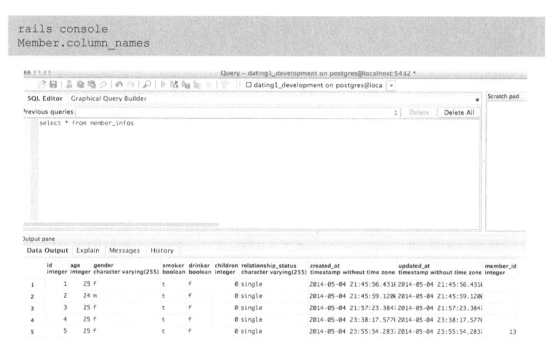

It is also good to see it in postgreSQL pgAdmin:

Next you need to tell active record this relationship exists:

```
class Member < ActiveRecord::Base
has_attached_file :avatar
# Validate content type
validates_attachment_content_type :avatar,
:content_type => /\Aimage/
# Validate filename
validates_attachment_file_name :avatar,
:matches => [/png\Z/, /jpe?g\Z/]
```

```
  has_one :member_info, autosave: true
end
class MemberInfo < ActiveRecord::Base
  belongs_to :member
end
```

Next test the relationship works:

```
rails console
memberinfo1 = MemberInfo.new({age: 25, gender: 'f', smoker: 't',
drinker: 'f', children: 0, relationship_status: 'single'})

memberinfo1.save
member1 = Member.new({ first_name: 'paul', last_name: 'smith',
description: 'outgoing person, looking for a friend'})
member1.member_info=memberinfo1
member1.member_info.smoker
```

Reference guide on associations:

http://guides.rubyonrails.org/association_basics.html#the-has-one-association

We have the member model created, assigning an object to a belongs_to association does not automatically save the object but when you assign an object to a has_one association, that object is automatically saved (in order to update its foreign key).

If you want to set up a 1-1 relationship between two models, you'll need to add belongs_to to one, and has_one to the other. How do you know which is which?

The distinction is in where you place the foreign key (it goes on the table for the class declaring the belongs_to association), but you should give some thought to the actual meaning of the data as well. The has_one relationship says that one of something is yours – that is, that something points back to you. For example, it makes more sense to say that a member owns a member_info than that a member_info owns a member.

```
class Member < ActiveRecord::Base
  has_one :member_info
end
class MemberInfo < ActiveRecord::Base
  belongs_to :member
end
```

The corresponding migration might look like this:

```ruby
class CreateMembers < ActiveRecord::Migration
  def self.up
    create_table :members do |t|
      t.string :name
      t.timestamps
    end
    create_table :member_infos do |t|
      t.integer :member_id
      t.string :member_info_number
      t.timestamps
    end
  end
  def self.down
    drop_table :member_infos
    drop_table :members
  end
end
```

ActiveRecord belongs_to associations have the ability to be autosaved along with the parent model, but the functionality is off by default, likewise for delete. To enable it:

```ruby
class Message < ActiveRecord::Base
  has_many :from_member, :class_name => 'Member'
  belongs_to :member, :autosave => true
end
```

If you set the :dependent option to :destroy, then deleting this object will call the destroy method on the associated object to delete that object. If you set the :dependent option to :delete, then deleting this object will delete the associated object without calling its destroy method.

You will need to prepare the Member model so that it knows to create one or more hobbies if it receives their attributes from the view form when creating a normal Member. This is done by adding a method to your Member model called #accepts_nested_attributes_for which accepts the name of an association, e.g:

```ruby
# app/models/member.rb
class Member < ActiveRecord::Base
  has_many :shipping_addresses
  accepts_nested_attributes_for :member_info, :hobbies
end
```

Note: accepts_nested_attributes_for, It allows you to combine more than one model in your forms while keeping the same basic code pattern that you use with simple single model forms. Nested attributes allow you to save attributes on associated records through the parent.

include versus join

The difference between joins and include is that using the include statement generates a much larger SQL query loading into memory all the attributes from the other table(s).

Assume we have a member created where age=24 [we will create members shortly]

include

```
c = Member.includes(:member_info).where('member_infos.age=24')
```

translates in SQL to

```
SELECT "members"."id" AS t0_r0, "members"."first_name" AS t0_r1, 
"members"."last_name" AS t0_r2, "members"."description" AS t0_r3, 
"members"."created_at" AS t0_r4, "members"."updated_at" AS t0_r5, 
"members"."avatar_file_name" AS t0_r6, 
"members"."avatar_content_type" AS t0_r7, 
"members"."avatar_file_size" AS t0_r8, 
"members"."avatar_updated_at" AS t0_r9, "members"."memberinfo_id" 
AS t0_r10, "members"."user_id" AS t0_r11, "member_infos"."id" AS 
t1_r0, "member_infos"."age" AS t1_r1, "member_infos"."gender" AS 
t1_r2, "member_infos"."smoker" AS t1_r3, "member_infos"."drinker" 
AS t1_r4, "member_infos"."children" AS t1_r5, 
"member_infos"."relationship_status" AS t1_r6, 
"member_infos"."created_at" AS t1_r7, "member_infos"."updated_at" 
AS t1_r8, "member_infos"."member_id" AS t1_r9 FROM "members" LEFT 
OUTER JOIN "member_infos" ON "member_infos"."member_id" = 
"members"."id" WHERE (member_infos.age>=24)
```

Result:

```
=> #<ActiveRecord::Relation [#<Member id: 1, first_name: "anthony", 
last_name: "oleary", description: "dsadasada", created_at: "2014-
06-27 21:38:50", updated_at: "2014-06-27 21:38:50", 
avatar_file_name: nil, avatar_content_type: nil, avatar_file_size: 
nil, avatar_updated_at: nil, memberinfo_id: nil, user_id: 1>]>
```

join

```
c = Member.joins(:user_info).where('member_infos.age=24')
```

Translates in SQL to

```
SELECT "members".* FROM "members" INNER JOIN "member_infos" ON
"member_infos"."member_id" = "members"."id" WHERE
(member_infos.age>=24)
```

Result:

```
#<ActiveRecord::Relation [#<Member id: 1, first_name: "anthony",
last_name: "oleary", description: "dsadasada", created_at: "2014-
06-27 21:38:50", updated_at: "2014-06-27 21:38:50",
avatar_file_name: nil, avatar_content_type: nil, avatar_file_size:
nil, avatar_updated_at: nil, memberinfo_id: nil, user_id: 1>]>
```

Note:

```
c = Member.includes(:member_info).where('member_infos.age=24')
```

can be also written as

```
c = Member.includes(:member_info).where(member_infos: { :age=>24})
```

or

```
c = Member.includes(:member_info).where(member_infos: { age: 24})
```

or this syntax for multiple parameters:

```
User.joins(:user_info).where(user_infos:{ :age => 2..26, :gender =>
"f"})
```

and

```
c = Member.includes(:member_info).where(member_infos: { age: 24,
gender: 'f'})
```

Eager loading

Eager loading loads all association in a single query using a left outer join. Active Record lets you eager load any number of associations with a single Model.find() using the includes method as shown above. Another example is:

```
clients = Client.limit(10)
clients.each do |client|
puts client.address.postcode
end
```

The problem lies within the total number of queries executed. The above code executes 1 (to find 10 clients) + 10 (one per each client to load the address) = 11 queries in total.

we could rewrite Client.limit(10) to use eager load addresses:

```
clients = Client.includes(:address).limit(10)
clients.each do |client|
puts client.address.postcode
end
```

The above code will execute just 2 queries, as opposed to 11 queries in the previous case:

```
SELECT * FROM clients LIMIT 10
SELECT addresses.* FROM addresses
WHERE (addresses.client_id IN (1,2,3,4,5,6,7,8,9,10))
```

In Rails 4 you should use #references combined with #includes if you have the additional condition for one of the eager loaded table.

```
Member.includes(:member_info)
 . where("member_infos.age =24").references(:member_infos)
```

Batch find

Looping through a collection of records from the database (using the all method, for example) is very inefficient since it will try to instantiate all the objects at once. In that case, batch processing methods allow you to work with the records in batches, thereby greatly reducing memory consumption. The find_each method uses find_in_batches with a batch size of 1000 (or as specified by the :batch_size option):

```
Person.find_each do |person|
person.do_some_method
end
```

Foreign key

A foreign key is a column or group of columns in a relational database table that provides a link between data in two tables. Normally in Rails this is not enforced by the database but by the Rails activerecord. In Rails 3, to add a foreign key and an index you would write a migration like this:

```
class AddUserToBooks < ActiveRecord::Migration
def change
add_column :books, :user_id, :integer
add_index :books, :user_id
end
end
```

It requires two method calls, one to add the user_id column to the Books table, and another to add an index to user_id. In Rails 4, you can accomplish the same thing with add_reference. add_reference for cleaner foreign key migrations.

```
class AddUserToBooks < ActiveRecord::Migration
def change
add_reference :books, :user, index: true
end
end
```

Transactions

We use transactions as a protective wrapper around SQL statements to ensure changes to the database only occur when all actions succeed together. The typical example of transactions is the banking method where funds are withdrawn from one account and deposited into the next. If either of these steps fail, then the entire process should be reset.

```
ActiveRecord::Base.transaction do
sam.withdrawal(100)
mike.deposit(100)
end
```

In Rails transactions are available as class and instance methods for all ActiveRecord models. It is perfectly fine to mix model types inside a single transaction block. This is because the transaction is bound to the database connection not the model instance.

As a rule, transactions are only needed when changes to multiple records must succeed as a single unit. Additionally, Rails already wraps the #save and #destroy methods in a transaction, therefore a transaction is never needed when updating a single record.

Rollback

In Rails, rollbacks are only triggered by an exception. This is a crucial point to understand; A coding problem is a transaction block that would never rollback because the containing code could not throw an exception. For example:

```
ActiveRecord::Base.transaction do
sam.update_attribute(:amount, david.amount -100)
mike.update_attribute(:amount, 100)
end
```

update_attribute is designed not to throw an exception when an update fails. It returns false, and for this reason you should ensure that the methods used throw an exception upon failure. A better way to write the previous example would be:

```
ActiveRecord::Base.transaction do
sam.update_attributes!(:amount => -100)
mike.update_attributes!(:amount => 100)
end
```

The bang modifier (!) is a rails convention for a method which will throw an exception upon failure.

Send messages

Add the ability to send messages to any member in the dating app. To store messages for each message:

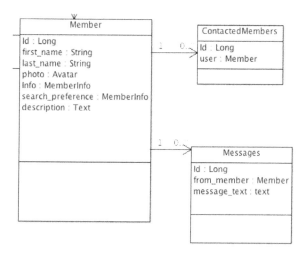

```
rails g model Message message_text:text
```

Add a reference to member manually to the generated migration file, this is the member that owns the message.

```
t.belongs_to :member, index: true
```

Also we need to store who sent the message, you can just paste this into the migration file before running it:

```
t.integer :from_member
class CreateMessages < ActiveRecord::Migration
  def change
    create_table :messages do |t|
      t.text :message_text
      t.belongs_to :member, index: true
      t.belongs_to :from_member
      t.timestamps
    end
  end
end
```

change the message model:
```
class Message < ActiveRecord::Base
has_many :from_member, :class_name => 'Member'
belongs_to :member
end
```

Alternatively you could have used:

```
rails g model Message message_text:text member:integer:index from_member:integer
```

Add the reference to Messages in the Member model:

```
class Member < ActiveRecord::Base
...
has_many :messages
...
end
```

note: if you need to delete a generate command that you used, you could use:

```
rails destroy model message
```

now to implement the changes run:

```
rake db:migrate
```

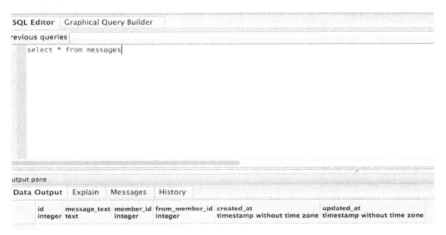

Test that the messages work in practice:

```
message1=Message.new
message1.message_text='test msg'
```

```
message1.save
member1 = Member.new({ first_name: 'paul', last_name: 'smith',
description: 'outgoing person, looking for a friend'})
message1.from_member_id = member1.id
message1.from_member = member1
```

Store members you have messaged

This table is to store which other members have been contacted by the specific member, nothing worse than sending another 'hello' message to a hot single girl and forgetting you already send one [it's faster to calculate this than going through the messages table to calculate it, a design choice for performance versus duplicate information.

```
rails g model ContactedMember member:integer:index

invoke  active_record
create    db/migrate/20140911224851_create_contacted_members.rb
create    app/models/contacted_member.rb
invoke  rspec
create    spec/models/contacted_member_spec.rb
invoke  factory_girl
create    spec/factories/contacted_members.rb
class CreateContactedMembers < ActiveRecord::Migration
def change
create_table :contacted_members do |t|
t.integer :member
t.timestamps
end
add_index :contacted_members, :member
end
end
```

Now create the database changes:

```
rake db:migrate
```

To Member model store your contacted members:

```
add has_many :contacted_members
class Member < ActiveRecord::Base
has_attached_file :avatar
# Validate content type
validates_attachment_content_type :avatar,
:content_type => /\Aimage/
```

```
# Validate filename
validates_attachment_file_name :avatar,
:matches => [/png\Z/, /jpe?g\Z/]
has_one :member_info, autosave: true
has_many :messages
has_many :contacted_members
end
```

To test it:

```
member = Member.new({ first_name: 'paul', last_name: 'smith',
description: 'outgoing person, looking for a friend'})
member.save
contactedmember1 = ContactedMember.new
contactedmember2 = ContactedMember.new
member.contacted_members[0]= contactedmember1
member.contacted_members[1]= contactedmember2
```

Store hobbies

For a list of hobbies to store in the database we could use enums supported in rails 4.1, here the values map to integers in the database, but can be queried by name. Which could help with performance or internationalisation for example how to search for users in spanish who like reading. You can then lookup those keys using the I18n.tranlsate method like t("status.#{review.status}").

Seed data could be used to initialise the hobbies table, or we could store all the hobbies in a table of their own and just reference a row in this table. The point of using enums is to save database space, have faster lookups, and to make your code more readable.

Reference: http://edgeapi.rubyonrails.org/classes/ActiveRecord/Enum.html

For example:

```
class Hobby < ActiveRecord::Base
enum interests: [ :cycling, :reading ]
end
class AddEnumToHobby < ActiveRecord::Migration
def change
add_column :hobbies, :interests, :integer, default: 0
end
end
```

```
hobby.interests = :reading
```

But I will keep using string for the hobby for simplicity here.

```
class HobbyConstant
HOBBIES=['reading','running', 'travel', 'cafe']
end
```

To app/views/members add:

```
<% HobbyConstant::HOBBIES.each do |hobbyconst| %>
<label class="li"><%= check_box_tag :hobby, :name => hobbyconst %>
<u><%= hobbyconst %></u></label><br />
<% end %>
```

Add the hobbies model:

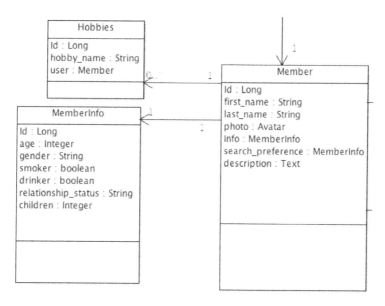

```
rails g model Hobby hobby_name:string member_id:integer:index
invoke  active_record
create    db/migrate/20140911225745_create_hobbies.rb
create    app/models/hobby.rb
invoke    rspec
create      spec/models/hobby_spec.rb
invoke      factory_girl
create        spec/factories/hobbies.rb
```

Creates:

```
class CreateHobbies < ActiveRecord::Migration
def change
create_table :hobbies do |t|
t.string :hobby_name
t.integer :member_id
t.timestamps
end
add_index :hobbies, :member_id
end
end
```

Again notice the name of the actual database table created is called hobbies. now implement the changes into the database:

```
rake db:migrate
```

Add a reference to hobbies in Member:

```
class Member < ActiveRecord::Base
has_attached_file :avatar
# Validate content type
validates_attachment_content_type :avatar,
:content_type => /\Aimage/
# Validate filename
validates_attachment_file_name :avatar,
:matches => [/png\Z/, /jpe?g\Z/]
has_one :user_info
has_many :contacted_members
has_many :messages
has_many :hobbies
end
```

To test:

```
hobby1 = Hobby.new({hobby_name: "fff"})
hobby1.save
member1 = Member.new({ first_name: 'paul', last_name: 'smith',
description: 'outgoing person, looking for a friend'})
member1.hobbies[0]=hobby1
```

Schema.rb

By running the db:migrate task it invokes the db:schema:dump task, which will update your db/schema.rb file to match the structure of your database. You can even delete your migration files once schema.rb is uptodate.

The rake db:reset task will drop the database and set it up again. This is functionally equivalent to rake db:drop, and rake db:setup, this uses the contents of the schema.rb file.

Schema.rb is created by inspecting the database and expressing it's structure using create_table, add_index, and so on. Because this is database-independent, it could be loaded into any database that Active Record supports, such as:

```
create_table "hobbies", force: true do |t|
t.string "hobby_name"
t.string "string"
t.integer "member_id"
t.datetime "created_at"
t.datetime "updated_at"
end
```

But database specific items such as foreign key constraints ((except rails > 4.2), triggers, or stored procedures are not stored in schema.rb, if in config/application.rb the config.active_record.schema_format setting is :ruby, by default. If you are using features like this, then you should set the schema format to :sql.

Instead of using Active Record's schema dumper, the database's structure will be dumped using a tool specific to the database (via the db:structure:dump Rake task) into db/structure.sql. For example, for PostgreSQL, the pg_dump utility is used. Loading these schemas is simply a question of executing the SQL statements they contain. Or a simpler way is to use the foreigner gem when adds foreign key helpers to migrations and correctly dumps foreign keys to schema.rb. This schema.rb should be checked into git.

Allow members to view all member profiles in the dating app

Next add the code for members to view the profile of other members.

Add the ability to log in.

Devise is the most popular gem for rails authentication to allow a user to login. Authentication and authorisation are frequently used terms, Authentication verifies who you are to allow you to log in, Authorisation verifies what you are authorised to do after you are logged in for example only an administrator can delete all members.

Reference: https://github.com/plataformatec/devise

Note: It would be useful to look at CanCan, an authorisation library which restricts what resources a given user is allowed to access. All permissions are defined in a single location (the Ability class) and not duplicated across controllers, views, and database queries.

https://github.com/ryanb/cancan

add devise gem to Gemfile: gem 'devise'

```
bundle install
```

```
rails g devise:install
create config/initializers/devise.rb
create config/locales/devise.en.yml
```

Open up config/environments/development.rb and add this line:

```
config.action_mailer.default_url_options = { :host => 'localhost:3000' }
```

Open up app/views/layouts/application.html.erb and add:

```
<% if notice %>
<p class="alert alert-notice"><%= notice %></p>
<% end %>
<% if alert %>
<p class="alert alert-error"><%= alert %></p>
<% end %>
```

Generate the required files for Devise:

```
rails g devise User
```

```
       invoke  active_record
       create    db/migrate/20140905140753_devise_create_users.rb
       create    app/models/user.rb
       invoke  rspec
       create    spec/models/user_spec.rb
       insert  app/models/user.rb
        route  devise_for :users
```

```
rake db:migrate
--  create_table(:users)
-> 0.0705s
--  add_index(:users, :email, {:unique=>true})
-> 0.0080s
--  add_index(:users, :reset_password_token, {:unique=>true})
-> 0.0045s
== DeviseCreateUsers: migrated (0.0834s)
```

To routes.rb add:

```
root to: "members#index"
```

To make the members index page as the default project page. Users is the account created by devise for each member who will sign up.

To test in your browser enter: http://localhost:3000/users/

Note: You could copy Devise views (for customisation) to your app by running, rails g devise:views, but we will not do it in our app.

To relate the devise user to the actual dating member information they can be linked together. You could always add your member fields to the user table and delete the member table then, but for here we will keep user and member tables. Add the login user account to the member table:

rails generate migration AddUserBelongsToMembers user:belongs_to

```
class AddUserBelongsToMembers < ActiveRecord::Migration
def change
add_reference :members, :user, index: true
end
end
```

Change model/user.rb to link to the devise user to the dating member

```ruby
class User < ActiveRecord::Base
# Include default devise modules. Others available are:
# :confirmable, :lockable, :timeoutable and :omniauthable
devise :database_authenticatable, :registerable,
:recoverable, :rememberable, :trackable, :validatable
has_one :member
end
class Member < ActiveRecord::Base
has_attached_file :avatar
# Validate content type
validates_attachment_content_type :avatar,
:content_type => /\Aimage/
# Validate filename
validates_attachment_file_name :avatar,
:matches => [/png\Z/, /jpe?g\Z/]
has_one :member_info, autosave: true
has_many :messages
has_many :contacted_members
has_many :hobbies
belongs_to :user
end
```

To test the relationship:

```ruby
user1 = User.new
user1.member
```

Store the devise user when a new dating member is created, in members controller:

```ruby
def create
@member = Member.new(member_params)
respond_to do |format|
if @member.save
current_user.member = @member
current_user.save
format.html { redirect_to @member,
notice: 'Member was successfully created.' }
format.json { render action: 'show', status: :created,
location: @member }
else
format.html { render action: 'new' }
```

```ruby
format.json { render json: @member.errors, 
status: :unprocessable_entity }
end
end
end
```

We need to check if a new member needs to be created after login and to set the current dating member. in application_controller.rb:

```ruby
class ApplicationController < ActionController::Base
# Prevent CSRF attacks by raising an exception.
# For APIs, you may want to use :null_session instead.
protect_from_forgery with: :exception

before_action :authenticate_user!
before_action :set_member
private
def set_member
if @member ==nil
@member=current_user.member
end
end
end
```

In UsersController add:

```ruby
class UsersController < ApplicationController
before_filter :check_user_created, only: [:index]

private
def check_member_created
if current_user.member==nil
puts 'no user created'
redirect_to new_member_path
end
end
```

Finally change the header to add the devise login/logout links. In views/layouts/_header.html.erb replace:

```
<ul class="nav navbar-nav navbar-right">
<li class="active"><a href="../navbar-static-top/">Inbox</a></li>
<li><a href="../navbar-fixed-top/">Logout</a></li>
</ul>
with
```

```erb
<p class="nav navbar-nav navbar-right">
<% if user_signed_in? %>
Logged in as <strong><%= current_user.email %></strong>.
<%= link_to 'Edit profile', ed-it_user_registration_path, :class =>
'navbar-link' %> |
<%= link_to "Logout", destroy_user_session_path,
method: :delete, :class => 'navbar-link' %>
<% else %>
<%= link_to "Sign up", new_user_registration_path,
:class => 'navbar-link' %> |
<%= link_to "Login", new_user_session_path,
:class => 'navbar-link' %>
<% end %>
```

Test by logging and and verify you are directed to the form to fill in the new member [log out from previous session].

For a new member profile on login, add the fields required in views/members/_form.html.erb:

```erb
<%= form_for @member, :url => members_path,
:html => { :multipart => true } do |f| %>
<% if @member.errors.any? %>
<div id="error_explanation">
<h2><%= pluralize(@member.errors.count, "error") %>
prohibited this member from being saved:</h2>
<ul>
<% @member.errors.full_messages.each do |msg| %>
<li><%= msg %></li>
<% end %>
</ul>
</div>
<% end %>
<div class="field">
<%= f.label :first_name %><br>
<%= f.text_field :first_name %>
</div>
<div class="field">
<%= f.label :last_name %><br>
<%= f.text_field :last_name %>
</div>
<div class="field">
<%= f.label :description %><br>
<%= f.text_area :description %>
</div>
```

```erb
<div class="field">
<%= f.label :avatar %><br>
<%= f.file_field :avatar %>
</div>
<%= f.fields_for :member_info do |memberinfo_f| %>
<div class="field">
<%= memberinfo_f.label :gender %><br>
gender:
<%= memberinfo_f.select(:gender, [['f', 'f'], ['m', 'm']],
:selected => @member.member_info.gender) %>
</div>
<div class="field">
<%= memberinfo_f.label :relationship_status %><br>
status:
<%= memberinfo_f.select(:relationship_status,
[['single', 'single'], ['married', 'married']],
:selected => @member.member_info.relationship_status) %>
</div>
<div class="field">
<%= memberinfo_f.label :smoker %>
<%= memberinfo_f.check_box :smoker,
:value => @member.member_info.smoker %>
</div>
<div class="field">
<%= memberinfo_f.label :drinker %>
<%= memberinfo_f.check_box :drinker,
:value => @member.member_info.drinker%>
</div>
<div class="field">
<%= memberinfo_f.label :age %><br>
<%= memberinfo_f.number_field "age",:min => 18,
:value => @member.member_info.age %>
</div>
<div class="field">
<%= memberinfo_f.label :children %><br>
<%= memberinfo_f.number_field "children",
:value =>@member.member_info.children %>
</div>
<% end %>
<%= fields_for :hobbies do |hobbies_f| %>
<div class="field">
Hobbies</br>
<% HobbyConstant::HOBBIES.each do |hobbyconst| %>
<label class="li"><%= check_box_tag :hobby,
:name => hobbyconst %> <u><%= hobbyconst %></u></label><br />
<% end %>
```

```
</div>
<% end %>
<div class="actions">
<%= f.submit %>
</div>
<% end %>
```

Note: **field_for** Like form_for, it yields a FormBuilder object associated with a particular model object to a block, and within the block allows methods to be called on the builder to generate fields associated with the model object.

Change member model to access hobbies in the form

Hobbies will become a nest form for member, This is done by adding a method to your Member model called #accepts_nested_attributes_for which accepts the name of an association:

```
accepts_nested_attributes_for :member_info,:hobbies
In members_controller.rb:
```

Make sure you've allowed your params to include the nested attributes by appropriately including them in your Strong Parameters controller method. Permit nested attributes:

```
def member_params
params.require(:member).permit(:first_name, :last_name,
:description, :avatar, member_info_attributes:
[:smoker, :gender, :relationship_status, :age, :drinker])
end
```

Create a member_info for it's parent member model to store the member information:

```
# GET /members/new
def new
@member = Member.new
@member.build_member_info
end
```

Add the ability to find other members

We will add search preferences to find other singles. We will store the preferences selected by the member in a browser cookie. Add a left hand search column, just use basic CSS3 for now, we will replace it with a grid later. We will use Rails layouts.

Reference: http://guides.rubyonrails.org/layouts_and_rendering.html

In general, views will be rendered in the main layout. create a new file: app/views/layouts/list_members.html.erb

Add the search if the member changes their dating preferences

We will store the preferences is a session variable, @searchMemberInfo, and create a new model class to store the search preferences. It is not an active record but, using ActiveModel gives you access to find methods etc..

Reference: http://edgeguides.rubyonrails.org/active_model_basics.html

```
create a new file app/models/member_preferences.rb
create an ActiveModel::Model to store preferences, change the file
member_preferences.rb
class MemberPreference
include ActiveModel::Model
attr_accessor :minage, :maxage, :gender, :smoker, :drinker,
:hobbies
end
```

Store the search in cookies

Store the search preferences in the browser's cookie so the search preferences are remembered:

```
preferences = MemberPreferences.new(member_preferences_params)
#Sets a permanent cookie
cookies.permanent[:memberpreferences]= preferences.to_json
```

Note: although we will store the activeModel for the search configuration in the cookie, in general be careful when storing a model in a session. It will behave differently than you expect and can easily get out of sync with the database. Instead of storing the model directly in the session, store the id to the model and use that to fetch it from the database, but there is a try off because each time a database access is need for a new session.

Search action

For the search action you are not limited to the seven routes that RESTful routing creates by default.

HTTP Verb	Path	action	used for
GET	/photos	index	display a list of all photos
GET	/photos/new	new	return an HTML form for creating a new photo
POST	/photos	create	create a new photo
GET	/photos/:id	show	display a specific photo
GET	/photos/:id/edit	edit	return an HTML form for editing a photo
PUT	/photos/:id	update	update a specific photo
DELETE	/photos/:id	destroy	delete a specific photo

If you like, you may add additional routes that apply to the collection or individual members of the collection. The decision is if to create a new controller to keep your code cleaner or add a custom action, in this case I will create one custom controller as it is just one action, if more custom actions were needed I would create a new controller. To create a custom action, in routes.rb change:

```
resources :members
```

to

```
resources :members do
collection do
get 'search'
end
end
```

This will enable Rails to recognise paths such as /members/search with GET, and route to the search action of MembersController. It will also create the search_members_url and search_members_path route helpers.

In app/controllers/members_controller.rb add the custom action:

```
def search
preferences = MemberPreferences.new(member_preferences_params)
cookies.permanent[:memberpreferences]= preferences.to_json
redirect_to members_path
end
```

Add the search preferences to the page in app/views/members/index.html.erb :

```erb
<% content_for :sidebar do %>
search preferences

<%= form_for @newmemberpreferences, :url => search_members_path,
:method => :get, :remote => true do |f| %>
<%= f.label :smoker%>
<%= f.check_box :smoker %> <br />
</br>

<%= f.label :gender%>
</br>
<%=f.radio_button :gender,@newmemberpreferences.gender=='m' %>
<%= f.radio_button :gender, @newmemberpreferences.gender=='f'%>
<%= f.radio_button :gender, @newmemberpreferences.gender==nil %>

</br>
<%= label_tag(:minage, "min age:") %>
<%= f.number_field :min_age, value: @newmemberpreferences.minage%>
</br>
<%= label_tag(:maxage, "max age:") %>
<%= f.number_field :max_age, value: @newmemberpreferences.maxage
</br>
<%= f.submit "Search" %>
<% end %>
<% end %>

<% content_for :content do %>
<h1>Listing members</h1>
<table>
<thead>
<tr>
<th>First name</th>
<th>Last name</th>
<th>Description</th>
<th></th>
<th></th>
```

```erb
<th></th>
</tr>
</thead>

<tbody>
<% @members.each do |member| %>
<%= render partial: "show_member", locals: {member: member} %>
<% end %>
</tbody>
</table>
<br>
<%= link_to 'New Member', new_member_path %>
<% end %>
```

In the index action add the search filter for the selected preferences

```ruby
def search
preferences = MemberPreferences.new(member_preferences_params)
cookies.permanent[:memberpreferences]= preferences.to_json

# build search query
search = {}

if preferences.smoker !=nil
smoker= {smoker: preferences.smoker}
search.merge!(smoker)
end

if preferences.gender !=nil
gender= {gender: preferences.gender}
search.merge!(gender)
end

if preferences.minage !=nil
age= {age:preferences.minage..preferences.maxage}
search.merge!(age)
end
@members= Member.joins(:member_info).where(member_infos:search)
render :action => 'index', layout: "list_members"
end
```

To test the search: http://localhost:3000/members/

Add helpers to view

You can create helpers in app/helpers/application_helper.rb to be used in all view pages. For example instead of:

```
<tr class="activeRow">
<td><%= number_to_currency(@value1, separator: ",", delimiter: "", format: '%n') %></td>
<td><%= number_to_currency(@value2, separator: ",", delimiter: "", format: '%n') %></td>
</tr>
```

You could use:

```
<tr class="activeRow">
<td><%= my_formatted_number(@value1) %></td>
<td><%= my_formatted_number(@value2) %></td>
</tr>
```

By adding the helper:

```
module ApplicationHelper
def my_formatted_number number
number_to_currency(number, separator: ",", delimiter: "", format: '%n')
end
```

Add Ajax to the search

Now let us update the search results using Ajax so the page does not need to be refreshed, in index.html.erb. Change the members area by adding an 'id' so we can update it with query.

```
<tbody>
<% @members.each do |member| %>
```

To:

```
<tbody id="tbodyid">
<% @members.each do |member| %>
```

Create a new file app/views/members/index.js.erb. Use jquery to append the members details:

```
$("#tbodyid").empty();
$('#tbodyid').append('<%= j render 'show_all_members', locals: {members: @members} %>')
```

Create a new file app/views/members/_show_all_members.html.erb

```
<% @members.each do |member| %>
<%= render partial: "show_member", locals: {member: member} %>
<% end %>
```

Add pagination to display all the members if say many existed once deployed.

to Gemfile add the gem 'will_paginate'

```
bundle install
```

To controllers/members_controller.rb, in def index, change

```
@members= Member.joins(:member_info)
```

to

```
@members= Member.joins(:member_info).paginate(
:page => params[:page], :per_page => 20)
```

In the search action, def search, change

```
@members= Member.joins(:member_info).where(member_infos: search)
```

to

```
@members= Member.joins(:member_info).where(member_infos: search ).paginate(:page => params[:page], :per_page => 20)
```

Add to index.html.erb

```
<%= will_paginate @members %>
```

Message people to invite say you like them, chat

We only need the show and delete actions for each message. Remember for members we used scaffolding but now we will go through adding each component manually with no scaffolding. By using generators the unit tests are generated.

To see all generates enter:

```
rails generator
```

Note the capital letter for Messages:

```
rails g controller Messages
```

For messages we only need a index page as the delete will be done by Ajax, and the only actions needed are show, delete, new:

#Note: no view files are created.

rails g controller Messages

```
create  app/controllers/message_controller.rb
invoke  erb
create   app/views/message
invoke  rspec
create   spec/controllers/message_controller_spec.rb
invoke  helper
create   app/helpers/message_helper.rb
invoke  rspec
create   spec/helpers/message_helper_spec.rb
invoke  assets
invoke  coffee
create   app/assets/javascripts/message.js.coffee
invoke  scss
create   app/assets/stylesheets/message.css.scss
```

Note: if you also wanted to generate a controller, view and route use

rails scaffold_controller g Messages, but his also generates some unneeded views.

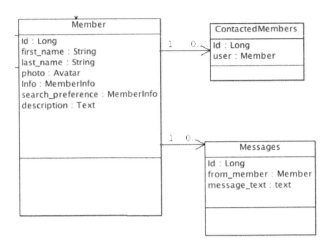

Create a model for the message

```
rails g model Message message_text:text member_id:integer from_member_id:integer
class CreateMessages < ActiveRecord::Migration
def change
create_table :messages do |t|
t.text :message_text
t.integer :member_id
t.integer :from_member_id
t.timestamps
end
end
end
```

We have to add the messages model as a reference to the members model, so we store who send the message [member] and who the message is for [from_member]:

```
rails g migration AddMemberToMessages
```

Generates:

```
class AddMemberToMessages < ActiveRecord::Migration
def change
add_reference :messages, :member
add_reference :messages, :from_member
end
end
```

Add to the message model a reference to members:

```
class Message < ActiveRecord::Base
has_many :from_member, :class_name => 'Member'
belongs_to :member
end
```

To members add a reference to message:

```
Class Member
has_many :messages
```

To test it in rails console:

```
member = Member.new
messagelist = Array.new
messagelist[0] = Message.new
messagelist[1] = Message.new
member.messages = messagelist
member.messages
```

Add the routes for message to routes.rb:

```
resources :messages, :path => '/messages',
:only => [:index, :new, :create, :destroy]
```

Add the header link to view any messages to layouts/_header.html.erb:

```
<% if user_signed_in? %>
<%= link_to 'Inbox', message_path %>
```

You also could have used:

```
<% if user_signed_in? %>
<%= link_to "inbox", {controller: "messages", action: "index"} %>
```

Create the message views

Manually create a test for message index view page:

```
rails g rspec:view messages index
create spec/views/messages
create spec/views/messages/index.html.erb_spec.rb
```

Create the index page to allow adding new message for a member, create a new file app/views/messages/index.html.erb:

```erb
<% if @messages == nil %>
no messages
<% end %>
<table>
<% @messages.each do |message| %>
<tr><td>
<td><%= link_to 'Destroy', message, method: :delete %>   <%= message.message_text %>
</td></tr>
<% end %>
</table>
```

Create the view for a new message

Create a new file app/views/messages/new.html.erb, You can also create a rspec test like for the index view:

```erb
<h1>New Message</h1>
<%= render 'form' %>
<%= link_to 'Back', members_path, :rel => "modal:close" %>
```

Create the shared message form, app/views/messages/_form.html.erb

```erb
<%= form_for(@message) do |f| %>
<% if @message.errors.any? %>
<div id="error_explanation">
<h2><%= pluralize(@user.errors.count, "error") %> prohibited this message from being saved:</h2>
<ul>
<% @message.errors.full_messages.each do |msg| %>
<li><%= msg %></li>
<% end %>
</ul>
</div>
<% end %>
<div class="field">
<%= f.label :message_text %><br />
<%= f.text_field :message_text %>
</div>
<div class="actions">
<%= f.submit %>
</div>
<% end %>
```

The messages will be updated with Ajax so we need a javascript file for this. Create a new file, app/views/messages/create.js.erb:

```
<%- if @message.errors.any? %>
console.log('Error');
$('#dialog-form').html('<%= escape_javascript(render('form')) %>');
<%- else %>
console.log('Created');
$('#dialog-form').dialog('close');
$('#dialog-form').remove();
$('table').append('<%= escape_javascript(render(@message)) %>');
<%- end %>
```

Add a link next to each member to allow a person to message them, for views/members/_show_user.html.erb add:

```
<td><%= link_to_modal "New Message",
new_message_path(member: member), :class=>"button" %></td>
```

Display all messages

To display all the messages for a member we will display them in a popup using a jquery modal popup form https://github.com/dei79/jquery-modal-rails

To Gemfile add:

```
gem 'jquery-ui-rails'
gem 'jquery-modal-rails'
```

To require the jQuery modal modules, add the following to your app/assets/javascripts/application.js:

```
//= require jquery.ui.all
//= require jquery.modal
```

Also add the jQuery modal CSS to your app/aassets/stylesheets/application.css:

```
/*
*= require jquery.ui.all
*= require jquery.modal
*/
```

The controller/messages_controller.erb file will now look like this, we are using format.json

```
{ head :no_content } for the ajax:
class MessagesController < ApplicationController
def index
@member = current_user.member
@messages = @member.messages
end

# DELETE /members/1
# DELETE /members/1.json
def destroy
@member.destroy
respond_to do |format|
format.html { redirect_to messages_url }
#head :no_content will create a HTTP response 204 success with
#an empty body, returning this response header:
format.json { head :no_content }
end
end

def new
@message = Message.new
end

# POST /members
# POST /members.json
def create
@message = Message.new(message_params)

# message belongs to the person you are sending it to
@message.member = params[:member]
@message.from_member_id = current_user.member
respond_to do |format|
if @message.save
format.html {redirect_to :back}
format.xml { render :xml => @message,
:status => :created, :location => @message}
format.js
else
format.html { render :action => "new" }
format.xml { render :xml => @message.errors,
:status => :unprocessable_entity }
format.js
```

```
    end
  end
end

private
def message_params
  params.require(:message).permit(:message_text )
end
end
```

Store number of messages for performance

The **:counter_cache** option can be used to make finding the number of belonging objects more efficient. Consider these models: Rails will keep the cache value up to date, and then return that value in response to the size method.

Reference: http://guides.rubyonrails.org/association_basics.html

For example:

```
class Order < ActiveRecord::Base
  belongs_to :customer, counter_cache: true
end
class Customer < ActiveRecord::Base
  has_many :orders
end
```

In the case above, you would need to add a column named orders_count to the Customer model.

Indicate number of messages in your inbox icon.

Twitter bootstrap have a nice feature to add the badges class, for example to indicate number of messages in your inbox:

Reference: http://getbootstrap.com/components/#badges

Badges

Name	Example	Markup
Default	1	`<span class="badge">1</span>`
Success	2	`<span class="badge badge-success">2</span>`
Warning	4	`<span class="badge badge-warning">4</span>`
Important	6	`<span class="badge badge-important">6</span>`
Info	8	`<span class="badge badge-info">8</span>`
Inverse	10	`<span class="badge badge-inverse">10</span>`

Live streaming

Rails 4 introduced live streaming which allow you to update a browser's web data without any action from the user. It enables Rails to open and close a stream explicitly. For example live reporting of revenue generated, live chat room between members. We could use the Unicorn app server, but it is meant for fast responses as unicorn will kill our connection after 30 seconds. Some good Ruby servers to look at for live streaming would be either Rainbows!, Puma, or Thin.

Server-Sent Events

Server-Sent Events (SSE) is a feature of HTML5 that allows long polling, but is built in to the browser. Basically, the browser keeps a connection open to the server, and fires an event in JavaScript every time the server sends data. You can use Server-Sent Events in conjunction with the Live API to achieve full-duplex communication. By default Rails provides a one-way communication process by writing the stream to the client when data is available. However, if we can add SSEs, we can enable events and responses, thus making it two-way.

Stream Data

Another use of streaming is for rendering the layout first and streaming each part of the layout as they are processed. Useful for expensive actions that, for example, do a lot of queries on the database. In such actions, you want to delay queries execution as much as you can and have lazy execution.

Reference: http://api.rubyonrails.org/classes/ActionController/Streaming.html

Consider a query-intensive view, such as a displaying tickets sold:

```
class TicketsController
def index
@users = User.all
@tickets = Ticket.all
@attachments = Attachment.all
end
end
```

In this case, streaming seems to be a good fit. In a typical Rails scenario, this page takes longer to load than usual because it has to retrieve all the data first. Let's add streaming:

```
class TicketsController
def index
@users = User.all
@tickets = Ticket.all
@attachments = Attachment.all
render stream: true
end
end
```

The Rails method render stream: true will lazily load the queries and allow them to run after the assets and layout have been rendered. Streaming only works with templates and not any other forms (such as json or xml). Since the database calls have not happened when the templates are rendered, references to instance variables will fail. Hence, in order to load attributes like title or meta we need to use content_for instead of the regular yield method. yield, however, still works for the body. instead of

```
<%= yield :title %>,
it will now look like:
<%= content_for :title, "My Awesome Title" %>
```

RESPONSIVE DESIGN

Designers have it tougher now than before. We not only have to design for stationary devices, but also mobile devices like the tablet and smartphones, and since we are talking about a lot of different screen sizes and resolutions here. Responsive design is when a website adapts the device' screen using it to give the user the possible possible viewing experience, you could have a different HTML layout based on the screen dimensions, it responds to the device. CSS3 media queries are mostly used to build the layouts for the different devices, it is normal to design for mobile, tablet, web - for a simple design you could have the same layout for all. The goal is to support all devices including iOS, android, windows, blackberry and others. For example, http://www.bostonglobe.com/, as you change the screen size at various points [mobile/tablet/web] their design snaps to a different layout.

Responsive design from a programming side, is where you detect the user's browser (via user-agent) or the size of their screen, and actually show them a different view based on the size of their device. For example, you might use a three column layout for desktops, a two column layout for tablets, and a single column layout on smartphones. In this case, the view on each device looks very different, because you are actually changing the view based on the device.

Web Layout:

Tablet Layout: [the right hand column is moved under the first two columns]

Mobile layout: [single column]

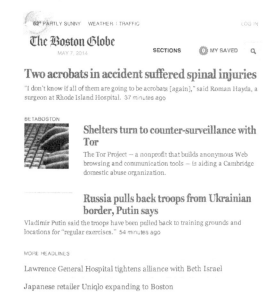

Some good example responsive sites are:

- http://www.visitlondon.com/
- http://www.sony.com/
- http://www.salesforce.com/
- http://www.mulberry.com/

Useful tools to test pages on multiple devices are:

http://deviceponsive.com/

For quick tests I just manually change the width of my browser [I use chrome mostly], also there is Chrome device emulation.

Reference: https://developer.chrome.com/devtools/docs/mobile-emulation

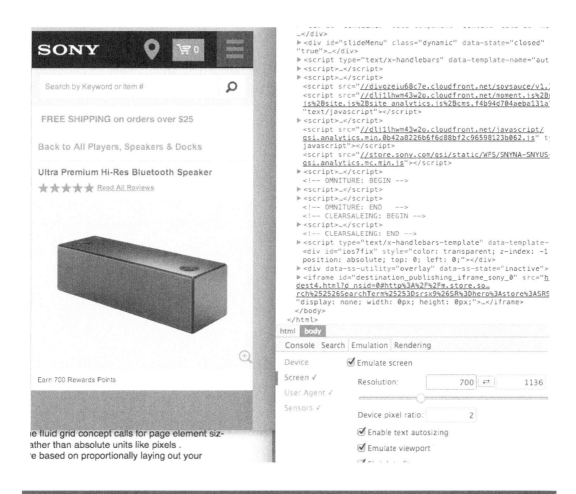

Fluid versus adaptive and responsive design

Commonly used terms are fluid and responsive. Traditionally web sites had fixed pixel widths, No matter what screen resolution the visitor has, he or she will see the same width as other visitors. Fixed-width layouts are much easier to design for a web designer - 'pixel perfect'.

In a fluid website layout, the page adjusts to the user's screen resolution. Fluid Design was possible long before Responsive Design. The fluid grid concept calls for page element sizing to be in relative units like percentages, rather than absolute units like pixels.

Fluid Layouts (also called Liquid Layouts) are based on proportionally laying out your website so elements take up the same percent of space on different screen sizes. Fluid Design means that different sections of the site are defined relatively (e.g. an element is 50% of the page width). No matter which browser you're using: Smartphone, Tablet, Desktop, the site will look (mostly) the same and have the same proportions (this element will take up half the screen). This is because in your CSS, everything is defined in terms of percent, or some other metric that scales nicely from device to device (Whereas defining fixed sizes in pixels might make and element take up half the screen on a desktop, the whole screen on a tablet, and be bigger than the screen on a smartphone).

Breakpoints is where the design changes to a different layout for a different device.

Fixed Design:

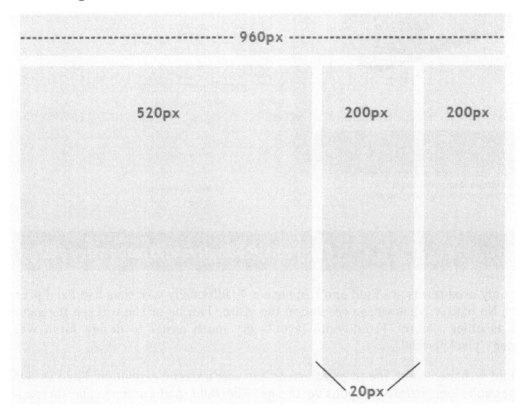

Fluid design:

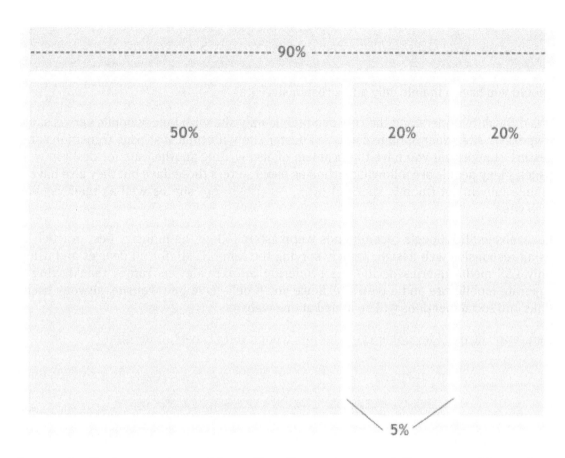

Responsive Design wasn't possible until media queries were fully supported by modern browsers with CSS3. Media queries made it possible to change CSS properties at different breakpoints (usually the size of the browser's width).

Responsive Design and Adaptive Design often get lumped together too, but they have some major differences. The adaptive layout is based on the idea: instead of using percentage we will give our layout fixe sizes, but we will adapt those sizes depending of the width of the browser/viewport, thus creating a layout with different "break points". For each of those break point, we will use media queries

We could define the responsive layout, as a mix between the fluid and adaptive layouts. It will use the relative units of the fluid layout and the break points of the adaptive one. Responsive design is the recommended practice, one page that adapts to all devices.

Responsive site versus mobile and responsive sites

Should you have a mobile only and a responsive site?

It is difficult to understand the role of a mobile only site with jquerymobile versus say a responsive site. Jquerymobile can give a faster site with their fast page transitions and gesture support but you have the problem of also writing another site for desktop web pages. Many people are following airbnb as trend setters these days but they also have a mobile only m.dot (mobile specific) http://m.airbnb.com site as well as their regular web site.

For website SEO, Google recommends webmasters follow the industry best practice of using responsive web design, namely serving the same HTML for all devices and using only CSS media queries decide the rendering on each device, rather than having a separate mobile site and a web site. Since you'll only have one website, all your back-links and social mentions will be aimed at one website.

Reference: https://developers.google.com/webmasters/smartphone-sites/

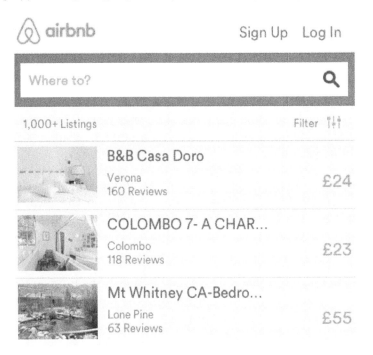

A mobile only site, using for example jquerymobile, might be useful whereby you only want a mobile phone web site,, if you want to convert your jquerymobile site to a native mobile application using phone gap or maybe if you have a site which does not have a complicated content layout such as a utility tool - currency converter or a lightweight UI. Building a separate mobile version of a site may lead to a better user experience.

A responsive site might not be the best solution if for example you do not want to modify your existing site, maybe it works great as it current is, and a mobile only may be cheaper to develop, or responsive design can compromise the desktop user experience. When you weigh the pros and cons, responsive design really comes out on top. Not only is it much better for SEO, but it provides visitors with a better user experience. As more and more websites become responsive, people have come to expect it.

A mobile only website negatives are:

- Two code bases to maintain
- You have to manage cross-linking and redirecting of users between the two sites.

A responsive website negatives are:

- Harder to develop.
- Larger code and longer to load.

Network latency

We usually think of mobile cellular network speeds in terms of bandwidth. With 3G, we get up to 5 Mbps; with 4G, we get up to 50 Mbps, but mobile latency on a mobile is high compared to a home broadband. Latency is delay, Latency is the round-trip time that the first byte of every package takes to get to a device after a request. The lower the latency (the fewer the milliseconds) the better the network performance. While more bandwidth is useful for transferring big files (such as a YouTube video), it doesn't add much value when you're downloading a lot of small files and the latency is high and fixed.

While the latency on a DSL connection in a home is between 20 and 45 milliseconds, on 3G it can be between 150 and 450 milliseconds, and on 4G between 100 and 180. In other words, latency is 5 to 10 times higher on a 3G cellular connection than on a home network. A lot of attention and interest has been paid to wireless network speeds, but little light has been focused on wireless network latency. The following is a simplified introduction to the components and conventions of mobile cellular networks that factor into the latency:

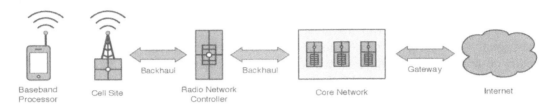

Unfortunately research has shown, most responsive websites deliver the same number of bytes regardless of screen size, even on slow mobile network connections. Not all users will wait for your website to load. Does a mobile device with 3G latency deserve the same data size as desktop? So responsive can be bad for responsive.

Grid frameworks

It is usual to design a responsive design imagining vertical lines across your website in order to align the content. Two of the most popular frameworks to help with responsive design are Twitter Bootstrap and Zurb foundation [they also supply menus, navigation etc.]. There are many more, if you are looking for a more basic smaller solution then libraries such as http://goldengridsystem.com/ may suit.

Top Core Differences Between Bootstrap and Foundation

- UI Elements : Foundation has a very limited number of UI elements. Bootstrap websites can look similar to each other as they use the same UI elements.
- REMs VS Pixels : Foundation uses REMs (to avoid the cascading issue of EM's), Bootstrap uses pixels.
- Flexible grids : Both are 12 column grids by default.
- Foundation uses SASS while Boostrap uses LESS. Bootstrap default grid mode is bound to breakpoints, meaning that it will give you static sized widths that will be reduced when the viewport reaches its limit. But you can also use the class. row-fluid and the width will use percentages, behaving the same way as Foundation's grid. So with Zurb as you reduce the browser screen will scale

down with more 'style' rather than just jump to a smaller size when you reach a breakpoint.
- Mobile first - Foundation encourages you to design mobile first by adding a simple rule: anything that is not under a media query will be considered mobile. If you want it to look differently on a tablet or computer, then you will want to specify the media query. Bootstrap is also now mobile fist by default since bootstrap 3.
- Community : Bootstrap has the larger community. You'll have to get your hands dirty when using Foundation.
- Tools : Zurb provides other great tools such as Solidify for prototyping and Ink for email templates.

I prefer Zurb Foundation as it is more fluid, the font sizes are not fixed as in Bootstrap and the screen sizes are not hard coded in pixels, but Bootstrap is easier to get going with better UI elements provided so for popularity I will use Bootstrap here. You can recompile Foundation or Bootstrap with your required layout tweaks if required.

Bootstrap grid

The default Bootstrap grid system utilises 12 columns, making for a 940px wide container without responsive features enabled, for example if you only wanted to support a typical large screen. With the responsive CSS file added, the grid adapts to be 724px and 1170px wide depending on your viewport. Below 767px viewports, the columns become fluid and stack vertically.

Supported devices

Bootstrap supports a handful of media queries in a single file to help make your projects more appropriate on different devices and screen resolutions. Here's what's included:

Label	Layout width	Column width	Gutter width
Large display	1200px and up	70px	30px
Default	980px and up	60px	20px
Portrait tablets	768px and above	42px	20px
Phones to tablets	767px and below	Fluid columns, no fixed widths	
Phones	480px and below	Fluid columns, no fixed widths	

Note: the gutter is the space between the columns.

Zurb uses different screen width breakpoints It also has a default 12-column.

Reference: http://foundation.zurb.com/docs/media-queries.html

```
// Small screens
@media only screen { } /* Define mobile styles */

@media only screen and (max-width: 40em) { } /* max-width 640px, mobile-only styles, use wh
// Medium screens
@media only screen and (min-width: 40.063em) { } /* min-width 641px, medium screens */

@media only screen and (min-width: 40.063em) and (max-width: 64em) { } /* min-width 641px a
// Large screens
@media only screen and (min-width: 64.063em) { } /* min-width 1025px, large screens */

@media only screen and (min-width: 64.063em) and (max-width: 90em) { } /* min-width 1025px
// XLarge screens
@media only screen and (min-width: 90.063em) { } /* min-width 1441px, xlarge screens */

@media only screen and (min-width: 90.063em) and (max-width: 120em) { } /* min-width 1441px
// XXLarge screens
@media only screen and (min-width: 120.063em) { } /* min-width 1921px, xlarge screens */
```

The problem I have with bootstrap (Zurb to a lesser extent) is that it's minimum width is 768pixels, which is not granular enough for say smaller mobile devices and you may need to customize it to create a new group size with a maximum of 480pixels for example.

Gesture support

To add touch/swip gesture support, some useful libraries are:

- http://hammerjs.github.io/
- http://labs.rampinteractive.co.uk/touchSwipe/demos/

Browser versus server side device detection

A responsive website is not automatically a mobile-friendly website. so optimisation is required. Traditionally device detection was done by detecting the HTTP user-agent, media queries did not exist before CSS3. in each HTML request, HTTP is the protocol layer below HTML. With the advent of smartphones and CSS3 support, a few things have changed. This has allowed developers to take development shortcuts and create websites that partially adapt themselves to mobile devices, using client-side adaptation. Creating mobile websites with a pure client-side approach, including techniques such as progressive enhancement and responsive Web design is often enough for most sites.

Using Chrome developer to view the HTTP user-agent:

Most smart phone websites use client side code to detect the screen size and orientation in CSS3. The CSS3 code is download into the browser and dynamically changes the layout using media queries. Libraries such as Bootstrap use browser client size media queries to detect the device type and screen.

There are two approaches for doing device detection on client side or server side:

Server-side detection based on user-agent string, Client-side detection based on features.

When you know the device or type of device you could deliver different Javascript/CSS files or implement different parts of the code as downloading and interpreting the same Javascript for each device can slow down the page rendering. The goal should be to download only the required Javascript/CSS files, but balancing this against how easy asset pipelines assembles all files together, you could by using logic; specify in each layout which CSS/javascript files to include.

Client side device detection

The first point to note is that not all devices support modern HTML5 and JavaScript features equally, so some of the problems from the early days of the mobile Web still exist. Client-side feature detection can help work around this issue, but browsers may return false positives for some feature support tests (such as Opera mini provides a false positive for CSS Gradients).

Reference: http://modernizr.com/news/modernizr-policy-feature-detects/

Media queries

You can specify different style sheets per media query as in:

```
<link rel="stylesheet" type="text/css" media="only screen and (max-device-width: 480px)" href="small-device.css" />
```

Zurb foundation 'interchange' can now pull in HTML partials so you can load different sections of your page for particular media queries but you still have to load all the Javascript/CSS files.

Reference: http://foundation.zurb.com/docs/components/interchange.html

Check if all css files are downloaded in Chrome developer:

If we have a HTML page which includes a different CSS file based on the screen size, the browser still downloads both files unfortunately, for example:

```
<!DOCTYPE HTML>
<html>
<head>
<link rel="stylesheet" media="screen and (min-width: 400px)" href="small.css">
<link rel="stylesheet" media="screen and (min-width: 6000px)" href="big.css">
<title>CSS files with media queries</title>
</head>
<body>
test loading
<h1>test h1</h1>
<h2>test h2</h2>
</body>
</html>
small.css:
body {
color: blue;
```

```
}
h1 {
color: #00ff00;
}
h2 {
color: rgb(255,0,0);
}
big.css:
body {
color: red;
}
h1 {
color: #00ff00;
}
h2 {
color: rgb(255,0,0);
}
```

You can see all three files are downloaded, I would have wished only two were downloaded:

So we really do not need to load small.css for a desktop. This seems wasteful but is based on how browsers worked in the past and, I assume, done to make rendering happen as early as possible.

Some Useful libraries to detect CSS features in order to decide if to include Javscript libaries are:

MatchMedia, https://github.com/paulirish/matchMedia.js/ allows CSS3 media queries to be tested directly within JavaScript.

Device.js, https://github.com/matthewhudson/device.js, allows you to write conditional CSS and/or JavaScript based on device operating system (iOS, Android, Blackberry, Windows), orientation (Portrait vs. Landscape), and type (Tablet vs. Mobile).

Server side device detection

Before smart phones and HTML5, mobile device detection was determined in the server side, it would render different layouts based on what the server decided the device was. Server side detection is done by checking the HTTP user-agent. With device detection, the HTTP headers that browsers send as part of every request they make are examined and are usually sufficient to uniquely identify the browser or mobile model and, hence, its properties. Device-detection solutions use various pattern-matching techniques to map these headers to data stores of devices and properties.

Server side detection also enables you to deliver a small contained experience to the older feature phones, a rich JavaScript-enhanced solution to smartphones, all from the same URL.

Media Queries have sparked the idea that client-side adaptation could ultimately make device detection unnecessary. However it is not quite that simple. Advantages of server side detection:

Rendering speed

Because device-detection solutions can prepare just the right package of HTML and resources on the server, the browser is left to do much less work in rendering the page. Typically in many solutions a mobile phone will download and process CSS styles meant for desktop devices, which could can extra download time.

Rails 4.1 mobile variants

We often want to render different HTML/JSON/XML templates for phones, tablets, and desktop browsers. Variants make it easy. You can set the variant in a before_action:

```
request.variant = :tablet if request.user_agent =~ /iPad/
```

Respond to variants in the action just like you respond to formats:

```
respond_to do |format|
  format.html do |html|
    html.tablet # renders app/views/projects/show.html+tablet.erb
    html.phone { extra_setup; render.. . }
  end
end
```

Provide separate templates for each format and variant:

```
app/views/projects/show.html.erb
app/views/projects/show.html+tablet.erb
app/views/projects/show.html+phone.erb
```

Other gems to detect service side devices are:

- https://github.com/jistr/mobvious-rails, which detects whether your website is being accessed by a phone, tablet or desktop.
- A basic Rails gem to detect general type of devices is https://github.com/brendanlim/mobile-fu, without each device model, it does not know iPhone 4 or iPhone 5, just that it is an iphone. You can then use different layouts for example
- The Detect Mobile Browsers project http://detectmobilebrowsers.com/ is another basic solution.

AWS cloudfront has the configurable option to detect the device and send it in the HTTP header to your site:
http://aws.amazon.com/about-aws/whats-new/2014/06/26/amazon-cloudfront-device-detection-geo-targeting-host-header-cors/ . Note: caching is improved if you do not forward any headers (which causes CloudFront to cache multiple versions of an object based on the device values.) CloudFront will match the header against an internal device list and will send an CloudFront-Is-Mobile-Viewer, CloudFront-Is-Desktop-Viewer, or CloudFront-Is-Tablet-Viewer header to give you a generic indication of the device type.

Performance

Server side device-detection solutions allow the developer to send only the content required to the requesting browser. The browser features are available only after the DOM has loaded and the CSS tests have run, by which time it is too late to make major changes to the page's content.

Doing as much optimisation on the server side as possible makes sense, to relieve the client of data transferring and the execution of logic in the browser.The main reason for doing this is performance. Much of the time taken by a page to load is caused by the browser trying to make sense of the data being received.

Support of business requirements, such as targeted business models and advertising and customised experiences for specific devices is best done from the server side.

Server side detection Pros/cons

The main disadvantages of server-side detection are the following:

- The device databases (to be discussed shortly) that they utilise need to be updated frequently and the cost. Vendors usually make this as easy as possible by providing sample cron scripts to download daily updates.
- Device databases might get out of date or contain bad information causing wrong data to be delivered to specific range of devices. Device-detection solutions are typically commercial products that must be licensed.

The main advantages:

- Source order, URL structure, media, and application designs can be finely optimised for a specific device class before ever reaching its browser, only send what a client needs. But server-side solutions generally rely on user agent redirects to device-specific code templates. Each device class that warrants adaptation needs its own set of templates and these templates may ultimately contain duplicative code that actually applies to every class of device.
- Server side device detection might seem to cost significantly more than responsive design to develop, but device detection is what gives total flexibility. it enables you to deliver a small contained experience to feature phones, a rich JavaScript-enhanced solution to smartphones.
- Because device-detection solutions can prepare just the right package of HTML and resources on the server, the browser is left to do much less work in rendering the page. This can make a big difference to the end-user experience.
- Another area where device detection has an advantage is in fine-tuning media formats and other resources delivered to the device in question.
- Some properties are not available at all via Javascript/CSS if you did client side detection; for example, whether a device is a phone, tablet or desktop, its model name, vendor name and maximum HTML size, and so on.

Server side detection Libraries

HTTP user-agent libraries are used to detect the device on the server side. This user-agent is compared it to a know devices in a database library such as Wurfl (it used to be free and you now pay for it), and DeviceAtlas, these can cost several thousand dollars on license terms.

Using server side you can also detect the network speed and say redirect to a settings using more image compression using DeviceAtlas. To test network performance:

```
quality=new DeviceAtlasNPC().getQuality()
```

There are simpler, free alternatives too, the drawback, of course, is that device detection will inevitably be less comprehensive such as:

- http://www.openddr.org/
- http://51degrees.com/ [this does not offer a free ruby lite version].

An example of server side detection to render different Javascript or CSS files. You could determine the screen width using server side detection then set a session variable with the device type, for example:

```
<% if (@highEndDevice) %>
<link href="css/bootstrap.css" rel="stylesheet">
<link href="css/bootstrap-responsive.css" rel="stylesheet">
<link href="css/additional.css" rel="stylesheet">
<% end %>
<% if (@highEndDevice): %>
<script src="js/jquery.js"></script>
.
.
<% end %>
```

RESS

Responsive design with server-side components (RESS) tries to bring together the best of both worlds - client and server side detection. RESS can make significant performance and reach improvements to a website. Instead of determining the device on the server side with the complexity of a device repository you can use media queries and Javascript to change the URL to resources such as images.

It is good to look at the RESS gem https://github.com/matthewrobertson/ress It adds a back end for adapting server responses based on client side feature detection.

This Rails gem basically sends the media query detected result to the server side, which sets server variables in the code so you can do conditional includes. Ress allows you to customise how your Rails application responds to mobile requests in two ways:

It adds controller and helper methods to detect which version of your site has been requested such as

```
<% if mobile_request? %>
<%= image_tag 'low-res.png' %>
<% else %>
<%= image_tag 'high-res.png' %>
<% end %>
```

It prepends a view path for each alternate version of your site, so that you can override the templates or partials that are rendered for certain requests. For example if you want to render a different html form for creating users on the mobile version of your site.

If the server detects a mobile browser is accessing the site, it can render the page template with the mobile components. Otherwise, it falls back to the "standard" ones. Each component set is rigorously optimised for the device classes it applies to thereby taking advantage of what server side solutions do best. Together we get an adaptive layout at a single URL that integrates components optimised. Doing as much optimisation on the server side as possible makes sense, to relieve the client of data transferring and the execution of logic in the browser.

Image rendering

Serving a large picture on a regular website is fine, but there are good reasons why sending the same picture to a mobile user is not ok: mobile devices have much smaller screens, (often) more limited bandwidth and more limited computation power. By providing a lower resolution and/or a smaller size of the picture, performance is improved. The best way to optimise images is still to resize and prepare them server side.

To limit the maximum width of an adaptive image on the device screen, you'd have to limit the maximum width of the image's container, rather than of the image itself. Let's say you've wrapped your logo image in a module with a class of branding. Here is the style that will do the trick:

```
.branding {
max-width: 150px;
}
```

So, now we have scalable responsive images in our website's fluid layout, but all devices are fed the same images. Browsers in order to provide the fastest loading time possible, browsers preload all of the images that they can identify in the source code before any CSS or JavaScript is processed. So, this approach would actually penalise mobile visitors more, by forcing them to download all of an image's variants. Because of this preloading, most solutions require either a back-end solution (to preempt the preloading) or special markup and JavaScript.

Another issue is some images just don't scale well; fine detail is lost, and dramatic impact is reduced. For some photos rendered on a mobile, it would be much nicer visually if the mobile version of the photo was zoomed in, cropped and focused. To solve this problem, we need a responsive image solution that enables you either to specify different versions of the image for different situations or to adjust the image on the fly.

Encode images with a different format

JPEG is used when small file size is more important than maximum image quality, worth experimenting with different formats.

Google webP is a format to compress images but only supported natively on the latest google browsers and opera. http://caniuse.com/webp

There are two approaches to server side image resizing:

- You generate different sized images, for example low res, high res and use a HTML tag to decide the best picture to use. Each published image can be created in multiple versions, with device detection used to serve a pointer to the most appropriate version for that device or browser. Software libraries such as http://www.imagemagick.org/RMagick/doc/ can be used to resize images on the fly, based on the properties of the requesting HTTP client.
- On the server generate an image to best suit the screen size.

Client side image detection

The goal is to deliver optimised, contextual image sizes in responsive layouts that utilise dramatically different image sizes at different resolutions. Ideally, this could enable developers to start with mobile-optimised images in their HTML and specify a larger size to be used for users with larger screen resolutions -- without requesting both image sizes, and without UA sniffing.

This amounts to media queries embedded in HTML. We'd also need to create different image sizes before runtime, which means either setting up a script or manually doing it, a tiresome job.

There are two proposed standards for using alternative image sizes in the HTML5 tag:

- picture element
- srcset img attribute

srcset has an advantage over <picture> in that it takes pixel density into consideration: the <picture> element only accounts for device width. For current browser support see:

- http://caniuse.com/#feat=srcset
- http://caniuse.com/#feat=picture

Thanks to increasingly aggressive prefetching in several of the major browsers, an image's src is requested long before we have a chance to apply any custom scripting.

HTML5 picture tag

The picture element couples HTML with media queries, but coupling CSS to HTML is bad for maintenance. This solution also doesn't cover high-definition displays.

```
<picture>
<source srcset="portrait-small.jpg">
<source media="(min-width: 480px)" srcset="portrait-small.jpg">
<source media="(min-width: 1024px)" srcset="portrait-large.jpg">
<img src="portrait-small.jpg" alt="A photo of London by night">
</picture>
```

HTML5 srcset tag

WebKit supports the srcset attribute allowing developers to specify a list of sources for an image attribute, to be delivered based on the pixel density of the user's display. For example:

```
<img src="low-res.jpg" srcset="high-res.jpg 2x">
```

Use low-res.jpg as the source for this img on low-resolution displays, and for any browser that doesn't understand the srcset attribute. Use high-res.jpg as the source for this img on high-resolution displays in browsers that understand the srcset attribute."

iOS 8 safari browser now supports srcset.

Javascript libraries

Picture element

Picturefill is a JavaScript file (or a polyfill to be more specific) that enables support for the picture element and associated features in browsers that do not yet support them,

http://scottjehl.github.io/picturefill/

Note: The HTML5 picture element has been superseded by the HTML5 embedded content.

```
<span data-picture data-alt="Descriptive alt tag">
<span data-src="images/myimage_sm.jpg"></span>
<span data-src="images/myimage_lg.jpg" data-media="(min-width: 600px)"></span>
</span>
```

HiSRC

HiSRC, https://github.com/teleject/hisrc, is a jQuery plugin that enables you to create low-, medium- and high-resolution versions of an image, and the script will show the appropriate one based on Retina-readiness and network speed.

```
<img src="http://placekitten.com/200/100" data-1x="http://placekitten.com/400/200" data-2x="http://placekitten.com/800/400" class="hisrc" />
```

Then after the DOM has loaded, just call the function on the image class that you're using, like so:

```
$(document).ready(function(){
$(".hisrc").hisrc();
});
```

In practice, the browser will first load the image source — i.e. the mobile version of the image. Then, the script checks to see whether the visitor is using mobile bandwidth (such as 3G). If so, it leaves the mobile-first image in place. If the connection is speedy and the browser supports a Retina image, then the @2x version is delivered. If the connection is speedy but Retina is not supported, then the @1x version is delivered.

Zurb Foundaton Interchange

Zurb foundation provide Interchange to load larger resources for devices that can handle it:

```
<img data-interchange="[/path/to/default.jpg, (only screen and 
(min-width: 1px))], [/path/to/bigger-image.jpg, (only screen and 
(min-width: 1280px))]">
```

Reference: http://foundation.zurb.com/docs/components/interchange.html

Responsive_image_tag

Responsive_image_tag gem, https://github.com/futurechimp/responsive_image_tag, allows you to specify two images in a responsive_image_tag, and includes a javascript generator which will rewrite the DOM, requesting the correct image based on the screen size of the current client device. The screen.width is detected by Javascript and then an image element is inserted in the page with a dynamically created src attribute.

Forsight.js

An interesting javascript library is https://github.com/adamdbradley/foresight.js, which gives webpages the ability to tell if the user's device is capable of viewing high-resolution images before the image has been requested from the server. Additionally, it judges if the user's device currently has a fast enough network connection for high-resolution images.

Modify

Mobify.js is an open source library for improving responsive sites by providing responsive images, JS/CSS optimization, Adaptive Templating and more. Mobify.js also provides a Capturing API for manipulating the DOM before any resources have loaded. Since this technique directly circumvents native browser preloading, it is a bit controversial in web performance circles. Capturing won't work in any version of IE lower than 10.

http://www.mobify.com/mobifyjs/v2/docs/image-resizer/

resrc

Paid for Javascript plugin that delivers responsive images from the cloud, adds image filters and bandwidth detection and doesn't rely on user-agent detection or cookies.

http://www.resrc.it/

Server side image servers

If you'd rather not use JavaScript to decide which image to serve, you could try sniffing out the user agent server-side and automatically send an appropriately sized image. There is a lot of debate about how accurate user agent detection is. On top of that, the sheer number of new devices and screen sizes coming out every month will lead you to maintenance hell.

An image server is web server software which specialises in delivering (and often modifying) images. This is usually done by including the desired dimensions of an image directly inside the request.

List of image servers:

Reference: https://github.com/adamdbradley/foresight.js/wiki/Server-Resizing-Images

- Ruby+ImageMagick: http://www.imagemagick.org/RMagick/doc/
- Dragonfly - A Ruby gem for on-the-fly processing - suitable for image uploading in Rails: https://github.com/markevans/dragonfly
- Ruby extension for the vips image processing library: https://github.com/jcupitt/ruby-vips
- ScaleDown - A Sinatra image processing web server: https://github.com/jweir/ScaleDown

Server side apache/nginx modules

mod_pagespeed from Google, the Optimise Images filter
https://developers.google.com/speed/pagespeed/module/filter-image-optimize

nginx ngx_http_image_filter_module s a filter that transforms images
http://nginx.org/en/docs/http/ngx_http_image_filter_module.html

Adaptive images

Adaptive Images is a PHP server solution which detects your visitor's screen size and automatically creates, caches, and delivers device appropriate re-scaled versions of your web page's embeded HTML images. No mark-up changes needed. http://adaptive-images.com/. A Ruby port is https://github.com/KimNorgaard/rai.

Moddims

Moddims is an Apache module that uses ImageMagick to convert pictures on the fly.

https://code.google.com/p/moddims/wiki/WebserviceApi

Use with Amazon AWS

To use AWS you can use an image server on EC2 to dynamically adaptive the image, alternatively you could use AWS cloudfront which has a device detection feature, Amazon CloudFront can determine whether the end user request came from a Desktop, Tablet or Mobile device and pass that information in the form of new HTTP Headers to your origin AWS server. You can use the device type information to generate different versions of the content based on the new headers. Amazon CloudFront will also cache the different versions of the content at that edge location.

AWS cloudfront has the configurable option to detect the device and send it in the HTTP header to your site: http://aws.amazon.com/about-aws/whats-new/2014/06/26/amazon-cloudfront-device-detection-geo-targeting-host-header-cors/. Note: caching is improved if you do not forward any headers (which causes CloudFront to cache multiple versions of an object based on the device values.) CloudFront will match the header against an internal device list and will send an CloudFront-Is-Mobile-Viewer, CloudFront-Is-Desktop-Viewer, or CloudFront-Is-Tablet-Viewer header to give you a generic indication of the device type.

GENERAL MOBILE OPTIMISATION TIPS

Some tools to measure the performance and how heavy your web site page are:

- http://tools.pingdom.com/fpt/
- https://developer.yahoo.com/yslow/
- http://www.webpagetest.org/
- http://developers.google.com/speed/pagespeed/insights/
- https://www.modern.ie/en-us/report

Pagespeed

PageSpeed is a Web server apache/nginx module that applies multiple best practices to a website without forcing the developer to change their workflow. These optimisations include combining and minifying JavaScript and CSS files, inlining small resources, removing unused meta data from each file, and re-encoding images to the most efficient format accessible to the user. PageSpeed is available for both Apache and NGINX.

PageSpeed speeds up your site and reduces page load time. This open-source web server module automatically applies web performance best practices to pages and associated assets (CSS, JavaScript, images) without requiring that you modify your existing content or workflow.

Reference: https://developers.google.com/speed/pagespeed/module

Pagespeed is available as a chome playstore plugin also to check the performance of your website.

Add Icons for iPhone, iPad & Android to Your Website

Many sites currently add a favicon before launch that is visible in your user's browser tabs and bookmarks, but lots of sites are still missing icons for iOS. By adding an iOS icon, anyone who decides to save your webpage to the home screen of their iPhone, iPad, or Android* will see a nice app-like icon rather than an image of your page. To support the newest high resolution iPhone and iPad you'll want to create several different sized PNG images (The device will take the nearest size larger than it's default size if you don't have them all).

```
iPhone/iPod  iPhone/iPod Retina  iPad  iPad Retina
60×60        120×120             76×76 152×152
```

Apple introduced a new meta tag named apple-touch-icon you can now display website icons on the iOS homescreen when you bookmark a site. Add this code to your HTML head section:

```
<link href="http://www.yoursite.com/apple-touch-icon.png" rel="apple-touch-icon" />
<link href="http://www.yoursite.com/apple-touch-icon-76x76.png" rel="apple-touch-icon" sizes="76x76" />
<link href="http://www.yoursite.com/apple-touch-icon-120x120.png" rel="apple-touch-icon" sizes="120x120" />
<link href="http://www.yoursite.com/apple-touch-icon-152x152.png" rel="apple-touch-icon" sizes="152x152" />
```

Android uses this format:

```
<link rel="icon" sizes="196x196" href="apple-touch-icon.png">
```

Viewport

Mobile browsers render pages in a virtual "window" (the viewport), usually wider than the screen, so they don't need to squeeze every page layout into a tiny window (which would break many non-mobile-optimized sites). Users can pan and zoom to see different areas of the page. The viewport is the section of the page in view.

Different mobile browsers have different default viewport's, most mobile browsers use a default of 980px width viewport which means it will render the webpage in a viewport 980px and will zoom out to fit all of the webpage on. The smaller device screen you view this website on the more zoomed out you will be. If you compare the same webpage on a iPhone and an iPad the iPhone page will zoomed out more than viewing the page on the iPad.

Applying a viewport is the most important step to make web pages presentable on mobile browsers. The fixed rectangular area within which touch-based smartphone browsers display larger web pages is called the viewport. Applying a viewport meta tag allows you to control how mobile browsers render content within this rectangle, and whether users can magnify the page.

The width that you define in the viewport is like telling the browser this webpage is best viewed in this width. If you have setup a webpage which is best viewed on a iPhone then you will set the viewport to be 320px.

```
<meta name="viewport" content="width=320">
```

But this isn't good for responsive designs as if you are viewing this page on a tablet your web page will be zoomed out to just view an area of 320px. The best thing to do for responsive design is to set the width of the viewport to be the same as whatever device is being used. This is the most widely applicable viewport:

```
<meta name='viewport' content='width=device-width, user-scalable=no, initial-scale=1, maximum-scale=1, minimum-scale=1, user-scalable=no'/>
```

On mobile devices you can use a pinch gesture to zoom the pages in and out, but if you set the viewport to be the width of the device you don't need to zoom in to see the web page. To make sure that you web page isn't zoomed in when initially displayed you can use a property initial-scale to set the default zoom. To make sure the user doesn't need to zoom when visiting your page set this to a ratio of 1.

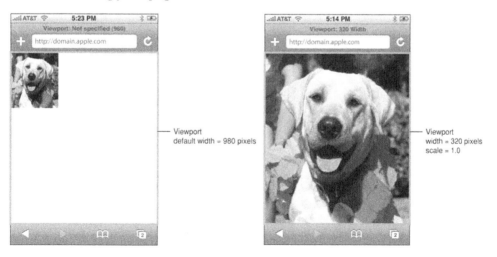

Viewporter is a open-source JavaScript project by Zynga to ease mobile viewport management. It specifically simplifies the part of setting up the right screen dimensions and removes the pain from handling the viewport meta tag manually.

Reference: https://github.com/zynga/viewporter

Accessing native mobile functionality

HTML5 is becoming more powerful allowing you to access the device level features directly from a web site with Javascript for example determining your location, or accessing the camera - getUserMedia API.

Access geo location

The geolocation API lets you share your location with trusted web sites. The latitude and longitude are available to JavaScript on the page, which in turn can send it back to the remote web server. Note: for usability testing that a user should be informed they will accept this setting:

```
function get_location() {
if (Modernizr.geolocation) {
navigator.geolocation.getCurrentPosition(show_map);
} else {
// no native support; maybe try a fallback?
}
}
```

Fonts

Typography is what separates good web sites apart. One of my favourite interview questions is discuss which font techniques should be used on mobile. Many people still use pixels for font sizes. There are three main techniques used to specify font sizes:

- Size with px
- Size with em
- Size with rems
- Size with percentages

Pixels offer a great deal of control for the designer/developer but very little control for the user. Em and Rems are much more fluid measures and will work more consistently in responsive projects.

Note: You might come across, http://fortawesome.github.io/Font-Awesome/, it gives you scalable vector icons with the power of CSS. Using icon fonts will be more and more relevant as more high resolution/density displays become available.

Chrome font resizing

The default chrome font size is medium, for example:

when you change the font to very large under settings /advanced:

Then the page appears as:

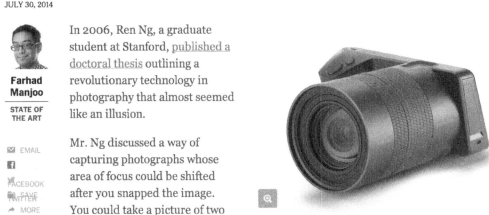

Not all sites adapt to font setting changes like this, try http://www.cnn.com.

Pixel (px)

The traditional choice of graphic designers. Use pixels for precision control, the are the most natural way to define screen measurements. But locking the font size with pixel or absolute values prevents the browser from changing the text size by zooming in/out.

Users can use the browser's "zoom" feature to read smaller text, although they are starting to cause some issues as a result of mobile devices with very high density screens.

ems

An em is a unit of measurement. Just like pixels, ems can determine the size of elements on a web page. Unlike pixels, which are absolute, ems are relative to their parent's font size. Em essentially works like percentage values. ems do not have an absolute size but take their size relative to the block they are in. The advantage to using em as a basis for type sizing is that by changing just the parent size, you can change all of the type sizes simultaneously. Most browsers have a default font size of 16px. So most of the time 1em = 16px. An em is equal to the current browser font-size.

If you set the font size of your web page to 12px, then:

```
0.5em = 6px
1em   = 12px
2em   = 24px
```

If you set the font size of your web page to 14px, then:

```
0.5em = 7px
1em   = 14px
2em   = 28px
```

Rem

CSS3 introduced the rem unit. Rem ultimately function in the same way as ems, but there is no defined parent font size. One of the problems with using "em" as font sizes is that they cascade, so you are forever writing rules that select nested elements to reset them back to 1em; CSS3 now has rem ("root em") to prevent that issue. The font-size will not responsively change, only by changing the browser settings.

The rem unit is relative to the root—or the html—element. That means that we can define a single font size on the HTML element and define all rem units to be a percentage of that.

Zurb foundation is now using Rem's. Zurb gives you a SASS mixim to convert pixels to REMs, so you can still think in pixels and up up with scalable em.

Browser support for Rem: http://caniuse.com/rem

Percentages

In theory, both the em and the percent units are identical, both have the compounding cascade, but they have a few minor differences that are important to consider. While using the percent unit, your text remains fully scalable for mobile devices and for accessibility.

```
<div style="font-size: 200%;"> your content here </div>
```

When the client's browser text size is set to "medium," there is no difference between ems and percent. When the setting is altered, however, the difference is quite large. On the "Smallest" setting, ems are much smaller than percent, and when on the "Largest" setting, it's quite the opposite, with ems displaying much larger than percent. While some could argue that the em units are scaling as they are truly intended, in practical application, the em text scales too abruptly, with the smallest text becoming hardly legible on some client machines.

vw, vh and vmin

These new properties allow you to scale font sizes according to the viewport dimensions, Browser support is a little patchy but it's coming. 100vw is equal to the width of the window and 100vh is equal to its height. We can scale something dependent on screen size.

Browser support: http://caniuse.com/viewport-units

```
1vw is 1% of the viewport width
1vh is 1% of the viewport height
1vmin is the smallest of 1vw and 1vh
```

The new units will revolutionise responsive design — text on mobile devices often appears a little large because you're holding the device closer than a monitor.

Font size suggestions

In practice, the percent unit seems to provide a more consistent and accessible display for users. When client settings have changed, percent text scales at a reasonable rate, allowing designers to preserve readability. it is recommended that you use a percentage value to set the font size for your page's body, and start defining the content size proportional to this value. By declaring your body's font size in percentages, you provide a flexible base-line from which you can size the text up or down using relative units like the em. Setting the font size on the body to 100% sets the text size to the browser's default font size, which is usually 16px. A lot of developers tend to, or prefer to, use a baseline value of 62.5% on the body instead of a 100%, because the resulting font size applied to it will be an even 10px, and so it becomes a lot easier to define other font sizes on the page relative to this number but 100% as a better baseline, one that ensures more consistent cross-browser results.

When people create a new design, you could use percent on the body element:

```
body { font-size: 62.5%; }
```

And then use the em unit to size it from there. As long as the body is set using the percent unit, you may choose to use either percent or rems on any other CSS rules and selectors and still retain the benefits of using percent as your base font size.

For responsive design fonts you could use media queries to change the font size, for example:

```
@media screen and (max-width: 768px) {
. lead {
font-size:2rem;
}
}
```

I find it useful to for example download Zurb foundation and see what they are doing in their code. People can find em confusing.

Font types

Font is a specialist area but a good tool to see what other sites are using is the Chrome plugin called 'Whatfont'.

Font face

With the CSS3 @font-face rule, web designers no longer have to use one of the "web-safe" fonts and you can easily install custom fonts. Start by putting your fonts into app/assets/fonts. add the fonts folder to the asset path, config/application.rb:

```
config.assets.paths << Rails.root.join("app", "assets", "fonts")
```

After that, you can include your fonts in a sass / scss file via the font-url('font.eot') helper.

A helper gem is: https://github.com/typekit/webfontloader

Font stack

When you decide on which fonts to use for your site, you should write a list of fonts that the browser can use, in order of preference – your font stack. This way, if your first choice of font is not available, perhaps your second choice is, and so on through your list.

http://cssfontstack.com/ shows which fonts are supported by which browsers.

http://typecast.com/ is a tool to see how fonts can look like in practice. Google fonts also has a try in typecast option for example http://www.google.com/fonts/specimen/Roboto. There is a helper gem at https://github.com/travishaynes/Google-Webfonts-Helper.

Some commercial fonts can be found at http://fontdeck.com/typefaces. An interesting gallery of site fonts is http://fontsinuse.com/

Mobile fonts

The default system font for Android is Roboto while iOS supports many others.

References:

- http://developer.android.com/design/style/typography.html
- http://iosfonts.com/

If you care about getting the same look and feel for a site across multiple platforms and devices, sticking with traditional "web safe fonts" will no longer do, also your default font may not be supported by mobile browsers. Use @font-face, or a web font service built on it, to push your specified fonts down to the user. You'll maintain brand consistency, and you'll have thousands (versus hundreds) of font choices. But be careful about the size of the font size downloaded to a mobile device.

A font stack based on system fonts is no longer as safe as it was before the mobile device growth. Where system fonts in the major mobile operating systems are concerned, there is barely any consistency at all. For example, the Android operating system only comes packaged with it's own system fonts — none of which appear on iOS or Windows Phone, and those two platforms only share a handful of fonts between themselves. There is no safe native typographic foundation on today's web. Web fonts do provide consistent typography across major mobile and desktop operating systems, but they come with the caveat that good typography isn't free in regard to page loading cost.

For responsive projects, we want to keep the page light in anticipation of the next user coming from one of any number of devices, and on a completely unpredictable connection speed.

If we think of web fonts as assets on the page—like images or any other asset—then we can use media queries to load different assets for different displays. For example, we can load high definition images for retina displays; why not do something similar for web fonts. You could have few fonts available for mobile devices, the fonts to load are decided by screen size.

UX Overview

The definition of UX is "User eXperience", people often use it incorrectly in the same context as User Interface (UI). UI which refers to "User Interface" and we have UX which refers to "User Experience". An Information Architect decides how information will be organised and presented on a web site. This would include navigation, aggregation, presentation (more what is presented than how). Think of them as responsible for "content design", as opposed to "site design". These are some of the various job titles in the UX world.

UI Design generally refers to the user facing side of any type of physical interface. The UX designer is responsible for the emotion of the user. They are responsible for how the user feels when interacting with the interface or product. UX is commonly used as a much broader term that encompasses the entire process from concept to completion. UX designers generally start by conducting user research and interviews. The goal with this is to understand exactly what the users' needs are. In most cases, the next step is to create a set of personas of each possible user and their needs. Once these first two steps have been completed, the UX designer will have the information needed to create the backbone of the product or "wireframes". The wireframes are essentially the blueprints of what the UI designer will use to create the interface that the user interacts with.

I will discuss the traditional approach to UX so you understand the terms, then the newer trend of by passing the wireframe by producing a working prototype.

MVP

In product development, the minimum viable product (MVP) is a strategy used for fast and quantitative market testing of a product or product feature. A Minimum Viable Product should be the minimum features in a product to validate that it is works, too many times over engineer products with unrequired features and wasted time in knowing if the product will actually sell and customers really want it. By just putting in the core features of the product you can change direction quicker to what a user really wants. Likewise in making the technology stack too heavy as it slows down output for new team members.

For startup's don't get carried away with feeling your product is not good enough until it has more bells/whistles, just get it to the market fast before your competitors swarm you and adjust your product based on the analytics gathers.

Do mobile first

The traditional product design process is to create a desktop site and then later add code for smaller screens, or for a UX person to only do the design for a desktop and leave it to the developers to interpret the design on a small screen. The argument that three screens are too many to maintain or even let's not do the tablet version nees to be taken on a case by case basis.

This problem exists because adding content to a Web site is relatively easy. Most of the time, you are overloading the smaller devices with far too information The problems then are the user interface on a mobile device can be confusing, ill thought out, and the pages can be really heavy causing slow time to download and render. Focus on the minimum requirements, with the maximum performance and best UI is a common sense approach.

There is the Mobile First design approach which is a different argument to the separate mobile site versus responsive web design argument, bot approaches still need to start the design from a mobile screen. A mobile first approach doesn't just concentrate on developing for mobile phones, it is also used to develop better usability of sites, develop better use of Web real estate and better reduce the amount unnecessary elements on pages. Let's stop trying to compress large amounts of information from the top-tiered tech devices into the lowest of the low tech devices.

Additional to slowed performance, by developing with desktops first, you omit the multitude of functions and features you can do with a mobile phone nowadays. With GPS and touch/swipe screens for example the mobile first design allows you to take all of these capabilities and put them in your design.

When you design for mobile first, a set of inherent constraints keeps you in check. Perhaps the most impactful of these constraints is screen space. When you are working with a 320x480 pixel screen, 80% of the screen space you had at 1024x768 is gone. Losing 80% of your screen space forces you to focus.

We simply start with the most minimal amount of mobile-tech development and build progressively upward to desktop. A mobile first approach doesn't just concentrate on developing for mobile phones, it is also used to develop better usability of sites, develop better use of Web real estate and better reduce the amount unnecessary elements from pages.

The advantage of mobile first is also to focus on performance, a desktop design can become heavy and over complicated making a site for example more difficult to cache etc. For example compare the ebay desktop to their mobile site:

See how their mobile page is more focused:

Note: Most designers assume that the majority of desktop users have a screen resolution of 1024x768 or higer. Although they choose a fixed width of 960pixels, which looks good for users with a 1024×768 resolution or above, with a bit of room for margins.

UX Design Steps

The traditional UX process is discussed along with more modern takes on it. Wireframes normally come quite early on in a product development process. You could typically hold a workshop to flesh out the details of an assignment with the client. One of the outcomes of this type of session would be a sitemap along with user stories, user journeys, or user case scenarios. Provided you have the necessary information about the target user, you're ready to begin on the wireframing process.

STEP1 : USER PERSONA & Stories

Different people want different goals from a web site for example from a car sales website an older person might want a value reliable car with a simple to use website while a younger driver might want a sportier model and more site features.

Personas are fictional characters created to represent the different user types within a targeted demographic, attitude and/or behaviour set that might use a site, brand or product in a similar way. Persona is a representation of a particular audience segment for a website / product / service you are designing, based on various types of qualitative and quantitative research. It captures a person's motivations, frustrations and the "essence" of who they are. Typically you will want to capture any number of the following attributes:

- A person's goals on your website / service / product.
- A person's motivations for using it.
- A person's current pain points or frustrations.

- Some demographic data such as age/location/male-female.
- A quote that captures their attitude in general towards the website.
- A short bio about their background.
- A person's technical ability along with which devices they use and how often.
- Other brands or websites they may like.
- A picture that captures that particular persona.

Personas are handy to pull out when you are trying to communicate what the user experience should be like to stakeholders, designers, developers and anyone else involved in the project. Normally personas are one of the main and first outputs from the initial discovery phase of a project.

How can a few fake people be sufficient to design a whole product? The personas you create will be highly representative of target users, their value is in the focus they give rather than trying to be all things to all people.The majority of your user base will share the same needs or at least be able to some with the features.

What does a persona look like?

Again there is no real set template, however in order to make sure the personas communicate their information quickly and clearly it is normally best to stick to a single page or post-it which can be easily stuck on the wall or shared with stakeholders. on paper stickies, e.g.

- singles/busy, income, 28-45, drinks - double income no kids, mobile.
- zoe - 18-33 single female living with friends.

Are personas still relevant

Personas have been a popular approach for guiding the design of Web sites and mobile apps. However, some in the UX community are now saying that personas have been superseded by the availability of more accurate data or by newer UX design and development methods. There are two main reasons that people give for saying that personas are no longer a useful tool for UX strategy:

- Analytics : you can track the journeys a user take on your site. With so many sites using Facebook to login in, you can easily extract user information to build your real personas.
- A/B and multivariate testing : When you perform an A/B test, you create two different versions of a web page, and split the traffic evenly between each

page. When you perform a multivariate test, you are performing a far more subtle test of the elements inside one web page.

STEP 2 : STORYBOARDING

A user journey storyboard is a series of steps which represent a scenario in which a user [persona] might interact with your product/feature, inspired by the filmmaking industry. Storyboarding makes for a very engaging and thought-provoking activity in research workshops. A storyboard can be a comic book style story of the user moving through the critical path. Storyboards work well because:

1. The act of drawing can help us think.
2. Images can speak more powerfully than just words by adding extra layers of meaning.

It is useful to specify scenarios which detail how users will interact with a feature, then turn those scenarios into storyboards. This means you can list all functional areas to be build to make the solution useful to users. Write out what your person persona will do, make the persona the voice of the story. The benefits of user journeys are:

- User journeys are a great way to communicate what you are trying to achieve with stakeholders.
- User journeys can help you work out how users are going to interact with your system and what they expect from it.
- By understanding the key tasks they will want to do to you can start to understand what sort of functional requirements will help enable those tasks.
- By understanding the 'flow' of the various tasks the user will want to undertake you can start to think about what kind of interface the user will be needing to accomplish them.

You will want to think broadly in each user journey step about things such as:

- How does each step enable them to get to the next?
- What device are they using? What features does the device have?

A user journey could look like:

STEP 3 : SITE MAPS

Sitemaps are used to "map" the major components of a website to a rather sparse-looking diagram. Sitemaps are normally produced after you have completed your persona and user journey work, and after you have completed your initial discovery period. They visualise what you have learnt about how users will navigate the site, what sort of content they will need to support them in their goals and what sort of language they use to identify things.

Sitemaps are a great tool to depict the navigational structure of your website. For this reason the sitemap provides the perfect overview in order to begin wireframing. Once the sitemap is established, wireframes allow you to think about the detail of each page, how information will be presented to the user, and the layout this will take. It allows you to think about where important elements and functionality needs to be added, such as navigational controls, call to actions, and user generated form fields.

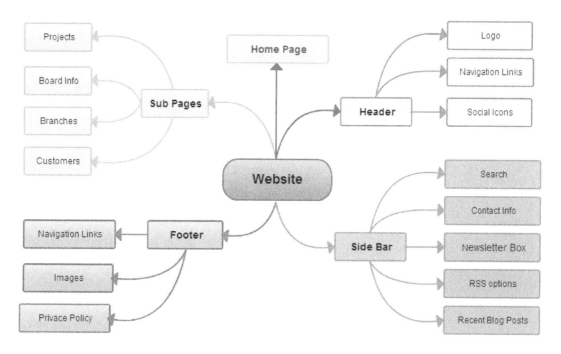

You could use a mindmap to group related content together, in order to think about the best sitemap. Your user journeys should have identified a few things which each persona will want to achieve on your site. Focus on needs not features. Instead of writing 'browse someone's profile', go for 'learn more about someone'. You will want to question your sitemap with these in mind. The output of the exercise would be a sitemap.

A mind map is a visual document which contains all of your related thoughts radiating outward from a central idea. I used http://mindnode.com/ to produce it. You can create your sitemap in any number of programs including Axure, Visio. By it's design, it structures your freeform thoughts. These can be further organised, prioritised or reshuffled based upon your needs. it's fast and easy for people to get engaged with. More commonly used for brainstorming.

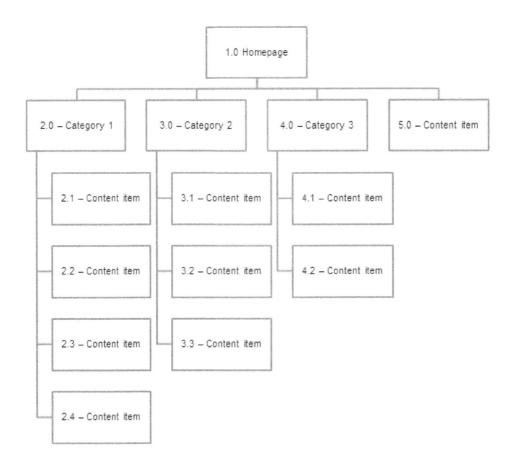

You will want to question your sitemap with these in mind along with a few other key questions:

- Does your proposed sitemap support your user journeys.
- Would your different personas understand the labelling you have come up with.
- Does the site map have any categories with only one item of content.
- Does the site map have more then 7 categories, If so can I group any together?

STEP 4 : Wireframe

A wireframe is a visual representation of a user interface, stripped of any visual design or branding elements. It is used by UX Designers to define the layout of items on a screen and communicate what the items on that page should be based on user needs.Wireframes typically outline the components for a screen, together with any associated behaviours, such as what happens when a button is click and where a hyperlink should go.

Wireframes are generally created after your initial persona, user journey, sitemap and other discovery activities are completed. Before you start to create a wireframe you will want to have a strong grasp on your user's goals, motivations and tasks they will want to achieve. You will also want to understand the structure of the website through your sitemap so that you know what the purpose of each page should be in terms of getting the user to their goal.

Pre-Wireframe tools

The first stage of UI/UX design should never be done in a mock-up or wireframing tool. It should be done with pen and paper. Black-grey-white are the typical colours used. Do the layout for a tablet, phone, and web.

Static pages can tell you how the layout will look, but they can't tell you how it's going to feel to use. That's where prototyping comes in, and it's an essential stage of UI development. Prototypes come in a few flavours, ranging from low-fi paper prototypes made from sketches, to mid-fi prototypes made with detailed wireframes in which users can use limited interactions, like taps or clicks, to hi-fi prototypes that are actually coded up to mimic as much of the full suite of interactions as possible.

Sketches

Sketches are the lowest fidelity in the world of UI/UX.They're the prep work you do before you do your best work. Now, it's at this juncture that mock-up tool lovers will inevitably tell me, "but I work faster in Balsamiq." No, you don't, you really don't. In the time it takes the average user to make a page mock-up in Balsamiq, you could easily generate and iterate on many thumbnails of many different ideas, some of which might not even be possible to mock-up in a tool with only so many boxes and buttons to use.

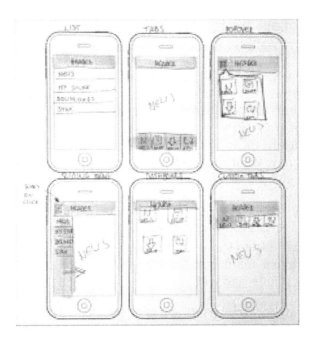

Use the sketching phase to generate a bunch of ideas, both good and bad, and let the good ones float to the top. Those will be the foundation for the next fidelity of UI work: the prototype. Have a pocket sized moleskin notepad and keep sketching, the small size will focus you on mobile first.Useful tools are:

- Onmigrapple for Mac, http://www.omnigroup.com/omnigraffle/, for Mac is a diagramming tool.
- http://graffletopia.com/ iOS/ android wireframes stencils for omnigraffle.

Paper prototyping

Paper prototyping is the most widely used design technique. Cut out elements from wireframe and put into a board:

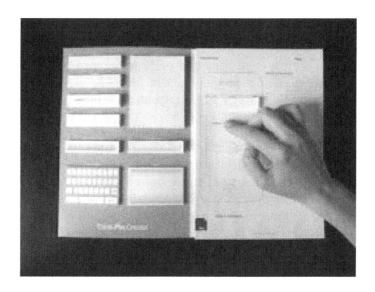

Mobile phone drill-down

In a very short period of time, a UI/UX designer can roughly sketch some screens, cut out some pieces of paper for elements on the screen that change, and put that in front of people to interact with as the designer plays the role of the computer.

Wireframes

If you've iterated quite a bit on sketches and early paper prototypes, and you've gone into the more detailed wireframe stage, you can later develop them into more high fidelity prototyping, or skip the wireframing stage all together.

Wireframes usually will come after the sketching phase, when you've rejected all of the bad ideas and the one or two good ideas have floated to the top. Those ideas usually get fleshed out in a wireframe. The wireframe is often the more polished version of the sketch, something you can deliver to a client or your stakeholders, and it looks like you spent some time on it. If wireframes are a part of your workflow, they usually will come after the sketching phase, when you've rejected all of the bad ideas and the one or two good ideas have floated to the top. Those ideas usually get fleshed out in a wireframe.

The wireframe - The tangible "deliverable" of UX work. There's a growing consensus in the UI/UX field that, with the coming of dynamic prototyping, the wireframe is dead—why do a static wireframe when the tools to make real UI screens and pages in your app or your game are frequently at your fingertips? We'll cover the wireframe briefly anyway, because it still has a place, although you may find that some of your UI/UX tasks don't require this phase.

Rapid prototyping

So what's so wrong with wireframes? Wireframes themselves are not necessarily bad; it's more the sort of design behaviour they encourage and the way they are often used (and abused) in projects. Here are some reasons why for the vast majority of projects wireframes should be consigned to the rubbish bin:

- Wireframes (which are static by nature) are not well suited to defining dynamic on-page interactions, such as expanding content, AJAX style reveals and animations. On-page interactions become more common place wireframes simply no longer hold up.
- Wireframes are not very user friendly (which is kind of ironic for a UX design tool). Project stakeholders are often intimidated by what they perceive to be very technical documentation and find it difficult to understand exactly what wireframes are, and what they show.
- Wireframes are typically very open to interpretation. Wireframes look like they're very exacting and specific but because behaviours and interactions have to be described they are by nature very open to interpretation. One project

stakeholder can read a wireframe very differently from another which can lead to confusion and misinterpretation.
- Wireframes often add unnecessary drag to the design process and can encourage death by documentation. Creating and annotating detailed wireframes takes considerable time and effort; time and effort that is usually better spent iterating and improving designs, rather than specifying them.

Bypassing wireframes with rapid prototyping

If wireframes are so flawed what's the alternative? The alternative is to bypass wireframes altogether and either go straight from sketch / outline designs to developing working code, or as is more use common use a rapid prototyping tool to create a prototype. There are now loads of great rapid prototyping tools out there. If you have got good web design skills you can also always create a prototype directly in HTML and CSS.

Creating static wireframes can be great but sometimes clients just don't understand how they function or change based on various devices. Building functional wireframes will help you communicate with clients better and work as a foundation for your fluid designs without losing sight of the importance of the content.

Rapid prototyping graphical tools

Invision is moy current tool of preference at the moment.

- A Mac Keynote plugin is http://keynotekungfu.com/ to create wireframes and clickable prototypes, for Powerpoint and Keynote use keynotopia.
- Balsamiq, http://balsamiq.com/ - an online platform to create wireframes - use comic font so stakeholders do not think the project is final. A user is more honest in their criticisms about a paper prototype. You can always give the client balsamic so they can do the wireframe themselves. some ready made libraries:
- https://mockupstogo.mybalsamiq.com/projects
- https://mockupstogo.mybalsamiq.com/projects/android/grid
- https://mockupstogo.mybalsamiq.com/projects/ios/grid
- Axure, http://www.axure.com/, gives you the power to quickly and easily deliver much more than typical mockup tools. What makes it so interactive is that it generates HTML wireframe prototypes which a pretty realistic functionally to the final product without any coding. A very powerful tool.

- Zurb Solidify, http://www.solidifyapp.com/, lets you create clickable prototypes from sketches, wireframe, or mockup.
- Quartz, http://facebook.github.io/origami/, is a freely-available Mac OS X application by Apple. without Origami, interaction prototyping with Quartz Composer is complicated. Origami provides a set of tools for Quartz Composer that make interaction prototyping a lot easier, created by the Facebook Design team.
- Adobe fireworks, https://creative.adobe.com/products/fireworks can be used to create a rapid prototype.
- Gomockingbird, https://gomockingbird.com/, is an online tool create interactive mockups.
- invision, http://www.invisionapp.com/, has become popular with a lot of companies: Create interactive prototypes complete with gestures, transitions & animations for web, iOS & Android. People can add comments to your design, create clickable mockups.

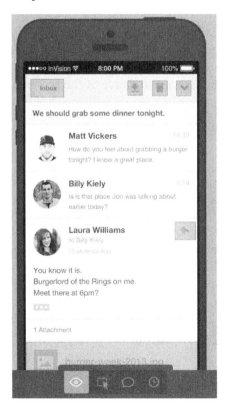

Mobile App prototyping tools

- https://www.flinto.com/, iOS and android prototypes from your existing screen designs.
- https://popapp.in -interesting ios/android app to make sketches interactive.
- http://www.realizerapp.com - iOS app to make sketches interactive.

Other online prototyping tools

- http://proto.io/en/examples/
- http://www.protoshare.com/
- http://www.hotgloo.com/
- https://www.fluidui.com/
- https://moqups.com/
- http://www.antetype.com/
- http://www.justinmind.com/
- https://codiqa.com/
- https://itunes.apple.com/us/app/fluid-designer/id437781563?mt=8

Rapid prototyping by coding

Prototyping is rather an expensive and time-consuming form of design communication. You could code the prototype, that can then be reused in development (it means that you need to code some HTML, CSS and probably Javascript on your own). Refine sketches into HTML CSS wireframes with frameworks such as:

- http://foundation.zurb.com/templates.html
- http://neat.bourbon.io/examples/
- http://bitters.bourbon.io /, http://refills.bourbon.io/
- A lesser know tools is http://getwirefy.com/

Hardcopy sketching prototypes

To draw your wireframes on paper, such tools are:

- http://sneakpeekit.com/wireframe-sketchsheets/
- http://www.uistencils.com/
- http://cohdoo.com/phonedoo.php

Design guidelines

Is is good to be aware of the iOS and android design guidelines when designing protoypes.

- apple human interface guidelines, https://developer.apple.com/library/iOS/design/index.html
- android guidelines, https://developer.android.com/design/index.html

UX usability study

Most people don't really put too much thought into what makes up a website; they just want good content and a site that works. Designers are often guilty of designing for themselves rather than a broader market who is not as in love with technology as we are. The earlier you test your site designs, the sooner you can find any problems and fix them. Once you've made a design, it gets harder to change, so it's best to test early and test often.

Usability testing in its most simple form is just running a design past one or more people to see if it works. There are a large number of methods for performing usability testing, from the hallway test (where you grab someone walking past you in the hallway or office), to eye-tracking systems (which monitor what part of a screen people's eyes are focusing on), heat map tracking (which shows where people have clicked on a screenshot or design).

Calibrate display

It is a good idea to calibrate your monitor frequently. You can either calibrate your display by eye or by using a device called a colour calibrator, alternatively for free:

- On Windows, open the Control Panel and search for "calibrate. Under Display, click on Calibrate display colour. A window will open with the Display Colour Calibration tool. It steps you through the following basic image settings.
- On a Mac, go to System Preferences > Display and click on the Colour tab. Next, click the Calibrate button, which opens the Display Calibrator Assistant, check the box for Expert Mode.

Usability tests even on sketches.

Clients often believe that you have to have a polished interface to show to users before you can get good feedback. Nothing is further from the truth. The most valuable feedback happens before you've even touched a computer. Paper prototyping is a great way to lay your ideas out on a page and see if they hang together. Nobody's judging artistic skills. Instead, the prototype gives a common understanding to everyone on the team.

And the same goes for usability test participants. Your paper prototype is an ideal test of whether your idea is simple enough to capture users' attention and whether it's complex enough to support their key tasks. If there's a problem, it's fast and simple to change a paper mockup. Paper testing allows you to show initial site layout and design at scale, without putting in a huge amount of work in the first instance. Once you have presented the sketches and given users the opportunity to tell you their initial thoughts, you can alter design appropriately.

Usability Testing Tools

- Paid for services : http://www.usertesting.com/ - Get videos of real people speaking their thoughts as they use your website or mobile app. http://verifyapp.com/ - Collect and analyze user feedback on screens or mockups.
- Zurb Solidify, http://www.solidifyapp.com/, is a prototyping tool but also validates user flows on any device by performing user tests in person, remotely or on your testers own time to get the feedback you need.
- Zurb Influence http://www.influenceapp.com/ is a way to get feedback from your mockups.
- Zurb Verify http://verifyapp.com/ lets you test screenshots of your design work.

Usability test script

User testing is a technique that always delivers useful information about how usable a web or mobile app really is. Design your usability test script to answer specific research questions. Steps in a usability test could be:

1. Line up at least 6 participants for a 30 minute session, over a couple of days. These participants should be from the target group.
2. Schedule these participants in for a 30 minute session.

3. Recording a video of the screen while the participants use the app. This can be used to back up your results to more senior team numbers.
4. Plan task for the uses to perform as part of a script, tasks should be written as scenarios that the reader can read themselves, or you read out to them.

You could create a survey to ask people after the test some more questions: http://survey.io/survey/demo

Test plan

It's both good practice and often necessary to have a test plan before beginning a usability test. Some sections in this plan could be:

- What you're testing : State the name, version of the interface you are testing, the functional area if necessary. decide a place - could do in specialist lab or else pick random people in a cafe
- Users (persona's): In addition to your target demographics (age, gender, geography), be sure to identify how much experience user's should have with the website or product.
- Sample size: Spell out your target sample sizes for the entire study and by participant profile if necessary. While there is a lot of controversy around sample sizes in usability studies, the best way to determine your sample sizes is to balance the math (what the equations say) and politics (what the stakeholders will expect).
- Methods : Identify the approach you'll use to collect the data. Will it be a moderated remote, moderated in-person, mobile or a mix of in-person and unmoderated studies.
- Tasks : For each task scenario you'll want to define at a minimum what information you'll give the user (the scenario) and the starting URL or screen. Ideally, you'll have a goal or objective for each task (e.g. can a member find a match).
- Metrics

Task metrics: Determine when to start and stop the time.

Task Difficulty: You will want to include at least one question on the perception of task difficulty.

Pre test questions: We usually collect standard demographic data prior to users attempting any tasks. This is also an opportunity to ask attitudinal and brand questions before users know what the study is about. You can then compare these to post-study questions to see if there is an increase or decrease in attitudes after exposure and use.

Post-Test Questions: include a few open-ended questions about what the users would improve and comments or issues they had.

- Record the users behaviour : It can be useful to record a person as they use your app to see their facial expression and hear their comments, Some good apps for this are:
    - http://silverbackapp.com/, Silverback is a cheap Mac-based software tool that enables the recording, analysis, editing and playback of usability testing sessions. For example you can see the person testing on the lower right hand corner of the screen.

    - iOS apps to recorder a user using your app:
        - http://www.uxrecorder.com/
        - http://www.magitest.com/
    - other tools
        - http://www.openhallway.com/, records a users movements on a desktop using your app but no video of the person.
        - http://www.techsmith.com/morae.html, records facial expression, eye movement, page duration, clicks, but it is expensive.

- Recruit people to test your site : The easiest but most expensive solution is to hire a re-cruiting company. You could just ask friends or strangers in a starbucks say their opinion for your site/app and buy them a coffee to spend a few minutes doing a test case, or puts ads up on https://www.mturk.com, ads on craigslist. Whether you use an agency or do it yourself, you need to know what type of people you're looking for. If you are using personas as a development aid, base your recruiting efforts around finding people who match your persona characteristics.
- Site analytics :It is very important to track a persons activity on our app in order to improve their experience and attract more users - measure conversion/funnel rates. Popular choices are:
    - http://www.google.com/analytics/mobile/
    - http://www.flurry.com/
    - http://aws.amazon.com/mobileanalytics/ (apps only)
- And specifically for event tracking are:
    - https://www.kissmetrics.com/
    - https://mixpanel.com/
- Some useful heat map tools to see where a user goes to on your site are:
    - http://www.google.com/analytics/
    - http://mouseflow.com/
    - http://www.clicktale.com/products/heatmap-suite
    - http://www.ghostrec.com/features/heatmaps/
    - https://vwo.com/features/
    - http://www.crazyegg.com/
    - http://www.inspectlet.com/
- A/B testing :The You can test which version of a web page gives the greatest improvement in conversions (i.e. completed activities that you measure as goals) by giving a different version of the web page to different users using tools such as:google analytics, kissmetrics. Compare how different web pages or app screens perform using a random sample of your users. Create different versions of your web pages to test: Headlines and headers, Images and icons, Text, Page layout etc.. Mixpanel also support A/B testing for native apps.

My preference for analytics is google analytics and mixpanel.

MAKE THE DATING SITE RESPONSIVE

Let's convert our dating application to be viewable on web, tablet and mobile devices.

UX process

Going through the steps we discussed above:

Step 1: persona

person, called Paul, 20-30, single, professional, uses a mobile to view web pages.

Step 2: storyboarding / user journey

Using https://www.storyboardthat.com/ storyboard-creator to create the storyboard.

For the user paul...I want to view all single girls between 20-25

Step 3 Sitemap : generated using http://writemaps.com/

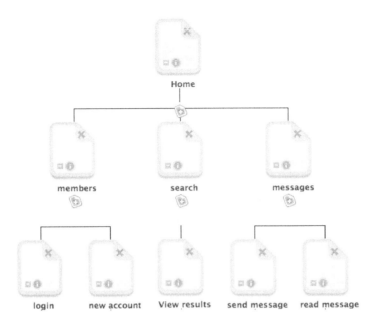

We will go straight from the story board to a sketch then to the low fidelity Balsamiq prot-type.

Sketch

The quickest way I get started is with a simple sketch – you don't have to be Picassco!

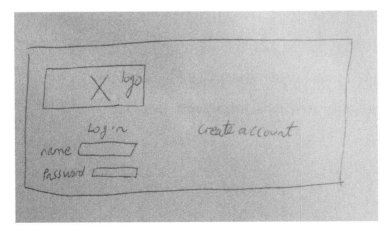

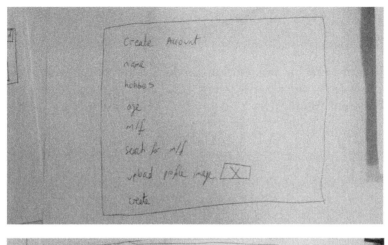

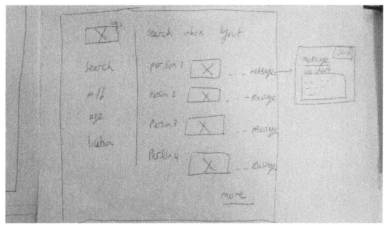

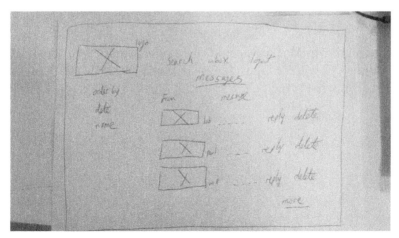

Low fidelity mockup

I will use balsamiq here for the mockups. add the bootstrap grid to your balsamic project. Do you need to document how the layout in every single view? - it would depend on the content complexity.

Reference:
https://mockupstogo.mybalsamiq.com/projects/layout/Bootstrap+Grid+Layout.bmml

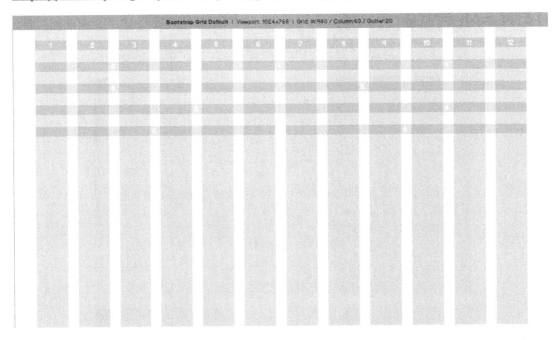

Some of the capabilities in Mockups could make it easier for you to communicate how your design would work with responsiveness in mind. Start with the grid system of your choice, and figure out what screen sizes you're going to target.

Web [default]:

```
Min-width: 780px
```

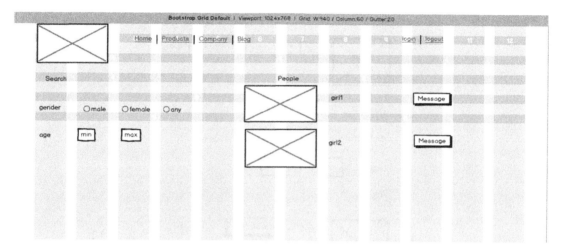

Tablet: The tablet will be the same as the web in this example

Tablet Portrait (to landscape and desktop)

```
Min-width: 768px / Max-width: 979px
```

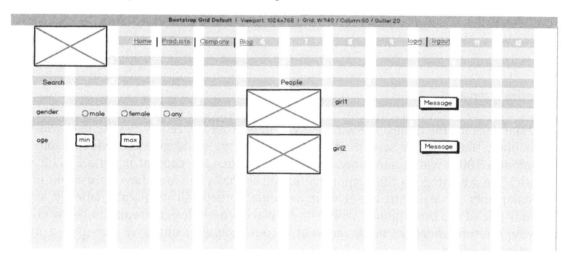

Mobile: Smartphone

```
Max-width: 480px
```

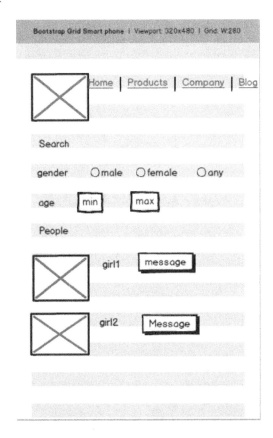

Media queries

All the sizes for the dating site will be given in percentage, relative to the max-width of our body. Note that for screen size under 540px, we could give the sidebars and the content a 100% width, and place the sidebars under the content using a CSS3 'clear: both'. The advantage of the responsive layout is that you won't have to use too many break points. Since the size are given in percentage, they will adapt automatically, so the major role of the break points will be to be place where design breaks, to re-order our layout (putting sidebars under content in our example) and give the user a more pleasant reading.

We could resize per device type with CSS, we will not be using this file as we have Boostrap instead but just for reference, for example in a file such as: app/stylesheets/devicelayout.css

```
#page{
max-width:1280px;
}
#header {
width: 100%;
margin: 0;
padding: 0;
}
#content {
float: left;
width: 60%;
margin: 0 0 20px 0;
padding: 0;
}
#content. bloc {
margin-right: 2%;
}
.sidebar{
float: left;
margin: 0 0 20px 1%;
padding: 0;
background-color: Aqua;
}
#bar1{
width:38%;
}
#footer {
clear: both;
width: 100%;
margin: 0;
padding: 0;
}
/* The media queries*/
@media screen and (max-width: 1000px) {
#bar1,
#bar2{
width:39%;
}
. sidebar{
float: left;
margin: 0 0 20px 1%;
```

```
padding: 0;
}
}
@media screen and (max-width: 540px) {
#bar1,
#bar2{
clear:both;
width:100%;
}
. sidebar{
float: left;
margin: 0 0 20px 1%;
padding: 0;
}
#content {
clear:both;
width:100%;
}
#content. bloc {
margin:0;
}
}
```

And you could then add this file to app/stylesheets/application.css

```
*= require devicelayout
```

Alternatively you could [as we will use now] use Twitter Bootstrap grid scaffolding, The Bootstrap grid system has four tiers of classes: xs (phones), sm (tablets), md (desktops), and lg (larger desktops). You can use nearly any combination of these classes to create more dynamic and flexible layouts.

Reference: http://getbootstrap.com/examples/grid/

In app/views/layouts/list_members.html.erb change the existing:

```
<div id="wrap">
<div id="sidebar" >
<%= yield :sidebar %>
</div>
<div id="content">
<%= yield :content %>
</div>
</div>
```

To:

```
<div class="row">
<div class="col-xs-6 col-lg-4"> <%= yield :sidebar %> </div>
<div class="col-xs-12 col-sm-6 col-lg-8"> <%= yield :content%>
</div>
</div>
```

RUBY RAILS SEO

SEO has traditionally divided into two main areas; on-page optimisation which covers what can be done on the pages of the website itself, and off-page optimisation which covers activity that takes place elsewhere (e.g. link-building, social media). on page will be discussed here. The first steps would be to install google analytics into your and create a Google webmaster account. [http://www.flurry.com/ is an option, but http://www.google.com/analytics/ is very good, both do funnel conversion goals]

Sitemap

Sitemaps are a way to tell Google/Yahoo about pages on your site we might not otherwise discover. In its simplest terms, an XML Sitemap. You could create one manually or use a gem such as Dynamic Sitemaps is a plugin for Ruby on Rails that enables you to easily create flexible, dynamic sitemaps. It creates sitemaps in the sitemaps.org standard which is supported by several crawlers including Google, Bing, and Yahoo.

Useful Gems:

- https://github.com/lassebunk/dynamic_sitemaps
- https://github.com/kjvarga/sitemap_generator

Valid HTML

It is good practice to validate your html code to keep Google happy. Enter your URL at: http://validator.w3.org/

Breadcrumbs

Breadcrumbs may help with SEO for Google to improve their search snippet, but it may unfortunately crowd a small mobile device, and with single page applications they are not really needed and make the site look old fashioned. A gem to help with creating bread-crumbs is:

https://github.com/lassebunk/gretel

Bootstrap has a class to assist:

```
<ol class="breadcrumb">
<li><a href="#">Home</a></li>
<li><a href="#">Library</a></li>
<li class="active">Data</li>
</ol>
```

Page URL slug name

Search engines give an important weight to URLs [called Url slugs] to draw up the page rank. Instead of http://example.com/states/4323454 we could have http://example.com/states/washington

Interesting that airbnb still has an unfriendly url such as:

https://www.airbnb.com/rooms/3011111

Perhaps because if a host changes their description how do you reflect this in any bookmarked url's etc. and if it has been bookmared. But eventbrite uses as an example:

http://www.eventbrite.com/e/tech-tuesdays-registration-9873754666?aff=es2&rank=1

Our goal is to use a slug as a parameter of the URLs so they are both more valuable for search engines and more comprehensible by human begins.

Instead of for example: http://localhost/dating/members/167

We could have: http://localhost/dating/members/bob-smith/167

One of the easiest way to add slugs is to override the to_param method in the model whose URLs we want to change:

```
class Member < ActiveRecord::Base
def to_param
#generate-slug
end
```

A useful gem to help with this is: https://github.com/norman/friendly_id

HTML5 markup

HTML5 elements such as <nav>, <footer>, <audio>, <video>, and many more. These new elements allow us to structure our websites in a more understandable manner for search engines.

Microdata

An important feature of HTML5 with regards to SEO is microdata supported by Google. Microdata uses simple attributes in HTML tags (often <span> or <div>) to assign brief and descriptive names to items and properties. Here's an example of a short HTML block showing information for Bob Smith.

```
<div>
My name is Bob Smith. My home page:
<a href="http://www.example.com">www.example.com</a>
</div>
```

Here is the same HTML marked up with microdata.

```
<div itemscope itemtype="http://data-vocabulary.org/Person">
My name is <span itemprop="name">Bob Smith</span>
Here is my home page:
<a href="http://www.example.com" item-
prop="url">www.example.com</a>
</div>
```

Some useful gems are:

- https://github.com/shadowmaru/microformats_helper/tree/master
- https://github.com/lancejpollard/html-schema

Dynamic Meta Tags

Meta tags invisible to users but quite useful for search engines to keep important information about our pages. They are tags invisible to users but quite useful for search engines to keep important information about our pages. The more they are related to content of the page the more they will be effective. So it's really important to have the ability to dynamically generate the meta tags of our web application, the more descriptive and different each metatag is per page the better.

The following method shows how to generate dynamic meta tags using content we have already added without using specific database fields. The first thing we have to do is to render a new partial in our application layout (and in every other layout we want to add meta tags):

```
<head>
<%= render 'shared/meta_tags' %>
...
</head>
```

The partial shared/_metatags.html.erb will contain the definition of meta tags we want to use. If meta tags will be present they will be used, otherwise a default value will be printed:

```
<title><%= yield(:title).presence || "Default title" %></title>
<meta name="keywords" content="<%= yield(:meta_keywords).presence || "default, keywords" %>" />
<meta name="description" content="<%= yield(:meta_description).presence || "Default description" %>" />
<meta name="author" content="<%= yield(:meta_author).presence || "Default Author" %>" />
```

Let's now create some methods inside the application_helper to easily pass custom meta tags to the layout:

```
#Meta tags helper methods
def meta_title(title)
content_for(:title, title)
end
def meta_description(description)
content_for(:meta_description, description)
end
def meta_keywords(keywords)
content_for(:meta_keywords, keywords)
```

```
end
def meta_author(author)
  content_for(:meta_author, author)
end
```

We can now generate the dynamic meta tags for our blog posts into resource views, for example into blog_posts/show.html.erb:

```
<%
meta_title "#{@blog_post.title} - MyCoolBlog"
meta_keywords "#{@blog_post.categories.join(", ")}"
meta_description truncate(strip_tags(@blog_post.teaser),
:length => 200)
meta_author @blog_post.user
%>
```

I choose to pass meta tags from views (instead of from the controller) because in this way we can use helper methods to customise them, as we have just done truncating and stripping HTML tags for the description meta tags.

Alternatively we could use an existing gem to add the title, descriptions meta tags such as:

1. https://github.com/kpumuk/meta-tags
2. https://github.com/lassebunk/metamagic

Note: considering Google doesn't use keywords as a ranking influence, it also give competitors the ability to understand the list of our keywords, it is best not to use them.

How responsive design affects SEO

There's been some debate in the past about which type of mobile optimisation is better: a separate mobile site, or a responsively designed site. However, Google, has recently made their stance on mobile optimisation clear. Google prefers responsive design to a separate mobile site.

Vary HTTP header for responsive SEO

In responsive wed pages the Vary HTTP header has two important and useful implications. Either configure nginx/apache to insert this or the Rails code.

- It signals to caching servers used in ISPs and elsewhere that they should consider the user agent when deciding whether to serve the page from cache or not. Without the Vary HTTP header, a cache may mistakenly serve mobile users the cache of the desktop HTML page or vice versa.
- It helps Googlebot discover your mobile-optimised content faster, as a valid Vary HTTP header is one of the signals we may use to crawl URLs that serve mobile-optimised content.

Reference: https://developers.google.com/webmasters/smartphone-sites/details

Deployment

The site is ready now, lets deploy it for users to start using it. The basic configuration is a nginx server in front of a Rails server (or nginx/rails combined on one server as typically on AWS) and a database server, or a load balancer in front of several rails servers.

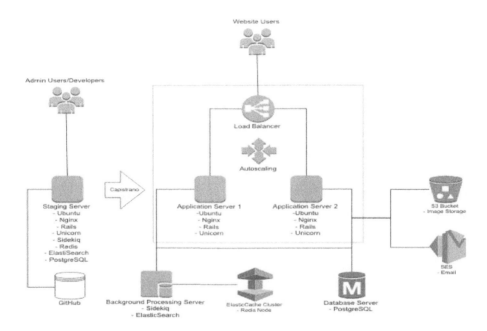

nginx/apache

Nginx HTTP server front-facing web server similar to Apache. A web server such as nignx or apache is used in front on the Rails server. It is capable of serving static files (e.g. images, text files, etc.) taking the load off your Rails server, balance connections as a load balancer, and deal with certain exploits attempts. It acts as the first entry point of all requests, and passes them to Unicorn for the web application to process and return a response. It queues up requests to the Rails server behind it.

Nignx has reached its popularity due it's performance. Thanks to its architecture, it is capable of handling a lot of requests, which - depending on your application or website load - could be really hard to tackle using some other, older alternatives such as apache.

Remember: "Handling" connections technically means not dropping them and being able to serve them with something. You still need your application and database functioning well in order to have Nginx serve clients responses that are not error messages.

Rails production server

The default Rails server is Webrick that comes with the rails download, but for production you will wants to use a more production ready server such as unicorn or puma. My preference is for Puma.

Database connections

When increasing concurrency by using a multi-threaded web server like Puma, or multi-process web server like Unicorn, you must be aware of the number of connections your app holds to the database and how many connections the database can accept. Each thread or process requires a different connection to the database. To accommodate this, Active Record provides a connection pool that can hold several connections at a time [5 by default].When scaling out, it is important to keep in mind how many active connections your application needs.

Connection pool: By default Rails (Active Record) will only create a connection when a new thread or process attempts to talk to the database through a SQL query. Active Record limits the total number of connections per application through a database setting pool; this is the maximum size of the connections your app can have to the database.

When scaling you application, it is important to keep in mind how many active connections your application needs. If you database purchased only allows say 20 connections, then if each say each of your your Heroku dyno allows 5 database connections, you can only scale out to four dynos before you need to provision a more robust database.

The Unicorn web server scales out using multiple processes, So in your unicorn config file if you have worker_processes set to 3. Then your app will use 3 connections for workers. This means each say Heroku dyno [or EC2 AWS instance] will require 3 connections. If you're on a database plan with 20 connections on Heroku, you can scale out to 6 dynos which will mean 18 active database connections, out of a maximum of 20 allowed for your database. AWS RDS has more generous connection limits dependibg on your database server size, but it is good to be aware of the limit.

Another web server, Puma, gets concurrency using threads (16 by default). This means it would require 16 connections in the pool to operate without exception.

Generally, PostgreSQL on good hardware can support a few hundred connections (Heroku limits the number you can use). If you want to have thousands instead, you should consider using connection pooling software to reduce the connection overhead.

You can see the number of connections to your postgres by running:

```
bundle exec rails dbconsole
select count(*) from pg_stat_activity where pid <> pg_backend_pid() and usename = current_user;
```

Since connections are opened lazily, you'll need to hit your running application at localhost several times until the count quits going up. To get an accurate count you should run that database query inside of a production database since your development setup may not allow you to generate load required for your app to create new connections. It is possible for connections to hang, or be placed in a "bad" state. This means that the connection will be unusable, but remain open.

Security

It is good to be aware of the security issues. Rails offers cross site scripting, cross site request forgery, sql injection, header injection.

Reference: http://guides.rubyonrails.org/security.html

Security offered by heroku: https://www.heroku.com/policy/security

With AWS, you have to configure the security groups yourself:

http://aws.amazon.com/security/

Security Attacks

To prevent attacks form individual I.P. addresses a useful gem is:
https://github.com/kickstarter/rack-attack

An example configuration for it is shown, for example to only aloow a few attemps to login, or fill in a form, or API calls for a map:

```
ack::Attack.throttle('req/ip', :limit => 30, :period => 30.second)
do |req|
# If the return value is truthy, the cache key for the return value
# is incremented and compared with the limit. In this case:
# "rack::attack:#{Time.now.to_i/1.second}:req/ip:#{req.ip}"
#
# If falsy, the cache key is neither incremented nor checked.
req.ip unless req.path.include?('assets')
end
Rack::Attack.whitelist('map_views') do |request|
request.path.include?("/refresh_map_display")
end

# throttle multiple login attempts from the same IP address
Rack::Attack.throttle('login_attempts', :limit => 10,
:period => 1.minute) do |request|
request.ip if request.path.include?("/users/sign_in")
&& request.post?
end

# throttle multiple login attempts for the same user
Rack::Attack.throttle('login_attempts', :limit => 10,
:period => 1.minute) do |request|
request.params['email'].presence
if request.path.include?("/users/sign_in") && request.post?
end

Rack::Attack.throttle('signup_attempts', :limit => 10,
:period => 1.minute) do |request|
request.ip if
request.path.include?("/registrations/create_guest")
&& request.put?
end

Rack::Attack.throttle('feedback_form', :limit => 2,
:period => 1.minute) do |request|
request.ip if request.path.include?("/contact_email")
```

```
             && request.post?
end

Rack::Attack.throttle('press_media_form', :limit => 2,
:period => 1.minute) do |request|
request.ip if request.path.include?("/contact_press_email")
&& request.post?
end

ActiveSupport::Notifications.subscribe('rack.attack')
do |name, start, finish, request_id, req|
# we don't log whitelisted requests because ick, log pollution!
unless req.env["rack.attack.match_type"] == :whitelist
Rails.logger.warn "RackAttack throttle event!
Event type: #{req.env["rack.attack.match_type"]} | " +
"Rule match:
#{req.env["rack.attack.matched"]} | " +
"Params: #{req.params} | " +
"Throttle data:
#{req.env["rack.attack.match_data"]}"
end
end
```

Site Scan

Some useful tools to scan your site for potential security risks are:

- https://code.google.com/p/skipfish/wiki/SkipfishDoc
- https://cirt.net/nikto2
- http://www.arachni-scanner.com/
- http://w3af.org/
- https://www.netsparker.com/ -pay for it
- https://suite.websecurify.com/plans -pay for it

Rails deployment environment

The Rails asset pipeline provides an 'assets:precompile' rake task to allow assets to be compiled and cached up front rather than compiled every time the app boots. You can precompile the assets locally, check them into git, and then push them to the production server along with the rest of the application.

RAILS_ENV=production rake assets:precompile

rails server -e production

A public/assets directory will be created. Inside this directory you'll find a manifest.yml which includes the md5sums of the compiled assets in Rails 3. In Rails 4 the file will be manifest-<md5 hash>.json. Adding public/assets to your git repository will make it available for deployment.

12 factor

The twelve-factor app is a methodology for building Software-As-A-Service apps:

- The twelve-factor app methodology stores application configuration in environment variables [for example the Url to your search server, which is different to what a lot of people do they store configuration as constants in the code - this is a violation of twelve-factor, which requires strict separation of configuration from code. Configuration varies substantially across deployments - development/staging/production, code does not.
https://github.com/bkeepers/ dotenv is a gem to store your environment variables in. env for development and you can then configure your environment variables for production.
- The code for a twelve-factor app makes no distinction between local and third party services. A deploy of the twelve-factor app should be able to swap out a local MySQL database with one managed by a third party (such as Amazon RDS) without any changes to the app's code.
- There is only one codebase per app, but there will be many deploys of the app. A deploy is a running instance of the app. This is typically a production site, and one or more staging sites. The codebase is the same across all deploys, although different versions may be active in each deploy.
- Backing services, is any service the app consumes over the network as part of its normal operation such as a database, elasticsearch, memcached. The code for a twelve-factor app makes no distinction between local and third party services. To the app, both are attached resources, accessed via a URL or other locator/credentials stored in the config. A deploy of the twelve-factor app should be able to swap out a local Postgres database with one managed by a third party (such as Amazon RDS) without any changes to the app's code.
- The twelve-factor app uses strict separation between the build, release, and run stages. Any change must create a new release.

- Twelve-factor processes are stateless and share nothing. Any data that needs to persist must be stored in a stateful backing service, typically a database. The memory space or filesystem of the process can be used as a brief, single-transaction cache. Sticky sessions are a violation of twelve-factor and should never be used or relied upon.
- Keep development, staging, and production as similar as possible. Historically, there have been substantial gaps between development and production deployment. The twelve-factor app is designed for continuous deployment by keeping the gap between development and production small. Looking at the three gaps described above:

Make the time gap small: a developer may write code and have it deployed hours or even just minutes later.

Make the personnel gap small: developers who wrote code are closely involved in deploying it and watching its behaviour in production.

Heroku also offer a 12 factor gem: https://github.com/heroku/rails_12factor. This gem adds two other gems rails_serve_static_assets and rails_stdout_logging. These gems are required to run your Rails app with both logging aggregation and static assets serving in production.

Application Hosting options

You can always run from your server from home if you have a public IP address from your ISP provider to demo your initial MVC if cost is an issue.

It is important to understand the difference between Infrastructure as a Service (Iaas) and Platform as a Service (PaaS). IaaS deals with Virtual Machines, storage (hard disks), servers, network, load balancers etc.. PaaS is a layer on top of IaaS where you don't have to worry about infrastructure such as load balancer, chef recipes to build servers etc. PaaS basically help developer to speed the development of app. But most large companies use IaaS to get the flexibility for massive scalability.

- Virtual servers such as https://www.linode.com/, https://www.digitalocean.com/, can work out cheaper than using say amazon AWS as you do not pay per time used.
- Heroku : Heroku is owned by Salesforce, it make scaling easier than AWS to set up but not as flexible. I have found their customer service good, databases are

expensive. they has excellent Rails documentation. Unlike AWS, you can't log into your server via SSH, you run the Heroku toolbelt from your own machines command line.

Heroku used the cedar runtime stack, https://devcenter.heroku.com/articles/cedar,

Heroku does by default not serve the compressed version of your assets to the client browser. It does not have a nginx server to compress/zip http responses but you can use the nginx build pack, https://github.com/ryandotsmith/nginx-buildpack, you have to add the nginx line to zgip the content, which serves up these compressed assets instead of the full uncompressed version, dramatically improving client download times.

Heroku has an equivalent of AWS's cloudfront to server static content more local to your customer using https://devcenter.heroku.com/articles/fastly. I really like Hero-ku but the fact that it does not have a powerful load balancer such as AWS elastic load balancer, and it has no region in Asia is a concern for some projects.

It has good features such as a production check button:

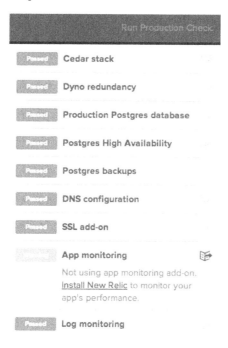

- Engineyard : Engine yard uses AWS to offer a Platform As A Service offering, but for example on AWS but they charge a lot more than AWS prices. I don't find there documentation so good as Heroku's. Heroku is similar to engine yard is a Platform As A Service.
- An interesting new PaaS I am watching lately is : http://www.pivotal.io/platform-as-a-service/pivotal-cf. It can use several infrasture providers such as Google cloud, AWS. They supply the tools to provision your hardware – in a way similar to AWS opsworks.
- Google cloud PaaS: Google compute engine, Infrastructure as a Service platform, is becoming more flexible in trying to compete with AWS. There have an interesting mobile backend end offering that makes integrating with mobile Android/iOS apps easy, especially with Android studio using Google endpoints. Google app engine was traditionally was focused on Java and python, but Google Cloud has a Ruby Rails solution now,
https://developers.google.com/cloud/ruby/

The Ruby stack provided is:

- Apache Web Server
- Passenger App Server
- Ruby on Rails Framework
- MySQL Database

Google Cloud now offers easy integration to MongoDB, Cassandra, RabbitMQ and a free GIT repository.

- **AWS Beanstalk PaaS** : AWS Elastic Beanstalk is a PaaS (Platform as a Service) service from Amazon Web Services that allows users to create applications and push them to a set of AWS services, including Amazon EC2, Amazon S3, Amazon Simple Notification Service (SNS), Amazon CloudWatch, auto scaling, and elastic load balancers.
- **Amazon web services [AWS] IaaS** : AWS, Infrastructure as a service platform, is the more flexible and powerful platform over Beanstalk. You can distribute your deployments across world regions, security configurations, ops management using Chef and AWS marketplace for configurations.

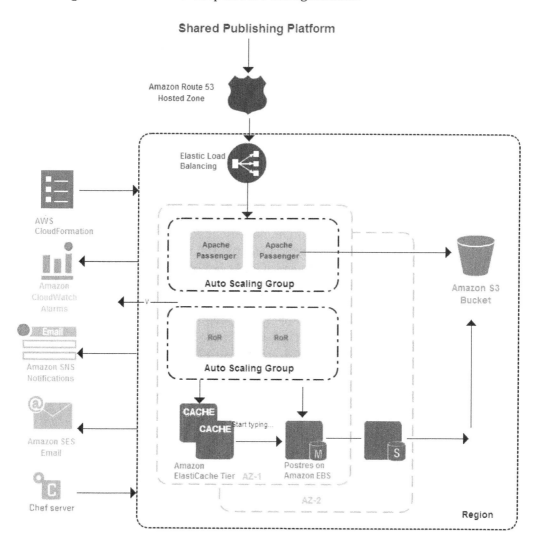

An AWS region is comprised of two or more availability zones, each zone consisting of one or more distinct data centers. Availability zones are designed to shield infrastructures from physical harm, for example. If one data center is damaged, you should be able to use another one by switching to another availability zone. Availability zones are, therefore, important in getting your apps resilient and reliable.

I have had problem with GoDaddy's DNS servers before, it worked in one location and went doen in another region of the world, so I replaced it with http://aws.amazon.com/route53/ with offers DNS redundancy and performance [remember to switch over your email MX record also].

Operations management

The objective of IT Operations Management is to monitor and control the services and infrastructure.

AWS

AWS has Opsworks and cloufFormation to help manage your apps.

- Opsworks :This is an application management service for building and managing servers using Chef recipes. It can talk a little time to become comfortable with Chef recipes. But you can find a lot of free Chef recipes in the community. Once a multitier application gets deployed through Opsworks, it's a tedious affair to try and move it out of AWS.
- CloudFormation : Using a coudFormation script you can build a complete application solution to include Opsworks stacks and other resources into one bundle. Good for example if you were selling a platform ad your product and you need to reproduce your entire stack for different customers.

Google Cloud

Gcloud, https://developers.google.com/cloud/sdk/gcloud/, can be used to manage both your development workflow and your Google Cloud Platform resources. You can use Puppet and Chef with google cloud, as well as http://www.ansible.com/home,http://www.saltstack.com/enterprise/.

Reference: https://cloud.google.com/products/cloud-deployment-manager/

HEROKU

Heroku used it's toolbelt, https://toolbelt.heroku.com/ to manage it's app.

Deployment Tools

Deployment to Heroku is easy, it generally means pushing an app to Heroku using Git. For AWS you could use a popular rails deployment tool called Capistrano, less popular alternatives to Capistrano are:

- https://github.com/mina-deploy/mina
- http://railsmachine.github.io/moonshine/
- https://github.com/mislav/git-deploy

Example of a Capistrano deployment script to Unicorn, created are scripts for staging and production is:

in Gemfile,

```
group :development,:test do
gem 'capistrano-unicorn', :require => false
```

In the config directory, create a new file, staging.rb :

```
set :rails_env, 'production'
server '194.117.29.74', :app, :db, :web, :primary => true
set :deploy_to, "/var/www/etestapp"
set :branch, "master"
logger.level = Logger::MAX_LEVEL
set :user, "root"
set :group, "root"
```

in the config directory, create a new file production.rb

```
set :rails_env, 'production'
server '192.192.27.83', :app, :db, :web, :primary => true
set :deploy_to, "/var/www/testapp"
set :branch, "master"
logger.level = Logger::MAX_LEVEL
```

```ruby
set :user, "mike"
set :group, "mike"
In the config directory, create deploy.rb
require 'bundler/capistrano'
require 'capistrano-unicorn'
set :keep_releases, 2
set :stages, %w(production staging)
set :default_stage, "staging"
set :stage_dir, "config"
require 'capistrano/ext/multistage'

set(:current_path) { File.join(deploy_to, current_dir) }

set :scm, :git
set :repository, "git@bitbucket.org:mycompany/testapp.git"
set :migrate_target, :current
set :ssh_options, { :forward_agent => true }
set :normalize_asset_timestamps, false
set :use_sudo, false
default_environment["RAILS_ENV"] = 'production'
namespace :deploy do
task :restart, :roles => :web do
run "touch #{ current_path }/tmp/restart.txt"
end
task :symlink_shared do
run "ln -nfs #{shared_path}/config/database.yml #{release_path}/config/database.yml"
end

task :restart_daemons, :roles => :app do
sudo "monit restart all -g daemons"
end

task :initial do
system "cap deploy:setup"
system "cap deploy"
system "cap deploy:db:create"
system "cap deploy:db:migrate"
end

namespace :db do
task :create do
run "cd #{current_path};
bundle exec rake db:create RAILS_ENV=#{rails_env}"
end
```

```
task :setup do
run "cd #{current_path};
bundle exec rake db:setup RAILS_ENV=#{rails_env}"
end

task :migrate do
run "cd #{current_path};
bundle exec rake db:migrate RAILS_ENV=#{rails_env}"
end

task :migrate_reset do
run "cd #{current_path};
bundle exec rake db:migrate:reset RAILS_ENV=#{rails_env}"
end

task :drop do
run "cd #{current_path};
bundle exec rake db:drop RAILS_ENV=#{rails_env}"
end

task :seed do
run "cd #{current_path};
bundle exec rake db:seed RAILS_ENV=#{rails_env}"
end
end
end
```

You would use the capistano commands like :

```
Cap deploy:setup
Cap deploy
```

Note: An advantage of Jruby is that just one WAR file is produced for deployment. In Facebook they use their own tool called HipHop which converts PHP into heavily optimized C++ code, which can then be compiled into an efficient native binary. Because Facebook's entire code base is compiled down to a single binary executable, which is then pushed to all the servers. Facebook typically rolls out a minor update on every single business day. Major updates are issued once a week,

Git deploy

An alternative to capistrano is to use a similar process like in Heroku, using Git to deploy.

Using this gem : https://github.com/mislav/git-deploy

Deployments are done simply by pushing to the branch that is currently checked out on the remote:

git push production master

On every deploy, the default deploy/after_push script performs the following:

1. updates git submodules (if there are any);
2. runs bundle install --deployment if there is a Gemfile;
3. runs rake db:migrate if new migrations have been added;
4. clears cached CSS/JS assets in "public/stylesheets" and "public/javascripts";
5. restarts the web application.

You can customize all this by editing generated scripts in the deploy/ directory of your app. After using the Heroku git push deploy process, you could find it hard to go back to Capistrano,

Options to deploy on AWS

For a typical deploy, the changes to the code are minimal and really don't require a new machine image to be built, rather we just need to be sure that when the machine boots it is serving the latest version of the application code. You could streamline the process such as an automated checkout of the latest code from version control when the machine boots. This is all very well but we host our code at GitHub, but I really don't want to build in a dependency of GitHub for our auto-scaling. A simple workflow for AWS deployment is:

1. Work on new feature, finish up and commit
2. Push code up to GitHub
3. Git 'archive' the repo locally, tar and zip it up
4. Push the git archive up to S3
5. Reboot each of the production nodes in turn
6. Done

You could use Capistrano for on-the-fly deployment.

Server build tools

The two most popular scripting tools for building server are Chef [AWS preferred] and Puppet. Opsworks is built on the Chef framework. Puppet's DSL is easier to learn and use as a CLI command tool, but offers less flexibility than the pure Ruby CLI of Chef/Opsworks; this together with Puppet's powerful and user-friendly GUI, also reveal that Puppet is really a sysadmin tool. Chef is difficult to learn.

Having been around for a long time, Puppet has a large user community. The two main differences between them are a philosophical one (a sysadmin tool in Puppet vs. a developer tool in Chef) and whether you are operating on AWS or not. Puppet can actually be used to manage EC2 instances, but now Amazon have their own product to compete with it.

If you can make an Amazon Machine Image (AMI), installing software at deploy time is not necessary anymore, just use an existing build [just like virtual box snapshots] rather than using a Chef script.

Stress test

For measuring performance Jmeter is a good free tool. Charles Proxy is useful for detecting say web traffic between your browser and the server. Charles is also great as a proxy to say simulate slow connection speeds, replace a CSS file from a site with your local copy etc..

Apache 'ab' is a more basic performance test tool:
http://httpd.apache.org/docs/2.2/programs/ab.html

Performance tune

People typically spent time tuning the garbage collection in Java for performance but in Ruby is it not very typical for people to do it. The most common way to check up on Ruby's Garbage Collector (GC) is probably calling GC.stat, which returns a hash of of information about the current state of the GC. Garbage collection (GC) finds unused data objects and reclaims that memory space for use by another process.

The memory Ruby manages and to which we have access is organized on the Ruby heap, which itself is split up into slots. Each slot is big enough to hold one Ruby object. In the context of Ruby's memory management and GC an object is represented as a simple struct called RVALUE. Each slot on the Ruby heap has the size of one RVALUE, which is 40 bytes.

For Ruby 2.1:

```
rails console
GC.stat
```

```
=> {:count=>49, :heap_used=>2343, :heap_length=>3320,
:heap_increment=>963, :heap_live_slot=>942536,
:heap_free_slot=>12465, :heap_final_slot=>0,
:heap_swept_slot=>354530, :heap_eden_page_length=>2332,
:heap_tomb_page_length=>11, :total_allocated_object=>5967776,
:total_freed_object=>5025240, :malloc_increase=>15418448,
:malloc_limit=>19584230, :minor_gc_count=>41, :major_gc_count=>8,
:remembered_shady_object=>8658,
:remembered_shady_object_limit=>9884, :old_object=>561864,
:old_object_limit=>727108, :oldmalloc_increase=>21081696,
:oldmalloc_limit=>34789233}
```

Ruby allows users to tweak its GC via environment variables. And since 2.1 there are a lot more variables to use than in previous versions.

- **RUBY_GC_HEAP_INIT_SLOTS :** The initial number of slots Ruby allocates on its heap. Default value is 10000. Increasing this number to cover the live objects after a process is fully booted can reduce the number of GC runs when booting and thus the boot time.
- **RUBY_GC_HEAP_FREE_SLOTS :** The minimum number of free slots that should be available after a GC run. Default value is 4096.
- **RUBY_GC_HEAP_GROWTH_FACTOR :** The factor by which the size of the heap grows when it needs to be expanded. Default value is 1.8. increasing this number increases the size of the Ruby heap and a larger heap triggers less GC runs. But it does make sense to lower this number when RUBY_GC_HEAP_INIT_SLOTS is already really high, since the memory consumption might be go through the roof.
- **RUBY_GC_HEAP_GROWTH_MAX_SLOTS :** The maximum number of slots on the Ruby heap. Default value is 0, which means the feature is disabled. But if the number is higher than 0 it sets the maximum number of slots Ruby is allowed to add to its heap at once. The higher the number the less GC runs does Ruby need for its heap to grow to the needed size.

- **RUBY_GC_HEAP_OLDOBJECT_LIMIT_FACTOR :** The factor by which Ruby increases GC.stat[:oldobject_limit] and GC.stat[:remembered_shady_object_limit] after each major GC. Default value is 2.0.
- **RUBY_GC_MALLOC_LIMIT :** The minimum value for GC.stat[:malloc_limit], which causes a minor GC when triggered. Default value is 16777216 (16mb).
- **RUBY_GC_MALLOC_LIMIT_MAX :** GC.stat[:malloc_limit] changes dynamically through a growth factor. This sets its maximum value. Default value is 33554432 (32mb).
- **RUBY_GC_MALLOC_LIMIT_GROWTH_FACTOR :** The growth factor by which GC.stat[:malloc_limit] is resized before every sweep. Default value is 1.4.
- **RUBY_GC_OLDMALLOC_LIMIT :** it is the minimum value for GC.stat[:oldmalloc_limit], which causes a major GC when triggered. Default value is 16777216 (16Mb).
- **RUBY_GC_OLDMALLOC_LIMIT_MAX :** The maximum value GC.stat[:oldmalloc_limit] can have. Default value is 33554432 (32mb).
- **RUBY_GC_OLDMALLOC_LIMIT_GROWTH_FACTOR :** The growth factor by which GC.stat[:oldmalloc_limit] is resized before every sweep. Default value is 1.2.

Newrelic

An excellent cloud based tool for measuring your server/rails/database performance is NewRelic. Newrelic can also report on the garbage collection statistics. Just add the following line to your environment.rb file:

```
GC.enable_stats if defined?(GC) && GC.respond_to?(:enable_stats)
```

It is easy to install:

https://docs.newrelic.com/docs/agents/ruby-agent/installation-configuration/ruby-agent-installation

It is very a powerful tool, even reporting on your slow SQL statements, and Javascript errors.

mini-profiler

A useful tool to help profile your code which displays speed badge for every HTML page:

https://github.com/miniprofiler/rack-mini-profiler

Logs gathered from different Rails servers

With AWS there is no need to log in to several machines and manually update your configuration by using CloudWatch Logs (alternatives are Splunk, Loggly and Logstash). Heroku can use several add ons including logentries.

A good cloud logging service is www.airbrake.io.

How to enable features as you require them

When Facebook or Google+ start rolling new features they release it in a phased manner - first releasing to a selective audience and progressively to everyone else. It also enables Facebook and Google+ to test things on early users and react to responses.

The basic idea is to have a configuration file that defines a bunch of toggles for various features you have pending. The running application then uses these toggles in order to decide whether or not to show the new feature. Most of these decisions occur in the user-interface of the application.

Making the test site the default for employees ensures that pending features get more exposure before they are merged as Facebook do. A typical Facebook deployment doesn't require scheduled downtime or cause any other disruption to the website. Instead of deploying a new built to all your users you could deploy to section of your user base to check the build does not break or to test usability. Feature toggles can be also used:

- for avoiding branching and merging.
- experimenting such as A/B tests.
- putting unfinished code in production.
- reducing risk associated with large change.
- turning a resources heavy feature OFF in high load conditions.

One danger with feature toggles is an accidental exposure, when someone forgets to wrap the UI feature in a toggle tag. This is awkward to test, since it's difficult to form a test that nothing that should be hidden is visible without calling out the individual elements - which are likely to be forgotten at the same time.

Feature toggle

Normally features toggles can have boolean states - ON or OFF. But depending on your requirements a feature toggle can be more than boolean states - lists, arrays, strings, conditions, logical statements, integers or any other value. State of toggles is either set statically using application configuration based toggles or dynamically using rules based toggles. Once a list of toggles are available in application context or namespace, you can use them your application code using simple if conditions.

```
if (ENV['enable_new_feature']) {
// do new feature here
}
```

We can then set the value of ENV['enable_new_feature'] on each environment (false for production, true for dev, etc.). For Rails, you can define feature flipping on all levels - Model, View, Templates and Controller.

Rule based Toggles

Rule based toggles can be applied to selected records using database queries - filter using a select condition and update toggle state to ON.

select all users where users.count > 1000 and TEST_FEATURE = ON

Another way to apply rule based toggles is to use performance parameters like number of users, average load time etc. Performance based toggles can help you to degrade your service under high load conditions gracefully.

```
set TEST_FEATURE = OFF when loadTime > 5s
```

Feature groups

Once your start using feature toggles regularly, it is good idea to group the features. For instance, you can group all features with positive impact on performance. Moreover, feature groups are very handy when one feature depends on another.

Part completed features

One of the most common arguments in favour of Feature Branch is that it provides a mechanism for pending features that take longer than a single release cycle. Imagine you are releasing into production every two weeks, but need to build a feature that's going to take three months to complete. How do you use Continuous Integration to keep everyone working on the mainline without revealing a half-implemented feature on your releases? We run into this issue quite a lot and feature toggles are a handy tool to deal with it.

Feature flags and flippers mean you don't have to do merges, and that all code (no matter how far it is from being released) is integrated as soon as it is committed. Deploys become smaller and more frequent; this leads to bugs that are easier to fix, since you can catch them earlier and the amount of changed code is minimised.

it's easy to imagine code that's in development going wrong and corrupting all your data. Also, after launching a feature, we have to go back in the code base and remove the old version

Process

Basically you need a CRUD life-cycle for feature toggles, otherwise they will become technical debt. So:

- Development team create toggles when required.
- Application read or expose toggled feature when they are switched ON.
- Development team update toggled features when they are buggy.
- A semi-automated process to destroy or remove toggles when job is done.
- Destroy or remove toggles when a feature.

It's very important to retire release toggles once the pending features have bedded down in production. This involves removing the definitions on the configuration file and all the code that uses them. Otherwise you will get a pile of toggles that nobody can remember how to use. Release toggles are a useful technique and lots of teams use them. However they should be your last choice when you're dealing with putting features into production.

Your first choice should be to break the feature down so you can safely introduce parts of the feature into the product. The advantages of doing this are the same ones as any strategy based on small, frequent releases. You reduce the risk of things going wrong and you get valuable feedback on how users actually use the feature that will improve the enhancements you make later.

Feature toggle gem's in Ruby include:

- https://github.com/pda/flip gem [thoughbot use this]
- https://github.com/FetLife/rollout gem
- https://github.com/balvig/chili
- https://github.com/mgsnova/feature
- https://github.com/jamesgolick/degrade : Keep track of service error rates using redis. Degrade functionality if they're too high.

Scalable Architecture

For most applications as they evolve over time, they grow into one large monolithic Rails app in the standard way with many models [tables] and their many corresponding controllers and views. Over time your application will grow in size as more functionality is created, you can either scale vertically [larger server] or horizontally [more servers]. Scaling vetically is slow to implement having to reinstall the code/tools, and expensive. Scale horizontal not vertical is the best solution. loose coupling is the key. If you design with a loosely coupled architecture, only a few parts of the application should be affected when requirements change.

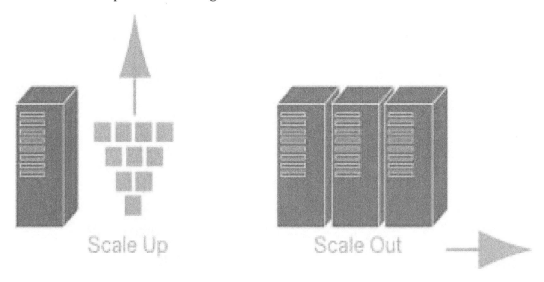

Typical large Rails monolithic applications can be successful, but increasingly people are feeling frustrations with them ; especially as more applications are being deployed to the cloud. A change made to a small part of the application, requires the entire monolith to be rebuilt and deployed. Over time it's often hard to keep a good modular structure, making it harder to keep changes that ought to only affect one module within that module. Scaling requires scaling of the entire application rather than parts of it that require greater resource. In a monolith, the components are executing in-process and communication between them is by function calls. Application's balloon and get out of control, leading us to try and find better ways of modularisation. Some approaches to architect the app could be:

- Move to several apps with their own logic and often using the big one via API. A service-oriented architecture approach.
- Single "app" made up of several Rails engines

But a lot of inefficiency comes from badly written code, terrible SQL statements designed without performance in mind. Companies like Airbnb often start out as monolithic applications – which performs all of the functions of the organization. As traffic (and the number of engineers working on the product) grows, this approach doesn't scale. The code base becomes too complicated, concerns are not cleanly separated, changes from many engineers touching many different parts of the codebase go out together, and performance is determined by the worst-performing sections in the application.

The solution to this problem is services: individual, smaller code bases, running on separate machines with separate deployment cycles, that more cleanly address more targeted problem domains. This is called a services-oriented architecture (SOA).

How to loosely couple your application

- For building loosely-coupled, highly-cohesive systems with Rails applications, there could be three choices:
- *All-in-one* app that could get more structure through namespacing of its interals. We could separated the monolith application into libraries [create gems], and then combined them as one API, but the issues with the approach are:
    - Scaling. When you want to scale, you have to scale the entire API at once.
    - Versioning. With the library approach, a single dependency can hold the entire application back. For instance, the upgrade from Rails 3 to Rails 4 is a difficult one.
    - Multiple languages and frameworks. Right now it is a Ruby application, but you might want to be able to experiment with new technologies and languages when they come along.
- *Services* (REST or message queue) running as separate apps and communicating via APIs. Having separate apps can have it's problems such as coordinating releases that spanned apps, making sure the API's work across the app's. The goal would be to make your application more modular so each module can be made more scalable.

- *Engines* are used to distribute a mini-app as a ruby gem which can then be mounted in an existing application.

Rails engines

Rails Engines is basically a whole Rails app that lives in the container of another one. engines and applications can be thought of almost the same thing, just with subtle differences.

If some front end components could be reused then consider rails engines, engines can be considered miniature applications. It can help you break up the monorail incrementally without the immediate investment in fully separate apps. An advantage with Rails engine is that it is one codebase and git repo.

We still get most of the modularisation that multiple apps have, for example the model in one engine is private from another engine and it's various helper methods.

By using engines we are getting many of the benefits of a component based architecture. In addition, The cost of maintaining individual applications that share a central database or one giant application with less defined components would be higher.

Reference: http://guides.rubyonrails.org/engines.html

Some disdavantages with engines, or even splitting you code into gems are:

1. Scaling. When you want to scale, you have to scale the entire API at once.
2. Versioning. With the library /engine approach, a single dependency can hold the entire application back. For instance, the upgrade from Rails 3 to Rails 4 is a difficult one. If you code was spread across multiple projects instead in a SOA, you then don't have to update everything at once, you could leave older APIs running, and upgrade them when we have meaningful changes to make.
3. Multiple languages and frameworks. If you are a Ruby shop, but we want to be able to experiment with new technologies and languages when they come along. For examppple with Go and Clojure, and because all the services expose REST APIs, communication isn't a problem — it's all just HTTP in the end.

Service Orientated Architecture

We can break our application into several service applications. The enterprise Service Orientated Architecture (SOA) concept with modules listening for a request on a 'bus'.

Rails does not have advanced frameworks like the enterprise Java SOA world [Enterprise Service buses as such http://www.mulesoft.org/, https://www.talend.com/ frameworks] but modularisation can be achieved by for example splitting you login service into its own module, this module could contain its own database with the user information.The request to this module is made via a REST API call. People sometimes develop these modules in Sinatra which is a cut down type of Rails framework with less features but with better performance.

Services are independently deployable and scalable, each service also provides a firm module boundary, even allowing for different services to be written in different programming languages. A consequence of using services as components, is that applications need to be designed so that they can tolerate the failure of services.

Another advantage of SOA is as Ruby/Rails versions regularly change so small apps can isolate changes so you don't have to say update a large app to a new rails version. Overtime your application's test coverage will decrease so by having smaller applications you can ensure the test coverage is higher and any requirement changes will affect less test code. services prefer letting each service manage its own database. Moreover, different services might use different types of database – a so-called polyglot persistence architecture. For example, a service that needs ACID [Atomicity/consistency/Isolation/Duability] transactions might use a relational database, whereas a service that is manipulating a social network might use a graph database.

There are two ways our services communicate with each other: HTTP requests, and a message bus. you could start out just using HTTP and Sinatra or Rails in the backend. The services passing messages through URL requests to one another. This works great for things that need to happen right now, but becomes exponentially more complicated the more services you have talking to each other.

Using services like this does have downsides. Remote calls are more expensive than in-process calls to develop, and thus remote APIs need to be coarser-grained (that simply returns all the value results), which is often more awkward to use. If you need to change the allocation of responsibilities between components, such movements of behavior are harder to do when you're crossing process boundaries.

SOA HTTP Requests

You could communicate between services with HTTP requests. The advantage is that requests are synchronous, you get a reply immediately.A negative is if you want to scale the service you need to keep an internal list of the service URL's. If you need asynchronous functionality or loosely coupled components like in case of publish-subscribe HTTP isn't usually a good choice. Another limitation is that both the client and the server must be simultaneously available, which is not always the case since distributed systems are prone to partial failures. Also, an HTTP client needs to know the host and the port of the server.

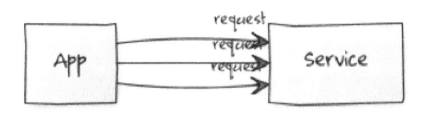

SOA messaging buses

Instead of using a RESTful API to connect your different services you could use a message bus for asynchronous communication. An alternative to synchronous HTTP is an asynchronous message-based mechanism such as an AMQP-based message broker. This approach has a number of benefits. It decouples message producers from message consumers. The message broker will buffer messages until the consumer is able to process them. Producers are completely unaware of the consumers. The producer simply talks to the message broker and does not need to use a service discovery mechanism. Message-based communication also supports a variety of communication patterns including one-way requests and publish-subscribe. One downside of using messaging is needing a message broker, which is yet another moving part that adds to the complexity of the system. Another downside is that request/reply-style communication is not a natural fit.

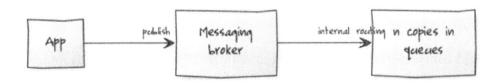

A popular option is RabbitMQ, you could also use Resque. Reasons for using a bus are:

- improve response times by doing some tasks asynchronously
- reduce complexity by decoupling and isolating applications
- build smaller apps that are easier to develop, debug, test, and scale
- build multiple apps that each use the most suitable language or framework versus one big monolithic app
- get robustness and reliability through message queue persistence
- potentially get zero-downtime redeploys
- distribute tasks across machines based on load

Most messaging software is implemented as a message broker which is a daemon connecting producers with consumers. Producers send messages and consumers process them. In Web development, a producer is usually a frontend which based on user actions generates tasks, whereas a consumer is usually a backend executing those tasks.

Resque:

Resque Bus uses Resque to create an asynchronous message bus system, based on https://github.com/taskrabbit/resque-bus. Application A can publish an event while Application B is subscribed to events.

RabbitMQ:

RabbitQA has advancing routing configuration capabilities. Note: Google cloud supports it: https://cloud.google.com/solutions/rabbitmq/

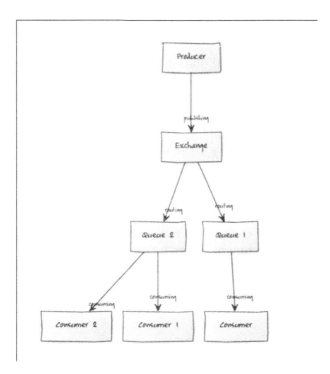

AWS SQS:

AWS uses SQS but with Amazon SQS, the message consumer is forced to poll the queue in order to determine whether or not a message is available. If a message is available, that's great, the consumer is happy and receives the message. If not, the consumer must idle for awhile, and then poll again. The pros of SQS is high availability comes along for free. Also SQS may be slower than rabbitMQ.

Potential AWS architecture

The services pass messages through URL requests to one another. This works great for things that need to happen right now, but becomes exponentially more complicated the more services you have talking to each other. You could use Amazon SNS (Simple Notification Service) for publishing events, and Amazon SQS (Simple Queue Service) to store the events. SNS takes a message passed to it by a service and publishes it to the appropriate queues via SQS.

We will discuss microservices shortly, we can equally use services instead. Microservices then can take jobs off a queue, process them, and delete them if successful.

When a new microservice is deployed, it includes a configuration file which describes what types of messages it wants to listen to, and what types of messages it wants to publish. You can use HTTP requests when we need an immediate response, like for logins.

An example architecture using AWS with the front end messaging the backend using SQS is:

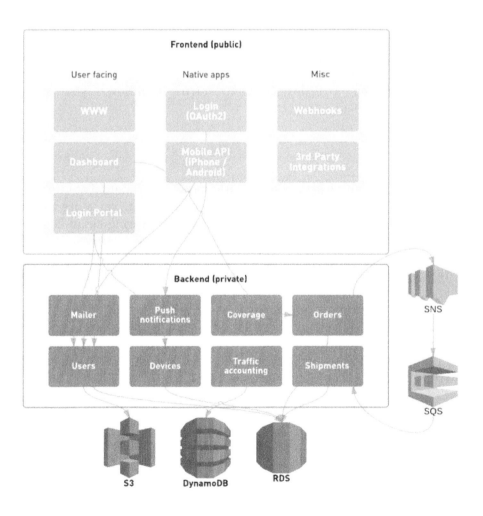

For example, when a member signs up: That's straight forward enough, but what if we want to do more after the user sign up such as generate recommendations for this user, send the member an email. That packs a lot of knowledge about the entire ecosystem into the dating application, and becomes difficult to work with. So you could start splitting off parts of the task into an event-based system. We could use Amazon SNS (Simple Notification Service) for publishing events, and Amazon SQS (Simple Queue Service) to store the events. SNS takes a message passed to it by a service and publishes it to the appropriate queues via SQS. Services then can take jobs off a queue, process them, and delete them if successful.

When a new service is deployed, it includes a configuration file which describes what types of messages it wants to listen to, and what types of messages it wants to publish. you could make a tool which reads this configuration and sets up the appropriate SQS and SNS queues. You could still use HTTP requests when we need an immediate response, like for logins.

Note: if you wanted to design your own workflow, you could use: http://aws.amazon.com/swf/details/flow/

Microservices

The current trend is for micro services. I feel it it more experimental at this stage as the complexity to deploy and manage many small services is not trival. More work is being done in Golang microservices frameworks than in Rails. Spring cloud is a good Java project addressing the needs of microservices http://projects.spring.io/spring-cloud/. Spring cloud brings together solutions from Netflex OSS components, https://github.com/spring-cloud/spring-cloud-netflix. When continuous delivery people and dev ops people came together, microservices was the result to real life deployment/code-maintenance issues. Small is beautiful, which adheres to the Unix philosophy of doing one thing well. Micro-services could be 500 lines of code according to a lot of blogs. But I feel there should be no code limit put on it, a microservice is something that does one thing well – if it is 200 lines or 2000 lines. So microservices is maybe a wrong name, as it does not have to be 'micro'.

How to manage the deployment off many microservices is not trivial. The microservice architectural style is an approach to developing a single application as a suite of small services, each running in its own process and communicating with lightweight mechanisms, often as an HTTP resource API.

The most common form of microservice today is probably one implemented via HTTP and JSON. However this form isn't a fixed rule, ProtocolBuffers (http://en.wikipedia.org/wiki/Protocol_Buffers) might be a better choice for an data exchange format and RabbitMQ might be a better choice for a transport.

But as our system grows, we end up with many scaled modules, each of them requiring a separate load balancer. This seems troublesome as our infrastructure is very complex even without them. If we use ZooKeeper as a service orchestration [as an example] and discovery tool we can use built-in load balancing capability without introducing any additional complexity into our microservice architecture. These tiny services have some major advantages over their heavier service counterparts:

- They have an inherently smaller surface area, and their development can be continually iterated until all bugs are squashed.
- Due to their small area of responsibility, they're rarely in the same state of constant change that's a matter of course many larger codebases. Less change is natural protection against new bugs or regressions.

The disadavantages are:

- The microservice architecture also introduces significant operational complexity. There are many more moving parts – multiple instances of different types of service – that must be managed in production. To do this successful you need a high-level of automation.
- Where a monolithic application might have been deployed to a small application server cluster, you now have tens of separate services to build, test, deploy and run, potentially in polyglot languages and environments.
- All of these services potentially need clustering for failover and resilience, turning your single monolithic system into, say, 20 services consisting of 40-60 processes after we've added resilience.

Throw in load balancers and messaging layers for plumbing between the services and the complexity starts to become pretty large when compared to that single monolithic application that delivered the equivalent business functionality.

Asgard is a tool for application deployments and cloud management in Amazon Web Services (AWS) - http://techblog.netflix.com/2012/06/asgard-web-based-cloud-management-and.html.

Duplication Of Effort

Imagine that there is a new business requirement to calculate profit percentage. We have a few choices in how to deliver this.

1. We could introduce a new service and allow the other services to call into this where needed.
2. We could duplicate the effort, adding the profit calculation into all of the services that need it.
3. The final option is to share resources such as a profit calculating library between the services.

It seems to me that all three of these options are sub-optimal as opposed to writing the piece of code once and making it available throughout the monolithic application

Distributed System Complexity

Once we have distributed a system, we have to consider a whole host of concerns that we didn't before. Network latency, fault tolerance, message serialisation, unreliable networks, asynchronicity, versioning, varying loads within our application tiers etc. The cost of this however is that the application developer has to think about all of these things that they didn't have to before.

Testability Challenges

With so many services all evolving at different paces and different services rolling out, it can be difficult to recreate environments in a consistent way for either manual or automated testing. We can test the individual service, but in this dynamic environment, very subtle behaviours can emerge from the interactions of the services which are hard to visualise and speculate on.

Service Discovery

How do clients determine the IP and port for a service that exist on multiple hosts? Usually, you start off with some static configuration which gets you pretty far. Things get more complicated as you start deploying more services. With a live system, service locations can change quite frequently due to auto or manual scaling, new deployments of services, as well as hosts failing or being replaced. There are two sides to the problem of locating services. Service Registration and Service Discovery. For your front end to automatically discover the services/microservices some tools to help are:

- http://zookeeper.apache.org/ : Apache zookeeper is a tool to register, manage and discover services working on different machines.
- https://github.com/coreos/etcd : A highly-available key value store for shared configuration and service discovery.
- Eureka is Netflix's middle-tier, load balancing and discovery service for AWS. https://github.com/Netflix/eureka. A load balancer for the instance/server/host level. You typically run in the AWS cloud and you have a host of middle tier services which you do not want to register with AWS ELB or expose traffic from outside world.
- SmartStack from AirBnB http://nerds.airbnb.com/smartstack-service-discovery-cloud/
- http://www.serfdom.io/ - Serf is a tool for cluster membership, failure detection, and or-chestration

Deployment of services

Docker, https://www.docker.com/, is an open platform for developers and sysadmins to build, ship, and run distributed applications. It works much like a virtual machine, wraps everything (filesystem, process management, environment variables, etc.) into a container. Unlike a VM, it uses LXC (Linux kernel container). For any reason, the Rails app needs to be moved to another server; I can just copy the whole docker repository instead of re-deploy the app and migrate the database and copy over the assets. It can be confusing – why have a virtual service inside another virtual machine – but it has become more popular.

Because you never know whether your application will work on the server even if you have run and tested it out on you localhost. That's because the environment on the server differs from your computer so much. The configuration of RVM, Ruby, gemsets differs. If we can test the application in our localhost before deploy, and we know that if it works on localhost, it works on the server, we can save a lot of time debugging deployment issues on the server.

Deploying onto 100 cloud servers becomes easy, because you just push the same container 100 times, potentially in parallel. A complex, polyglot, microservice based application is also much simpler in that you are just pushing a different set of docker containers around onto the right servers. They're all just containers to be moved with less consideration of what is inside them. What this means is that instead of manual work or complex scripting to package and deploy your application services and infrastructure, your deployment scripts become one or two lines of scripting to push or pull the relevant Docker image to the right endpoint server. For massive deployments, using an VM image is really handy. In the case of Docker.

- You don't have to upload the whole image again. Docker is based on AuFS, which tracks the diff of the whole filesystem.
- The performance loss is ignorable since it runs on the host kernel.
- You can run Docker on a VM because Docker is not a VM.

AWS Elastic Beanstalk supports the deployment of web applications from Docker containers. With Docker containers, you can define your own runtime environment.

Reference: http://aws.amazon.com/about-aws/whats-new/2014/04/23/aws-elastic-beanstalk-adds-docker-support/

Google cloud also supports docker:
https://developers.google.com/compute/docs/containers

Sinatra services

Sinatra essentially being a stripped down Rails is faster with less features but higher performance. You could have specific services running on sinatra applications. For example in the dating application we could put the image resizing service a Sinatra application.

Database scalability

Like the application server you could scale the database vertically or horizontally.

Master /slave

A good way to scale a database horizontally is to configure read replica's of your master database for tasks that require just to read, for example analytical purposes, or send out a weekly email, and say a one second delay is not critical such as sending out newsletters. a fully replicated application will send all writes queries to the primary database, and all reads queries to followers. To write your own custom code such as:

```
def with_slave_database
if ENV["SLAVE_DATABASE_URL"].present?
ActiveRecord::Base.establish_connection(slave_database_config)
begin
yield
ensure
ActiveRecord::Base.establish_connection(
VL::Application.config.database_configuration[Rails.env])
end
else
yield
end

end
def slave_database_config
begin
uri = URI.parse(ENV["SLAVE_DATABASE_URL"])
rescue URI::InvalidURIError
raise "Invalid DATABASE_URL"
end

{
adapter: uri.scheme,
database: (uri.path || "").split("/")[1],
username: uri.user,
password: uri.password,
host: uri.host,
port: uri.port
}
end
```

Alternatively you could use gems such as:

- https://github.com/tchandy/octopus
- http://dbcharmer.net/#master-slave

Google cloud support read replicate, https://developers.google.com/cloud-sql/docs/replication, for mySQL.

AWS RDS supports read replication for mySQL, http://aws.amazon.com/rds/mysql/, but not for Postgres.

Database backup

You can have high available database configuration but you should to do a database dump before each deployment in case migrations cause issues, you can roll back the SQL table changes but your data may have been deleted.

Sharding

To solve scaling problems you could create a database server for a group of users, In this scheme the data for User A is stored on one server and the data for User B is stored on another server [say users beginning with A-P on ine database and the remaining users on another database. Groups of users are stored together in what are called shards. The advantage is faster queries. Smaller amounts of data in each user group mean faster querying.

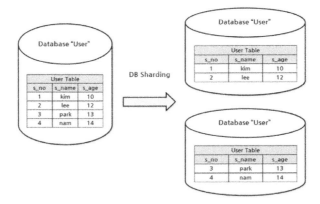

cons:

- Rebalancing data. What happens when a shard outgrows your storage and needs to be split.
- Joining data from multiple shards.

Gems for shading are:

- https://github.com/tchandy/octopus
- http://dbcharmer.net/#sharding

Note: MongoDB noSQL is really easy to setup for sharding, master/slave configurations, which is more difficult to configure for relational databases.

SINGLE PAGE APPLICATIONS (SPA)

Single-Page Applications (SPAs) are Web apps that load a single HTML page and dynamically update that page as the user interacts with the app. SPA has become a popular recent architecture whereby the frontend of the project is run in the browser with no Rails views [or perhaps part of the web page done in a Rails view], instead a user download's the javascript application to their browser as what happens in a typical web page viewing except the Javascript in the browser determines what is rendered in the page, not the server side view page.

The Javascript communicates to the server typically using RESTful API's. For example to list all the member's make a show API. Some negatives of this approach is the initial load time, for example you have to download the Javascript, then you have to make REST requests to the server for the information. Airbnb have an interesting library for this called rendr for backbone.js/node.js. Debugging is also more difficult, and having have some duplication of data models in the Rails model and also in the Javascript data model.

The most popular tools to write SPA's are with the backbone.js library, angularjs from Google, and ember.js. I really like angularjs, it has great test support, and less code to write than backbone.js. But it would be more appropriate to say compare angularjs and marionette.js [a layer on top of backbone.js to give better memory management and regions within a page]. Angualrjs makes two way data binding easy: https://docs.angularjs.org/guide/databinding.

For example to create a mobile only page with jquerymobile, it is more tricky to add angularjs, for if you plan never to go that route I would recommend angularjs. Also it is more difficult to use Zurb foundation with angularjs. Angular.js officially calls itself a framework as opposed to knockout and backbone which actually refer to themselves as libraries.

Trying to decide on backbone.js, angularjs, ember.js is like trying to decide on a MVC framework for Java, there is no easy straight forward path. meteor.js [www.meteor.com] is nice framework for rapid prototyping ideas with a nosql mongodb backend, sql support is difficult and not used in many large production sites yet.

Who uses SPA

Some sites using Backbone.js, http://backbonejs.org/#examples, are: USA Today, Hulu, airBnb.

Some sites using Angularjs, https://builtwith.angularjs.org/, are: msnbc.com, Virgin America.

Some sites using ember.js, http://emberjs.com/ember-users/ are: Yahoo, Groupon.

Problems with SPA

As good as SPA sounds there many issues to consider. For example, we used the login Devise gem, how to code the same functionality in a SPA needs to to be thought about. Other issues are:

- Cache
- Live updates
- SEO
- Pagination
- SPA touch swipe
- Page Load vs Perceived Page Load
- How to do internationalization
- Recruitment, staff needed with extra skills. Front end javascript person reliant on backend person for changes.

Single page application 'Perceived Page Load'

In a traditional page, measuring the page performance is quite easy; a request is made, the server responds with some HTML and the browser renders it. Done. A lot of the rendering logic is taken care of as part of the server processing and so looking at Window Load and DOMContentReady are good indicators of page performance.

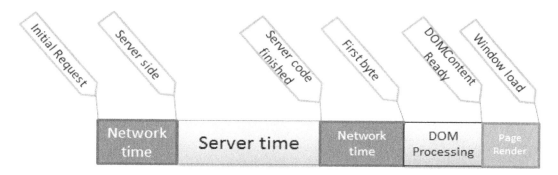

In a Single Page Application, things get trickier. The Window Load is only the beginning - that's when the JavaScript has been delivered to the browser, at which point the client-side logic - all the real work - kicks in and begins rendering the page, making API calls and setting up listeners, events, etc. The DOM is then continuously manipulated as part of user interaction or monitoring, polling and other events. As you can see, the traditional definition of a page being 'done' doesn't apply here.

The **perceived page** performance is how long the user thinks the major elements of the page took to load. By definition it is highly subjective - some users may think that the page is loaded just because the initial furniture appears. But for most users this will be the parts of the page they consider most important. The perceived page load is when all of the important dynamic parts of the page have been filled.

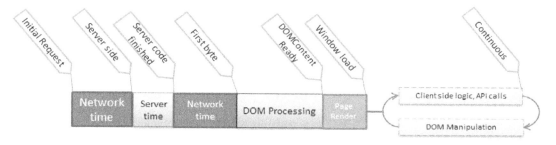

Google experiments show that a delay as small as a hundred milliseconds can have an adverse effect on users leaving your site. But how do we measure web page load speed? And what does "page load" actually mean?

In the past, web developers have used the JavaScript Date object for timing metrics.

```
var start = Date.now();
console.log("Page load took " + (Date.now() - start) +
"milliseconds");
```

Using inline JavaScript to measure performance in this way is limited and unreliable

The order of performance.timing events is shown in the image below from the Navigation Timing Recommendation:

Navigation Timing is a JavaScript API for accurately measuring performance on the web.

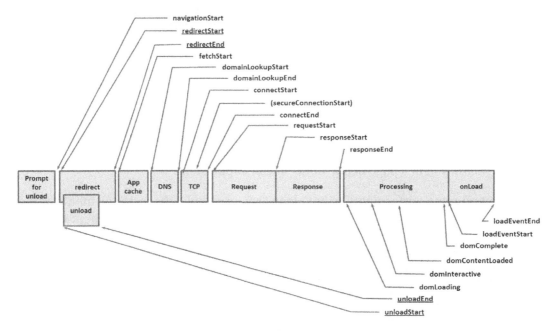

The natigation timing API provides a simple way to get accurate and detailed timing statistics—natively—for page navigation and load events. The API is accessed via the properties of the window.performance object.

Reference: http://www.w3.org/TR/navigation-timing/

Chrome also provides a performance.memory property that gives access to JavaScript memory usage data. The simplest way to try out the API is to take a look at window.performance in your browser's JavaScript console.

```
Q  Elements  Network  Sources  Timeline  Profiles  Resour
◎  ▽   <top frame>              ▼
            unwebkitresourcetimingbufferfull: null
       ▼ timing: PerformanceTiming
            connectEnd: 1402999343675
            connectStart: 1402999343632
            domComplete: 1402999352613
            domContentLoadedEventEnd: 1402999350466
            domContentLoadedEventStart: 1402999350422
            domInteractive: 1402999350422
            domLoading: 1402999348641
            domainLookupEnd: 1402999343632
            domainLookupStart: 1402999343340
            fetchStart: 1402999343336
            loadEventEnd: 1402999352738
            loadEventStart: 1402999352613
            navigationStart: 1402999343336
            redirectEnd: 0
            redirectStart: 0
            requestStart: 1402999343675
```

In the Google browser, select developer console and enter 'performance', or In Google Chrome, from any web page:

1. Select Tools -> JavaScript console from the menu at the top right of the Chrome window.
2. Type in the word 'performance' next to the > prompt at the bottom of the window and press return.
3. Click Performance to see the properties of the object: memory, navigation and timing. Click the arrow to the left of timing to view its properties.

Data from the API really comes to life when events are used in combination:

- Network latency = responseEnd-fetchStart
- The time taken for page load once the page is received from the server: loadEven-tEnd-responseEnd
- The whole process of navigation and page load: loadEventEnd-navigationStart.

Multi user server synchronization - live updates

How to sync your frontend when say the backend has changed - for example an iOS app changes values in the backend such as a user purchasing tickets and the concert is not sold out, that need to be updated in a desktop browser view for other users with open connections. Some choices are:

- You could do polling every few seconds –an AJAX polling solution, a client will setup a regular callback with setInterval and make an AJAX call to the server to a /sync/ endpoint. It will pass in its latest client_timestamp and the server will run the queries to detect what has changed and reply with the JSON structure to pass that information back to the client.
- You could create a service that uses some Websocket implementation.
- Use existing commercial services to sync data across devices such as:
    - https://www.firebase.com/
    - https://goinstant.com/
    - http://deployd.com/
    - http://pusher.com/

SPA Performance Monitoring

An issue with Single Page Applications is you will not be monitoring the Javascript code directly if you have monitoring configured for the Rails code.

- A useful gem for new Relic is to do this is: https://github.com/uken/newrelic-timing
- Alternatively you could monitor SPA's with this free tool http://github.hubspot.com/bucky/.
- there is a paid service called http://caliper.io/ which can automatically measure the performance of parts of your app.

Restful API versus Websocket Performance

The standard way to connect SPA's to the backend server controller is over RESTful API's, but there are performance benefits using websockets instead.

WebSockets is two way connection connection, It is something that neither SOAP nor REST have. Because the connection is persistent, the server can now initiate communication with the browser. The server can send alerts, updates and notifications. You could run JSON over it. Support for it is becoming more standard, http://caniuse.com/websockets A library for it is http://socket.io.

Single TCP connection

Typically a new TCP connection is initiated for a HTTP request and terminated after the response is received. A new TCP connection needs to be established for another HTTP request/response. For WebSocket, the client and server communicate over that same TCP connection for the lifecycle of WebSocket connection.

- WebSocket is a more efficient protocol than RESTful HTTP as there are less TCP connections to open. Websockets will not replace HTTP Restful connections for now, but good to be aware of it, an overview of websockets is:
- WebSocket is a low-level protocol. Every thing, including a simple request/response design pattern, how to create/update/delete resources need, status codes etc to be build on top of it. All of these are well defined for HTTP.
- WebSocket is a stateful protocol where as HTTP is a stateless protocol. WebSocket connections are know to scale vertically on a single server where as HTTP can scale horizontally. There are some proprietary solutions for WebSocket horizontal scaling, but they are not standards-based.
- HTTP comes with a lot of other goodies such as caching, routing, multiplexing, gzipping and lot more. All of these need to be defined on top of WebSocket.
- How will Search Engine Optimization (SEO) work with WebSocket ? Works very well for HTTP URLs.
- All proxy, DNS, firewalls are not yet fully aware of WebSocket traffic. They allow port 80 but might restrict traffic by snooping on it first.
- Security with WebSocket is all-or-nothing approach.

Feature Toggle

Feature toggles between Rails and SPA's can get more complicated. Previously adding a feature toggle to Rails was discussed, if part of this same feature in in the SPA then you will need to support both different mechanisms – Javascript and Rails feature toggling. Some feature libraries for SPA are:

- Emberjs http://emberjs.com/guides/configuring-ember/feature-flags/
- Angluarjs: https://github.com/mjt01/angular-feature-flags
- Backbone.js https://github.com/Starter4Ten/feature-flag-js

SPA Grid Layout

Keep an eye on http://zurb.com/article/1312/the-next-foundation, they are building a new grid layout, built just for Web apps with an emphasis on angularjs.

Reference: https://github.com/zurb/foundation-apps

REWRITE THE DATING APP SO FAR IN BACKBONE.JS

Next let's convert the Rails dating application as a Single Page Application (SPA) - using backbone.js. We will use the existing controllers/models from the dating application and use backbone.js Javascript front end instead of the Rails views.

The SPA sends RESTful API calls from the browser to the Rails controller to request data.

There are two options for the backbone.js development [likewise for angularjs]:

- Using the yeoman, http://yeoman.io/, solution which places the code into the Rails public directory. The Yeoman / Grunt way creates a nice minified build for you but you will then have two build environments.
- Or using a rails backbone gem such as https://github.com/codebrew/backbone-rails, which places the code in the assets directory. Use the Rails asset pipeline which works well but causes issues if you are using require.js AMD.

Personally I prefer the Yeoman way as it allows a front end developer to more easily get into a product design without having to have Rails knowledge, the Javascript is separate form your Rails, but it means you cannot mix Rails views, your frontend must be all in Javascript.

Turbolinks issues

Turbolinks will appeal to developers who decided not to develop an application's presentation entirely in a client-side stack. It you decide not to use turbolinks and use a SPA, check that your turbolinks is disabled.

Reference: https://github.com/rails/turbolinks

Reason to use a SPA

To provide the web site with even more responsiveness, speed, and enhanced user interaction, it requires bringing the logic closer to the client (browser). Web applications now-a-days require heavy use of JavaScript to generate content on the fly. The user does not need to wait between requests and page refreshes. A lot of the logic/code that used to be on the server side is being moved to the client side. JS allows web sites to render only content that changes without needing to reload the full-page on every request. A common problem with large JS web application developed is that they can become pretty messy really quickly. The lack of structure makes the code hard to maintain. This is where Backbone comes into play. It provides structure to organise the code and increase maintainability.

But it is not an easy decision to decide to use a SPA, you no longer have some of the advanced Rails caching, no turbolinks and many of these issues discussed above. Debugging Rails is difficult at times due to the typical lack of a good IDE, it gets a lot more complicated having a SPA involved. For a web site that needs to change how a user views the data then this is a good case for a SPA, but for a site where all a user does is basically page pagination view of data –it needs careful research of the advantages to be gained as pagination must be done server side when there is a lot of content data involved.

For a startup should you get your prototype working in Rails, then at a later stage replace the view with a SPA or just only use a SPA from the start with a Rails controller/model – sometimes it also depends on the skill set you have available.

SPA page Security

An exercise is to study how exisiting SPA site implement their RESTful API security with the Charles tool to examine HTTP traffic, unfortunately It is difficult as most of these sites use HTTPS, you may likewish have to implement HTTPS for your website. In a shift aimed at fostering wider use of encryption on the Web, Google is tweaking its search engine to favor sites that use HTTPS to protect end users' privacy and security.

RESTful API security

Ty to imagion a stranger monitoring your API's calls from your SPA (with the Charles proxy tool) and the potential damage they could do to your backend. To secure your RESTful API to your controllers as your browser clients will be accessing your backend code. Some companes offer a choice of two authentication strategies to customer- Token based authentication and 0Auth 2.0. My preference is oAuth 2.0 over HTTPS for each API with the API's using their own URL such as api.test.com.

Basic authentication

Basic authentication authenticates each individual request using a username and password pair. It should be used with TLS (formerly known as SSL) encryption because the username and password combination can be easily decoded otherwise.

Oauth

OAuth is an authentication protocol that allows users to approve application to act on their behalf without sharing their password. There are two standards for it.

Oauth 1.0 :

- https://github.com/oauth-xx/oauth-ruby
- https://github.com/pelle/oauth-plugin

Oauth 2 :

- https://github.com/intridea/oauth2
- https://github.com/doorkeeper-gem/doorkeeper

OAuth 2.0, the application can make a request using only the issued token over HTTPS. Although some people thing oAuth 1.0 is better, personally would only implement 0auth 2.0 as the protocol is simpler, easier to implement, more popular, some example API's are:

- http://developer.eventbrite.com/docs/auth/
- https://developers.facebook.com/docs/reference/dialogs/oauth
- https://developers.google.com/accounts/docs/OAuth2

Token based authentication

Token based authentication is when an API client uses a token identifier to make authenticated HTTP requests. A lot of popular services offer token based authentication for connecting with their web API. For Facebook, At the end of the login process, an access token is generated https://developers.facebook.com/docs/facebook-login/access-tokens. This access token is the thing that's passed along with every API call as proof that the call was made by a specific person from a specific app.

Rails offers the, authenticate_or_request_with_http_token, method which automatically checks the authorisation request header for a token and passes it as an argument to the given block: In the following example, we'll authenticate our requests for the Memberscontroller class:

```
Class MembersController < ApplicationController
Before_action :authenticate
def index
members = Members.all
render json: members, status: 200
end
protected
def authenticate
authenticate_or_request_with_http_token do | token, options|
Member.find_by(auth_token: token)
end
end
end
```

It is very important that the auth_token is unique across all users. In our Member model, we use a before_create callback to generate the token.

```
Class member < AuctiveRecord:Base
before_create :set_auth_token
private
def set_auth_token
return if auth_token.present?
begin
self.auth_token = SecureRandom.hex
end while self.class.exists?(auth_token: self.auth_token)
end
end
```

The token generation code is placed inside a while loop. If SecureRandom returns a token that's already being used, we'll keep on looping until it generates one that's unique. we could also add a unique constraint on the auth_token column in the database.

Using curl, we can test our token based authentication by passing a valid token in the Authorization header:

```
$curl -IH "Authorization: token token=24d8d081bgff33"
http://localhost:3000/members HTTP/1.1 200 OK Content-Type:
application/json; charset=utf-8
```

If the authentication fails and our block returns false, the request is halted and our application immediately responds with a 401 - Unauthorized status code

The authenicatate_or_request_with_http_token, automatically includes that header for us:

```
WWW-Authenicate: Token realm="Application"
```

Token based authentication is the simplest one as it only requires the developer to request an API credential (http://www.freesound.org/docs/api/authentication.html) and add a provided api key to all requests (see below). The flow for OAuth2 authentication is a little bit more complicated.

Session Security

In a normal web page session it is typical to have a session timeout but in a SPA is it not so easy. Fortypical web apps we need to have a concept of a logged in user and unauthenticated user. Web frameworks hide this in a Session abstraction. First a user will submit a login form to the backend. Instead of just returning a response, the backend will generate and remember a session id that it can use to look up this particular login for later requests. This session id is passed back to the client as a cookie value. Now whenever the client makes a request, the cookie will also be sent to the backend. The backend can then check to value to know whether the user is authenticated and authorized to access the resource they're requesting. You will need to decide if your SPA needs to have a timeout in the typical session timeout. You could use an access token to control your timeout.

Yeoman overview

Yeoman workflow, http://yeoman.io/, is comprised of three tools for improving your productivity and satisfaction when building a web app:

- Grunt (the build tool) which is a build tool for to perform your steps such as rake. It builds up on Node.js. Grunt is used to build, preview and test your project.
- Bower (for package management). Used for dependency management, so that you no longer have to manually download and manage your scripts.
- Yo (the scaffolding tool), scaffolds out a new application, writing your Grunt configuration and pulling in relevant Grunt tasks and Bower dependencies that you might need for your build.

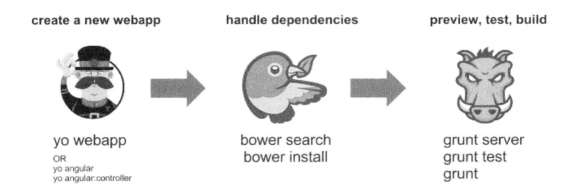

Using the Yeoman solution the Javascript application code is stored as a static files under the /public directory rather than having your front end HTML code served from a Rails view or having your assets compiled using the asset pipeline.

The code/review iteration speed is fast with Yeoman's workflow - add dependencies and make changes while LiveReload pushes all of your changes to the browser in realtime, allowing you to dial in and create some serious focus.

First Solution: Yeoman solution

We shall call the Rails controllers using JSON requests (instead of HTTP requests)

Use yeoman [grunt] to build it.

Use backbone.js for the view all members page, new member and delete member functionality. There are community made Yeoman generators, use the yeoman backbone generator: https://github.com/yeoman/generator-backbone

Install the required yeoman generator:

```
npm install -g generator-backbone
npm install -g generator-jasmine
gem install compass
```

Create a new directory called dating-backbone-yeoman inside the Rails dating application above into it, so they are all in the one project then.

```
/dating/
/dating-backbone-yeoman/
/app/
/assets/
/controllers/
/models/
....
```

Change to the directory: cd dating-backbone-yeoman

Yeoman defaults to mocha, change this to my preferred Jasmine.

```
yo backbone datingfrontend —test-framework=jasmine
```

The installation will ask you to select some options, select:

Twitter Bootstrap for Sass

```
Use RequireJs
```

To run the backbone code enter:

```
grunt serve
```

Into your browser enter: http://localhost:9000/

Yeoman generated these directgories:

`app/ directory`

The app directory contains your static app. It has your HTML, CSS and Javascript in it.

`package.json`

The package.json file helps npm to identify our project as well as to manage all of it's dependencies. It can also contain all sorts of other metadata relevant to your project.

`node_modules`

This one is self explanatory. This is where all the node modules that your project depends on are stored.

`Gruntfile.js`

The Gruntfile is a javascript file that is responsible for configuring your project as well as any tasks or plugins that your project requires. For instance, your gruntfile might specify that your project uses Uglify and that you want it to run uglify on a particular directory at build time. More about Grunt in a moment.

`component.json`

The component.json file is used to inform the Bower package manager of your projects dependencies as well as other metadata. In recent versions of Bower this file is called bower.json – more on that in a moment.

`.bowerrc`

The. bowerrc file is used to pass general config options to bower.

Getting around CORS issues

With the Yeoman solution there is an issue whereby the Rails app and the Javascript app are running on different ports [3000 and 9000] and need to communicate for debugging [on production they are all on the same port]. In production this would not be an issue.

Cross-origin resource sharing (CORS) s a mechanism that allows many resources (e.g. fonts, JavaScript, etc.) on a Web page to be requested from another domain outside the domain the resource originated from.JavaScript's AJAX calls can use the XMLHttpRequest mechanism. Such "cross-domain" requests would otherwise be forbidden by web browsers, per the same origin security policy. CORS defines a way in which the browser and the server can interact to determine whether or not to allow the cross-origin request.

Now fire up the two servers (rails server & grunt server). When you try to communicate with the rails API via the HTTP [or ngResource services provided by AngularJS] you will run into CORS issues. This occurs because the two servers run on different domains (localhost:3000 (rails) & localhost:9000 (backbone.js or angularjs).To solve it simply add the gem 'rack-cors' in your Gemfile's development group

```
gem 'rack-cors', :require => 'rack/cors'
```

and add this config to your development.rb config file:

```
config.middleware.use Rack::Cors do
allow do
origins 'localhost:9000'
resource '*', :headers => :any, :methods =>
[:get, :post, :options, :delete]
end
end
```

To connect to Rails, this library allows Grunt support for proxying API calls during development:

https://github.com/drewzboto/grunt-connect-proxy

```
npm install grunt-connect-proxy —save-dev
```

Modify the Gruntfile.js to deploy to the dating/public directory:

First add the following line to the Gruntfile:

```
var proxySnippet =
require('grunt-connect-proxy/lib/utils').proxyRequest;
```

And specify your proxy setting:

```
proxies: [
{
context: '/',
host: 'localhost',
port: 3000,
https: false,
changeOrigin: false
```

}

Then, configure the folder to which the 'grunt build' command will copy and compile the angular or backbone.js client app just before deployment. Currently we put the backbone client inside the 'public' folder within the rails root directory and have it served as a static files.

```
var yeomanConfig = {
app: 'dating',
dist: '../public'
};
```

Note: Grunt built can concatenated, minified, and even prefixed the javascript files with unique hashes to prevent browsers from caching outdated versions.

Second Solution

Alternatively use a Rails backbone gem inside your assets directory using https://github.com/codebrew/backbone-rails, But this uses coffeescript, theses are the generated files:

```
rails g backbone:install
insert app/assets/javascripts/application.js
create app/assets/javascripts/backbone/routers
create app/assets/javascripts/backbone/routers/.gitkeep
create app/assets/javascripts/backbone/models
create app/assets/javascripts/backbone/models/.gitkeep
create app/assets/javascripts/backbone/views
create app/assets/javascripts/backbone/views/.gitkeep
create app/assets/javascripts/backbone/templates
create app/assets/javascripts/backbone/templates/.gitkeep
create app/assets/javascripts/backbone/testapp.js.coffee
bundle install
rails g backbone:install
rails g scaffold Post title:string content:string
rake db:migrate
rails g backbone:scaffold Post title:string content:string
```

If you do not like coffeescript, try this alternative gem which you can use without coffee script:

https://github.com/meleyal/backbone-on-rails

Add gem 'backbone-on-rails' to your Gemfile

```
bundle install
rails generate backbone:install -j
rails generate backbone:scaffold user -j
#as an example create a Message view/controller/model
rails g scaffold Message title:string content:string
rake db:migrate
rails g backbone:scaffold Message title:string content:string -j
```

Dating code

Some example code for the dating app rewritten in backbone is shown here.

File backbone/app/index.html:

```
<button id="add-member">Add Member</button>
<script id="newMemberTemplate" type="text/template">
<div>
<h2>newmember</h2>
</div>
</script>
<script id="memberTemplate" type="text/template">
<div>
<h2><%= name %> <button>Delete Member</button> </h2>
</div>
</script>
<script src="scripts/main.js"></script>
<script src="scripts/templates.js"></script>
<script src="scripts/models/member.js"></script>
<script src="scripts/collections/member.js"></script>
<script src="scripts/routes/user.js"></script>
<script src="scripts/views/user.js"></script>
<script src="scripts/views/newUser.js"></script>
</body>
</html>
```

In dating/app/backbone/scripts/main.js , to kickstart backbone

```
window.backbone = {
Models: {},
Collections: {},
Views: {},
```

```
Routers: {},
init: function () {
'use strict';
console.log('Hello from Backbone!');
}
};
$(document).ready(function () {
'use strict';
backbone.init();
var app = new backbone.Routers.UserRouter();
Backbone.history.start({ pushState: true});
var routes = new backbone.Routers.MemberRouter();
});
```

In backbone/app/scripts/models/member.js to store the member model:

```
backbone.Models = backbone.Models || {};
(function () {
'use strict';
backbone.ModelsMemberrModel = Backbone.Model.extend({
urlRoot: 'http://localhost:3000/members/',
url: function() {
if (this.id==null || this.id==0)
return this.urlRoot;
else
return this.urlRoot + this.id;
}
})();
```

In backbone/app/scripts/collections/member.js to store the collection of member models:

```
backbone.Collections = backbone.Collections || {};
(function () {
'use strict';
backbone.Collections.MemberCollection =
Backbone.Collection.extend({
url: "http://localhost:3000/members.json",
model: backbone.Models.MemberModel
});
})();
```

In backbone/app/scripts/routes/member.js

```
backbone.Routers = backbone.Routers || {};
(function () {
```

```
'use strict';
backbone.Routers.MemberRouter = Backbone.Router.extend({
routes:{
"":"listmembers",
"list/:id":"memberDetails"
},
listmembers: function() {
var cart = new backbone.Views.MemberCollectionView();
},
memberDetails: function(id) {
//var newView = this.memberList.
},
initialize:function () {
}
});
})();
```

In backbone/app/scripts/views add newMember.js:

```
backbone.Views = backbone.Views || {};
(function () {
'use strict';
backbone.Views.NewMemberView = Backbone.View.extend({
tagName: "div",
className: "item-wrap",
template: $("#newMemberTemplate").html(),
initialize:function () {
},
render: function() {
var templ = _.template(this.template);
this.$el.html(templ(this.model.toJSON()));
return this;
}
});
})();
```

In backbone/app/scripts/views/member.js, add a view:

```
backbone.Views = backbone.Views || {};
(function () {
'use strict';
backbone.Views.MemberView = Backbone.View.extend({
tagName: "div",
className: "member-wrap",
template: $("#memberTemplate").html(),
initialize:function () {
```

```
this.model.on('destroy', this.$el.remove)
this.model.bind("change", this.render, this);
},
render: function() {
var templ = _.template(this.template);
this.$el.html(templ(this.model.toJSON()));
return this;
},
events: {
'click button': 'destroy'
},
destroy: function () {
this.model.destroy();
},
close:function () {
$(this.el).unbind();
$(this.el).remove();
}
});
})();
```

In backbone/app/scripts/views/MemberCollection.js create a view for the collection:

```
backbone.Views = backbone.Views || {};
(function () {
'use strict';
backbone.Views.MembercollectionView =
Backbone.View.extend({
el: '#container',
tagName: "div",
template: $("#memberTemplate").html(),
initialize: function(){
//this.collection = collection;
_.bindAll('destroy');
this.collection =
backbone.Collections.MemberCollection;
this.render();
},
events: {
"click #add-member": "newMember"
},
newMember: function() {
console.log('new member');
var newView = new backbone.Views.NewMemberView ();
},
renderItem: function(item) {
```

```
var userView = new backbone.Views.MemberView({
model: item });
this.$el.append(userView.render().el);
},
render: function(){
var collection = new
backbone.Collections.MemberCollection();
var self=this;
collection.fetch(
{ success: function() {
console.log('success');
collection.each(function(item) {
self.renderMember(item);
}, this);
},
error: function() {
console.log('no model');
}
}
);
}
}
);
})();
```

Implement Devise login authentication:

We used Devise for the Rails authentication login, we could use that instead of having to create custom backbone models [authentication, registration] and their corresponding backbone views but this is unnecessary as Devise ships with its own UI implementation.

Live update, push model changes to client side

With Rails views you could expire a cache for example on the server side controller when new data is available, with a SPA there is no direct link like this. You could push changes from Rails models to client-side Backbone.js collections with WebSockets. Using

https://github.com/jasonm/backbone_sync-rails, but it only supports publish/subscribe messaging system for the Faye messaging system (http://faye.jcoglan.com/).

Cache Results

To cache model data in backbone is tricky in terms of when to expire the cache. If for example member information changes on the server, how to push this to a backbone.js browser, how long to cache member information in the browser is a design decision.

Models can be cached in the browsers local storage. A useful library is https://github.com/mrappleton/backbone-fetch-cache.

Angularjs has an inbuilt $cacheFactory service.

Create SPA tests

Jasmine is a Behavior Driven Development framework for testing JavaScript code. It is similar to Rspec in syntax. A gem which installs generators for use with backbone and rails is:

https://github.com/wavell/backbone-jasmine

For angularjs you could use: https://github.com/pivotal/jasmine-gem

An example of a jasmine test is:

```
describe( "distance converter", function () {
it("converts inches to centimeters", function () {
expect(Convert(12, "in").to("cm")).toEqual(30.48);
});

it("converts centimeters to yards", function () {
expect(Convert(2000, "cm").to("yards")).toEqual(21.87);
});
});
```

Debugging SPA

Debugging is not trival for SPA, Google Chrome play store has a backbone.js (backbone debugger), and a anglarjs (angularJS Batarang) plugin to use with chrome developer. Otherwise you may need to look at Javascript objects through developer mode Javascript console. You will have to check for SPA memory leaks.

Chrome debugger [and safari] have good Javascript memory profiling tools. In Chrome developer you can look at the timeline as you clock around your site page, notice if the memory inceases a lot.

If you then need to drill down into the cause of increased memory [potentially a memory leak], you can create a profile snapshot to examine the data objects.

Add extra backbone functionality

There are libraries that site on top on backbone.js to provide extra functionality, namely:

- http://marionettejs.com/
- http://thoraxjs.org
- http://chaplinjs.org/

Angularjs is more self contaning framework and generally you do not need another layer onto of it like for backbone.js.

Javascript templating engine

Some of the most popular Javascript tempting engines are:

- Mustache : often considered the base for JavaScript templating.
- Mustache.render("Hello, {{name}}", { name: "Jack" });
- Returns: <p>Hello, Jack</p>
- Underscore : is a utlity belt library for JavaScript, providing all sorts of useful methods. It also provides simple templates. Used by backbone,
- _.template("Hello, <%= name %>", { name: "Jack" });

- Returns: Hello, Jack
- Embedded JS (EJS) : is inspired by ERB templates and acts much the same. It uses the same tags as ERB (and Underscore new EJS({ text: "Hello, <%= name %>" })

.render({ name: "Jack" });

- HandlebarsJS : this is one of the most popular templating engines and builds on top of Mustache. Handlebars add lots of helpers to Mustache. Anything that was valid in a Mustache template is valid in a Handlebars template, so I won't cover those basics again. Handlebars add lots of helpers to Mustache.

Rewrite in angularjs

An exericse is to rewrite the dating app in angularjs in order to better understand the choices between both. A Yeoman generator is https://github.com/yeoman/generator-angular

SPA SEO

One of the drawbacks with SPA's is SEO, normally Google can easily crawl pages in a HTML web site but with SPA's the view's are not generated unless Javascript is executed. The browser can execute JavaScript and produce content on the fly - the crawler cannot. The HTML content is tucked away in your SPA template, and Google can't find it easily. When Google crawls your website all it seems is empty tags:

```
<h1></h1>
```

The data is hidden in the template as the Javascript has not executed in a spider crawl,

```
_.template('You want Google to index this');
this.$el.html(this.template(this.model.attributes));
```

Your goal is to allow Google to see your final web page:

```
<h1>You want Google to index this</h1>
```

Google has been improving their indexing system and have been rendering a substantial number of web pages more like a typical user's browser which with JavaScript turned on. In Google webmaster, they have a 'Fetch as Google' button to see how your page will render according to their search bot (you could also change the user-agent in google developer to be the same as a google crawler and enter your url into the browser).

Google crawler

The Googlebot announces itself as a crawler to the server by making requests with a user-agent string. The user-agents used by Google for smartphone sites are listed at:

https://developers.google.com/webmasters/smartphone-sites/googlebot-mobile

And for desktop sites at:

https://developers.google.com/webmasters/control-crawl-index/docs/crawlers.

A Rails application can check for this user-agent string and send back the crawler-optimized home page if the user agent string matches. Otherwise, we can handle the request normally.

Solution for SPA page crawler indexing

Google released the idea of escaped fragments. The idea simply states that if a search engine should come across your JavaScript application then you have the permission to redirect the search engine to another URL that serves the fully rendered version of the page. We can program the server to respond to that request with an HTML snapshot of the page that would normally be rendered by JavaScript in the browser.

To make the crawler see what a user sees, the server needs to give a crawler a HTML snapshot, the result of executing the JavaScript on your page. This approach allows the site owner's own web server to return to the crawler this HTML -- created from static content pieces as well as by executing JavaScript -- for the application's pages. This is what we call an HTML snapshot.

Google came up with a solution. In order to make your AJAX/SPA application crawlable google recommend: the solution works as follows: the crawler finds a pretty AJAX URL (that is, a URL containing a #! hash fragment; if Hashbang used). It then requests the content for this URL from your server in a slightly modified form. Your web server returns the content in the form of an HTML snapshot, which is then processed by the crawler. The search results will show the original URL.

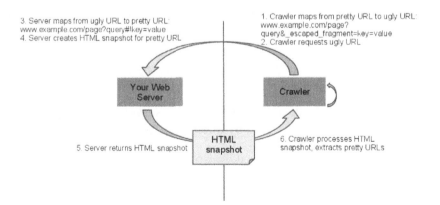

Step 1: Indicate to the crawler that your site supports the AJAX crawling scheme. The first step to getting your AJAX site indexed is to indicate to the crawler that your site supports the AJAX crawling scheme. The way to do this is to use a special token in your hash fragments (that is, everything after the # sign in a URL): hash fragments have to begin with an exclamation mark. For example, if your AJAX app contains a URL like this:

```
www.example.com/ajax.html#key=value
```

it should now become this:

```
www.example.com/ajax.html#!key=value
```

When your site adopts the scheme, it will be considered "AJAX crawlable." This means that the crawler will see the content of your app if your site supplies HTML snapshots.

Step 2. Set up your server to handle requests for URLs that contain _escaped_fragment_

Suppose you would like to get www.example.com/index.html#!key=value indexed. Your part of the agreement is to provide the crawler with an HTML snapshot of this URL, so that the crawler sees the content. How will your server know when to return an HTML snapshot instead of a regular page? The answer is the URL that is requested by the crawler: the crawler will modify each AJAX URL such as:

```
www.example.com/ajax.html#!key=value
```

to temporarily become:

```
www.example.com/ajax.html?_escaped_fragment_=key=value
```

In order to make pages without hash fragments crawlable (HTML5 PushState URLs) – such as your home page, you include a special meta tag in the head of the HTML of your page. The meta tag takes the following form:

```
<meta name="fragment" content="!">
```

SPA SEO Example implementation

You will configure you SPA to either use Pushstate or Hashbangs.

HTML5 Pushstate

Add this meta tag to the <head> of all of your pages:

```
<meta name="fragment" content="!">
```

Test it by adding _escaped_fragment_= to the query string of a url

```
http://testapp.com/
```

Turns into

```
http://testapp.com/?_escaped_fragment_=
```

We use _escaped_fragment_ for the crawlers that support it instead of checking the user agent to prevent cloaking penalties

Hashbang URLs with hashes (#)

Make sure you are using the hash-bang (#!) instead of just a hash (#)

Test it by adding the #! value to the query string using _escaped_fragment_=

```
http://testapp.com/#!/getting-started
```

Turns into

```
http://testapp.com/?_escaped_fragment_=/getting-started
```

Hashbang URLs are easier to implement and are compatible with older browsers, but many users find PushState URLs look more convenient. Hashbang URLs were an ugly stopgap requiring the developer to provide a pre-rendered version of the site at a special location. They still work, but you don't need to use them.

Text based browser

Lynx is a text based command line web editor, it only loads text and avoids Javascript and images. It can be used to test google defaults to seeing your website. To install it:

```
sudo port install lynx
```

SPA SEO Implementation

You can implement a solution yourself or use a commercial solution.

Implementation using Phantom.js

Phantom.js is a headless webkit browser. We are going to setup a node.js server that given a URL, it will fully render the page content. Then we will redirect bots to this server to retrieve the correct content.

You will need to install node.js and phantom.js onto your server. If you are using apache we can edit. htaccess such that Google requests are proxied to our middle man phantom.js server.

```
RewriteEngine on RewriteCond %{QUERY_STRING} ^_escaped_fragment_=(.*)$
RewriteRule (.*) http://webserver:3000/%1? [P]
```

We could also include other RewriteCond, such as user agent to redirect other search engines we wish to be indexed on.

Or for Nginx:

```
if ($args ~ _escaped_fragment_) {
# Proxy to PhantomJS instance here
}
```

Though Google won't use escapedfragment_ unless we tell it to by either including a meta tag; <meta name="fragment" content="!"> or using '#!' URLs in our links. You may likely have to use both.

But how do you know if your webpage is ready and the HTML returned from the headless browser is the final HTML for that given page? Well you need to set a flag in the DOM of your webpage that lets the headless browser know that it's ready. You can also wait for all JavaScript to be executed, but the problem here is that you do not know when any remote XHR requests have completed their job, nor do you know if there are any important asyn-chronous scripts going on in the background.

A reference guide applicable to any SPA is: http://backbonetutorials.com/seo-for-single-page-apps/. In practice implementing a node.js server along side your Rails server just for SEO could be a lot to maintain and make you think about using a commercial service instead.

For the https://prerender.io/ commercial service, you can add the following script snippet: window.prerenderReady = false; which will tell the Prerender service to wait until your entire page is fully rendered before taking a snapshot. You will need to set, window.prerenderReady = true, once you're sure your content has completed loading.

Some useful gems could be: https://github.com/benkitzelman/google-ajax-crawler

For angularjs: https://github.com/steeve/angular-seo

Commerical SPA index services

Services To allow your SPA to be crawled by search engines are:

- https://prerender.io/
- http://www.brombone.com/
- http://getseojs.com/

For example for prerender.io : When a crawler visits your page at: http://localhost:3000/#!/home, the URL will be converted to http://localhost:3000/?_escaped_fragment_=/home, once the Prerender middleware sees this type of URL, it will make a call to the Prerender service. Alternatively, if you are using HTML5 mode PushState, when a crawler visits your page at http://localhost:3000/home, the URL will be converted to http://localhost:3000/home/?_escaped_fragment_=. The Prerender service will check and see if it has a snapshot or already rendered page for that URL, if it does, it will send it to the crawler, if it does not, it will render a snapshot on the fly and send the rendered HTML to the crawler for correct indexing. Prerender provides a dashboard for you to see the different pages that have been rendered and crawled by bots.

Sitemaps

It is good to add the hashbang or HTML5 URL's to point to the content, Google and Bing will know they are AJAX generated pages. For example:

```
<urlset xmlns="http://www.sitemaps.org/schemas/sitemap/0.9">
. . .
<url>
<loc>http://www.yourwebsite.com/#!/home</loc>
<changefreq>daily</changefreq>
<priority>1.0</priority>
</url>
. . .
</urlset>
```

CONVERT TO A MOBILE APP

How would we start converting our dating application to a native iOS/android application? There are three principal ways to develop a mobile solution:

- native code
- hybrid mobile app
- mobile Web app

A popular question should you develop native or a hybrid mobile app. Native apps will always require more investment because they need to be written for each platform. Hybrid apps will always enable you to build for more platforms faster, if you are willing to sacrifice small amounts of performance, and a user interface which is not always native looking.

hybrid application

"Hybrid application" is a term often given to applications that are developed largely in HTML5 for the user interface and that rely on native code to access device-specific features that are not readily available to Web applications. Much of this native code is non-visual in nature, simply passing data back to the HTML5 layer of the app, where it is rendered to the user. Libraries such as Apache Cordova (formerly PhoneGap, Adobe purchased phonegap) provide this capability. Hybrid apps use a web view control (UIWeb-View on iOS, WebView on Android and others) to present the HTML and JavaScript files in a full-screen format, using the native browser rendering engine.

The secret of hybrid apps is the implementation of an abstraction layer that exposes the device capabilities (native APIs) to the hybrid app as a JavaScript API. This is something not possible with Mobile Web implementations because of the security boundary between the browser and the device APIs. Apache Cordova is an example of a JavaScript abstraction layer over native APIs. What this really means is that, for example if I build a mobile app with Apache Cordova, I can use JavaScript to access a native API, like the camera, using a single API call regardless of what platform the app will run on.

You may find that native controls, such as MapKit on iOS, provide superior performance to what can be achieved in HTML5.

Two GUI libraries to designing a hybrid app before passing it to phonegap are with using Bootstrap or jQuery Mobile.

jQuery Mobile is a mobile web application framework that aims to provide a cross-platform mobile application written entirely using JavaScript/HTML/CSS but it really focused on small screen devices. JQuery Mobile fits nicely with backbone.js [with angularjs it is more difficult]. jQuery Mobile does create more mobile-optimised form input interfaces (larger areas for clicking, etc.), but Twitter bootstrap creates clean CSS that I can easily add my own mobile-optimised CSS on top of when necessary. All of Bootstrap's nice responsive features come at a cost; to loading time and to the device's processing power.

Some negatives of hybrid apps are:

- Web views are typically not as good at performance as native code. Javascript can be noticeably slower than Java on android's VM or Objective-C compiled and running on iOS.
- Not all Web views render the same, extra testing would be needed for the different Android versions.

Phonegap

PhoneGap is essentially a wrapper around an existing web application that lets you access native device APIs (like camera, bluetooth, etc.) using JavaScript. The software underlying PhoneGap is Apache Cordova. PhoneGap is a distribution of Apache Cordova. Adobe purchased phoneGap so over time the two libraries will start to differ.It can be confusing to separate both at the moment for functionality.

A PhoneGap application may only use HTML5, CSS3, and JavaScript. However, you can make use of network protocols (XmlHTTPRequest, Web Sockets, etc) to easily communicate with backend services written in any language. This allows your PhoneGap app to remotely access existing business processes while the device is connected to the Internet. The way you can use PhoneGap with Rails is to request API's calls into a remote Rails application controller. So your mobile app (PhoneGap) make requests to your API to get/set data from database.

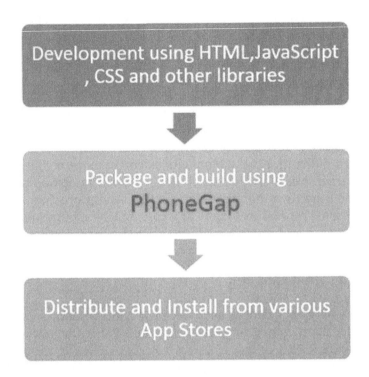

One architecture is to use an MV* Javascript framework like backbone.js, with jQuery Mobile and PhoneGap to send/receive JSON messages to/from API. Cross-platform is nice in that one phoneGap/jquerymobile codebase works on iOS/android, but most Android users don't want their apps to look like iOS apps and vice versa.

Use Rails with phonegap

An interesting gem to help integrate Rails SPA's and phonegap is: https://github.com/joscas/phonegap-rails

This gem provides generators for the Phonegap APIs. It is intended to be used within the scope of Single Page Applications that have a Ruby on Rails API backend.

Use phonegap with backbone.js

jQuery Mobile was (at least initially) intended as a full-stack framework as opposed to a pure UI toolkit like Twitter Bootstrap. As such, it overlaps with the Backbone.js infrastructure in some areas. In particular, the URL routing feature provided by both frameworks may clash. The approach typically used is to disable the routing and navigation capabilities of jQuery Mobile, and essentially use it as a pure UI framework on top of Backbone.js.

Use phonegap with angular.js

When our Cordova app is ready, the device has connected, and everything is ready to go, Cordova will fire the browser event called deviceready. With Angular, we can either boot-strap the app after this event has been fired or we can use promises to handle our logic after the deviceready event has been fired.

jquerymobile and boilerplate

An interesting combination for a mobile only site would be to use jquerymobile and html5boilerplate mobile, www.html5boilerplate.com/mobile.

Other interesting tools

Rubymotion is a commercial tool to develop iOS apps in Ruby. Personally i prefer to go the native iOS route as you have the superior Xcode tools.

Two good tools for generating native applications written from javascript are:

- Titanium appcelerator [generates native code directly].
- Sencha touch [uses phonegap but I find it more useful for enterprise type applications].

BIG DATA

We have our dating application but from a business point we need to generate reports to see what members are doing on the web site over time, for an eCommerce site what are the purchasing trends etc. These reports can come under the term 'big data', how big is 'big' is relative, I have seem companies use big data technology for only a few Mb of data (not recommended) to much later data sizes.

The most popular engine to process data is Hadoop. Hadoop is an open source framework for distributed processing and storage of Big Data on commodity machines. It uses HDFS as a dedicated file system that cuts data into small chunks and spreads them optimally over a cluster. The data is processed in parallel on the machines via MapReduce (Hadoop 2.0 aka YARN allows for other applications as well).

On top of this you can add a layer to simplify the analysis code instead of writing map/reduce jobs. Two popular addons are 'pig' and 'hive'. Pig is more like a procedure language and Hive is more like SQL.

Data warehouse Versus Big Data

When should I use Hadoop, and when should I put the data into a data warehouse?

A **Data Warehouse** is a structured relational database, where you aim to collect together all the interesting data from multiple systems. When putting data into a warehouse, you need to clean and structure it at the point of insertion. This cleaning and structuring process called ETL – Extract, Transform, and Load (such as with http://www.talend.com/resource/etl.html. The data warehouse approach is helpful because then your data looks clean and simple, but it is also very limiting:

The **Hadoop** ecosystem (could also be called the 'Big Data' approach) starts from the same aim of wanting to collect together as much interesting data as possible from different systems, but approaches it in a radically better way. With this approach, you dump all data of interest into a big data store (usually HDFS – Hadoop Distributed File System). This is often in cloud storage – cloud storage is good for the task, because it's cheap and flexible, and because it puts the data close to cheap cloud computing power.

You can still then do ETL and create a data warehouse using tools like Hive if you want, but more importantly you also still have all of the raw data available so you can also define new questions and do complex analyses over all of the raw historical data if you wish. The Hadoop toolset allows great flexibility and power of analysis, since it does big computation by splitting a task over large numbers of cheap commodity machines, letting you perform much more powerful, speculative, and rapid analyses than is possible in a traditional warehouse.

Big Data work flow

To demisify big data, a typical workflow could be for use 'Sqoop' to transfer data from a relational database into Hadoop's datastore called Hadoop Distributed File System (HDFS), and then run your Hive SQL like commands. The relational database rows could then be deleted once you are finished processing the data perhaps to save space and increase query performance on a smaller dataset size.

Cloud solutions

Google cloud support Hadoop: https://cloud.google.com/solutions/hadoop/, likewise AWS: http://aws.amazon.com/elasticmapreduce/.

Cloudera

Cloudera are the leaders on Big data consulting, they supply a free virtual machine with all the tools required to explore big data:

http://www.cloudera.com/content/cloudera-content/cloudera-docs/DemoVMs/Cloudera-QuickStart-VM/cloudera_quickstart_vm.html

Hadoop Alternatives

AWS Redshift

AWS offer a Hadoop solution but also a solution called Redshift, http://aws.amazon.com/redshift/, which they claim is more cost effective. Redshift's data warehouse-as-a-service is based on technology acquired from ParAccel. It is built on an old version of PostgreSQL with some major enhancements:

- Sharding - Redshift supports data sharding, that is partitioning the tables across different servers for better performance.
- scaling: when scaling Amazon's clusters, the data needs to be reshuffled amongst the machines. Scaling Hadoop doesn't require reshuffling since new data will simply be saved on the new machines., giving Hadoop the advantage is this is required.

Tests have shown that Redshift performs faster for terabytes of data. Nonetheless, there are some constraints to Redshift's super speed. Certain Redshift maintenance tasks have limited resources, so procedures like deleting old data could take a while.

Benchmark tests have shown that while Redshift performs faster for terabytes, Hadoop performs better for petabytes, that Hadoop does a better job of running big joins over billions of rows.

Redshift is maybe not a replacement for Hadoop due to its limitations, but rather it is a very good complement to Hadoop for interactive analytics.

Amazon Kinesis

Real-time processing of streaming data at massive scale. Amazon Kinesis takes in large streams of data for processing in real time. The most common Amazon Kinesis use case scenario is rapid and continuous data intake and aggregation. The type of data used in an Amazon Kinesis use case includes IT infrastructure log data, application logs, social media, market data feeds, web clickstream data, and more. Because the response time for the data intake and processing is in real time, the processing is typically lightweight.

Google BigQuery

BigQuery can run SQL type queries against terabytes of data: https://cloud.google.com/products/bigquery/.

Other tools

- Shark : Brings improved performance and advanced analytics to Hive users.
    - http://shark.cs.berkeley.edu/
- Apache flume allows you to stream data from multiple sources into Hadoop for analysis such as high volume log data from many servers.
    - http://flume.apache.org/FlumeUserGuide.html
- Apache mahout can be used as a recommendations engine on top of Hadoop.

- o https://mahout.apache.org/
- Apache Drill is used for low-latency interactive analysis of large-scale datasets.
  - o https://incubator.apache.org/drill/drill_overview.html
- Cloudera impala - cloudera allows Real-Time Queries in Apache Hadoop. you can query data, whether stored in HDFS or Apache HBase.

Column databases

Cassandra [or HBase] are considered column databases, which run on top of HDFS. These are suited when you need random, realtime read/write access to your Big Data, as Hadoop is more suited to processing all data in one go, rather than selecting which fields to process. Cassandra is generally easier to setup and maintain than HBase, and it handles failures better.

A columnar database is a database management system (DBMS) that stores data in columns instead of rows. It has better performance for aggregating large sets of data, perfect for analytical querying. In a columnar database, all the column 1 values are physically together, followed by all the column 2 values, etc. The data is stored in record order, so the 100th entry for column 1 and the 100th entry for column 2 belong to the same input record. This allows individual data elements, such as customer name for instance, to be accessed in columns as a group, rather than individually row-by-row.

Here is an example of a simple database table with 4 columns and 3 rows:

ID Last First Bonus

1 Doe John 8000

2 Smith Jane 4000

3 Beck Sam 1000

In a row-oriented database management system, the data would be stored like this: 1, Doe, John, 8000; 2, Smith, Jane, 4000; 3, Beck, Sam, 1000;

In a column-oriented database management system, the data would be stored like this: 1, 2, 3; Doe, Smith, Beck; John, Jane, Sam; 8000, 4000, 1000;

One of the main benefits of a columnar database is that data can be highlycompressed. The compression permits columnar operations — like MIN, MAX, SUM, COUNT and

AVG— to be performed very rapidly. Another benefit is that because a column-based DBMSs is self-indexing, it uses less disk space than a relational database management system (RDBMS) containing the same data.

CONCLUSION

Is there a tipping point for when not to use Ruby Rails? The case of Twitter switching for Rails due to performance issues is well know, although Rails performance has improved since, how much of that was also due to poor architecture and implementation.

For example for a typical web site, after a fixed number of users should you consider switching to Java, Scala or Node.js? There are in London far more Java developers than Ruby which will affect decisions also.

Ruby encourages a lot of test coverage, but at the same time any major redesign will also involve throwing this test suite out. Ruby does not have a good IDE, adding print statements is what most people do. Rubymine is great, but IntelliJ is just on another level. setting a break point, seeing what's going, changing values on the fly, is just invaluable.

There are a lot of great Ruby gems but the problem is that many projects are (actively) maintained by one guy. Most Java Jars are maintained by companies and also used by many companies.

The famous famous 15-min Blog post for Rails, has been copied by other languages now with good project generators such as Spring Boot, http://projects.spring.io/spring-boot/. People are using SPA's more often now in their design, which makes the advanced Rails view/templates/layouts/caching not as important.

Some companies such as Foursquare use Jruby, which is Ruby running in a Java environment, giving better Java multithreading performance with the TorqueBox framework, http://torquebox.org/. A roadmap path could be to switch from Ruby MRI to JRuby to use the JVM and its ecosystem from Tomcat such as using the Trindad web server to run Jruby on Tomcat, but in practice for most startups adding extra cloud servers is enough until they prove their business model. But keep a close watch on performance from day one as inefficient SQL queries, and lack of caching will be more expensive to undo later on.

With the popularity of SPA's the backend choice is not as important as it used to, once you have a RESTful API replacing Rails controller with a node.js controller, then the backend language is not such a critical move as it would have been previously. But SPA design is not trival with issues such as how to invalidate cached data, initial rendering performance, SEO, log gathering, and debugging.

Java has also come along from previously with the popularly of the Spring framework, functional programming, and Gradle for build management, Scala is another good but less popular choice for multithreading applications. Python [dyango framework] as liked by Google, perhaps has an advantage for a more mathematical application. Node.js, the Play framework or use a Javascript fronted and node.js as a REST server controller, is a good option for a non blocking asynchronous application such as for file uploads. Google cloud offer a pure Javascript node.js/angularjs stack with https://developers.google.com/cloud/mean/. Linkedin switched from Rails to node.js for performance, scalability, using the same Javascript team for front end and backend reasons. Uber taxi also uses node.js. Iron.io decided to switch from Rails to Golang [Hailo cabs also use Go] saying they reduced their server count alot.

But I still think Rails has the edge for development speed, built in testing, comes with features that decrease the burden on the programmer for some security issues, and existing code for reuse in the community. Rails has a lower total cost of ownership beause it is hghly conventional, one Rails app's codebase looks very similar to other Rails app's codebases. There is also a strong overlap between agile and Ruby communites. Rails is now a mature framework with lots of solutions to most problems. When your monolithic Rails application grows to an unmangable size you could rearchitect into services. With service orientated architecture we can mix match different languages and have fun doing it.

CPSIA information can be obtained at www.ICGtesting.com
Printed in the USA
LVOW03s2245211014

409914LV00007B/88/P